The Many Faces of Anne Boleyn

The Many Faces of Anne Boleyn

Interpreting Image and Perception

Helene Harrison

First published in Great Britain in 2025 by
Pen & Sword History
An imprint of Pen & Sword Books Limited
Yorkshire – Philadelphia

ISBN 978 1 03610 502 0

A CIP catalogue record for this book is
available from the British Library.

Typeset by Mac Style
Printed in the UK by CPI Group (UK) Ltd, Croydon, CR0 4YY.

The Publisher's authorised representative in the EU for product safety is Authorised Rep Compliance Ltd., Ground Floor, 71 Lower Baggot Street, Dublin D02 P593, Ireland.
www.arccompliance.com

For a complete list of Pen & Sword titles please contact

PEN & SWORD BOOKS LIMITED
47 Church Street, Barnsley, South Yorkshire, S70 2AS, England
E-mail: enquiries@pen-and-sword.co.uk
Website: www.pen-and-sword.co.uk
or
PEN AND SWORD BOOKS
1950 Lawrence Road, Havertown, PA 19083, USA
E-mail: uspen-and-sword@casematepublishers.com
Website: www.penandswordbooks.com

To Anne,
Your incredible bravery and strength is inspiring.
May we always 'judge the best'.

Contents

Acknowledgements

A big thanks to everyone at Pen and Sword, especially Sarah-Beth Watkins, Lucy May, and Laura Hirst, as well as Rosie Crofts and the amazing social media team. Thanks also to my fantastic editor, Sarah Hodder. I cannot believe this is now my third book!

Massive thanks to my friends and family. To Laura, editor extraordinaire and friend, for checking my grammar, that it made sense, and for continually rating my typos in order of hilarity – I do not think we have had too many this time around though! To Mark, as always, for continually being there for me and nudging me out of my comfort zone to do things that scare me, as well as for the coaching and boosting my confidence. To Ben, for also giving me confidence, making me laugh, relieving the tension when I'm stressed, and letting me talk about my writing and problems I may be having. To Hattie, for always being there and coming over for a chat and taking me out for McDonalds. To mum, dad, and Matilda for supporting my writing. Also, to my gran and grandad, for always asking how I'm getting on and what I'm writing next; I love you very much.

Thanks also have to go to my dissertation supervisor, Gaby Mahlberg, from when I was studying at Northumbria University. It was with your help and guidance that the idea for this book first took root in both my undergraduate and master's dissertations. It has taken nearly fifteen years before I have truly felt able to do Anne and her story justice, but I hope this book does build on the original vision and expands on the ideas we first developed. Being able to go back through that work has been absolutely invaluable.

It is also important to acknowledge the ruling of the Court of Appeal (THJ v Sheridan, 2023) which says that for copyright to arise on an image, the author has to be able to express their creative abilities. This cannot be applied to faithful reproduction photographs of portraits and other images on which the original copyright period has expired. This makes things much clearer for writers like me trying to acquire permissions for images and not wanting to break the bank. A landmark ruling. And thanks to Bendor Grosvenor who has been pushing for a ruling like this for so many years.

A big thank you has to go to fellow Pen and Sword authors and historians who have been so supportive and kind. It's a lovely community to be a part of

– special thanks to Carol Ann Lloyd, Amy McElroy, Brigitte Webster, Rebecca Batley, and Sharon Bennett Connolly for their help and support. Thanks also to Adrienne Dillard for her kindness. Big thanks to Lucy Churchill for her kind permission to share the fruits of her labour and for giving us all a clearer idea of what Anne Boleyn may have looked like. Also, thanks to the Tudor Trio (Owen Emmerson, Kate McCaffrey, and Nicola Tallis) for putting on so many wonderful events and sharing so much of their research and historical visits with us all, and for giving permission for me to share the results of *The Retrial of Anne Boleyn* event here. Special thanks go to Owen Emmerson for always being so willing to share his wisdom and answering questions, for his wonderful endorsement of my work and writing a brilliant foreword to this very book.

Illustration Credits

1. Anne Boleyn, Hever Rose portrait, late sixteenth century by an unknown artist, based on a lost original. Located at Hever Castle and Gardens. Photograph: Author's Own.
2. Anne Boleyn, NPG portrait, late sixteenth century by an unknown artist, based on a lost original. Located at the National Portrait Gallery NPG 668. Photograph: Author's Own.
3. Portrait medal of Anne Boleyn, 1534. British Museum M.9010. Photograph: Author's Own.
4. Reconstruction of the Anne Boleyn portrait medal by Lucy Churchill. With kind permission from Lucy Churchill.
5. Chequer's ring, *c.*1575. Cared for by the Chequer's Trust. Wikimedia Commons: Daniel Newman, CC BY-SA 2.0.
6. Sketch by Hans Holbein labelled 'Anna Bollein Queen'. Royal Collection Trust RCIN 912189. Wikimedia Commons, Public Domain.
7. Sketch thought to possibly be of Anne Boleyn, by Hans Holbein. Royal Collection Trust RCIN 600878. Wikimedia Commons, Public Domain.
8. Nidd Hall portrait, said to be Anne Boleyn. Kept in Bradford Art Galleries & Museums. Wikimedia Commons, Public Domain.
9. Hoskins miniature of Anne Boleyn, seventeenth century. Kept in the collection of the Duke of Buccleuch and Queensberry. Wikimedia Commons, Public Domain.
10. Horenbout miniature, from the workshop of the Horenbout family, said to possibly be Anne Boleyn though once identified as Katherine of Aragon, *c.*1525–1527. Kept in the Collection of the Duke of Buccleuch and Queensberry. Photograph: Author's Own.
11. Hever Castle. Photograph: Author's Own.
12. Anne Boleyn Gateway at Hampton Court Palace. Photograph: Author's Own.
13. The ceiling of the Anne Boleyn Gateway at Hampton Court Palace. Wikimedia Commons: John S. Turner, CC BY-SA 2.0.
14. Traitor's Gate at the Tower of London. Photograph: Author's Own.
15. Bell Tower at the Tower of London. Wikimedia Commons: Ethan Doyle White, CC BY-SA 4.0.

16. Chapel of St Peter ad Vincula in the Tower of London. Photograph: Author's Own.
17. Tomb marker for Anne Boleyn in the Chapel of St Peter ad Vincula in the Tower of London. Wikimedia Commons: AloeVera95, CC BY-SA 4.0.
18. Memorial on Tower Green in the Tower of London to those executed, including Anne Boleyn. Photograph: Author's Own.
19. Print of Anne Boleyn's execution by Jan Luyken, *c.*1664–1712. Kept in the British Museum 1872.1012.5138. Wikimedia Commons, Public Domain.
20. Painting of Anne Boleyn in the Tower of London by Eduoard Cibot, 1835. Musée Rolin. Wikimedia Commons, Public Domain.
21. Painting of Anne Boleyn and Henry VIII shooting deer in Windsor Forest by William Powell Frith, 1903. Private collection. Wikimedia Commons, Public Domain.
22. Painting of Anne Boleyn saying a final goodbye to Princess Elizabeth by Gustav Wappers, *c.*1803–1874. Kept in a private collection. Wikimedia Commons, Public Domain.
23. Painting of Henry VIII's first interview with Anne Boleyn by Daniel Maclise, 1835. Kept in a private collection. Wikimedia Commons, Public Domain.
24. Anne Boleyn's Book of Hours *c.*1527 with her inscription. With kind permission from Hever Castle and Gardens.
25. Close-up of Anne Boleyn's Book of Hours *c.*1527 with her inscription. With kind permission from Hever Castle and Gardens.

Foreword

by Dr Owen Emmerson

It is an honour to introduce *The Many Faces of Anne Boleyn* by Helene Harrison, a remarkable new study that masterfully examines how Anne Boleyn, one of the most captivating figures in British history, has been perceived and represented across time. As a fellow historian who has dedicated years to studying Anne Boleyn, I find Harrison's work comprehensive and astute. She brilliantly reveals not only Anne's agency in cultivating her image during her life but also how that image has been reimagined and reinterpreted by succeeding generations. Harrison's meticulous research into both English and international primary sources offers a fresh perspective on Anne's efforts to establish her legacy in an era when women rarely had such control. Through these sources, she uncovers Anne's careful construction of her public image, showing her as a highly strategic figure who harnessed her allure, intellect, and political acumen to navigate the treacherous waters of the Tudor court. This significant contribution highlights Anne's influence over her narrative and underscores her resilience in a male-dominated society.

Yet the genius of Harrison's work lies in its wide-ranging scope. The study goes beyond Anne's lifetime to explore how her image has been reshaped over the centuries. Harrison takes readers on a journey through evolving interpretations of Anne, from her portrayal in Elizabethan plays, Victorian romantic literature, and modern novels to her representations in popular films and television shows like *The Tudors* and *SIX The Musical*. Harrison's examination of Anne's portraiture is particularly compelling, as she demonstrates how visual depictions, too, have contributed to the enduring fascination with Anne's life and death. Harrison eloquently and candidly addresses the inherent challenge of writing about a historical figure who lived five centuries ago. As she points out, Anne Boleyn's story is continually filtered through modern lenses, and the cultural history of her image often reflects the values of the time in which each retelling is produced. Harrison encourages us to reconsider our own interpretations and to appreciate Anne in the context of her world – an era vastly different from our own.

The Many Faces of Anne Boleyn is a triumph of historical scholarship, skillfully blending rigorous analysis with a narrative that brings Anne Boleyn to life. Harrison has crafted a work that will inspire academic readers and a broader audience who continue to be captivated by Anne's story. With this book, Harrison reminds us why Anne Boleyn remains a figure of fascination, admiration, and debate – a remarkable woman whose story will never cease to intrigue.

Dr Owen Emmerson
Hever Castle, October 2024.

Preface

Anne Boleyn is an absolutely fascinating figure in English history. This book is the culmination of over a decade of research which began with my undergraduate and postgraduate dissertations. My master's dissertation was entitled *The Many Faces of Anne Boleyn: Perceptions in History, Literature and Film*, so it is easy to see where the inspiration for the title of this book has come from. Of course, there has been new research conducted and new discoveries made since I wrote that work and this book will examine some of these, building and expanding on my original research. I was determined to examine Anne Boleyn from a different angle. There have been numerous biographies written about her, including those by Eric Ives, G.W. Bernard, Josephine Wilkinson, Elizabeth Norton, Joanna Denny, and Amy Licence, among many others. This book is different. It is not a traditional biography, but a discussion of Anne Boleyn through a cultural lens.

With chapters on Anne in portraiture, as a mistress, as a queen and mother, as a traitor, through foreign eyes, and as a reformer, I cover her life through the letters, poems, acts, and literature that was written to or about her, as well as debatably by Anne herself. Later chapters about Anne as a tragic heroine, on stage, on film, on the small screen, on the page, and in historiography discuss how perceptions of Anne have changed over the centuries since her death. It was eye-opening to write and I hope you will discover something new within these pages, whether it is a new novel you want to go and read, a new source you have not really considered before, or a new viewpoint you have not previously thought about. Examining primary sources like letters and poetry alongside stage and screen productions, and novelisations can feel quite consuming, and I have loved getting lost in the sixteenth century through so many different eyes.

My previous two books – *Elizabethan Rebellions: Conspiracy, Intrigue and Treason*, and *Tudor Executions: From Nobility to the Block* – were exciting to write, but this one has been a real passion project, and it is quite overwhelming to see it finally coming to fruition. I have wanted to write it for so long, but it has felt a little out of reach. This felt like the right time to tackle it. I believe that I have done Anne Boleyn, and her life and reign, justice. It was so interesting to write and see all of these different interpretations of Anne come together in a single project.

I have had such positive responses to my previous books that I hope readers will enjoy this one just as much. I could have written so much more on this topic, but for the sake of space some things have had to be limited. I have covered the full scope of Anne's life and the huge variety of cultural influences surrounding her in this book. Anne Boleyn has always been quite a divisive figure, but I hope I have given plenty of opinions from all sides of the various arguments which will allow you to form your own opinions of this controversial queen.

Helene Harrison, June 2024.

Anne Boleyn Family Tree

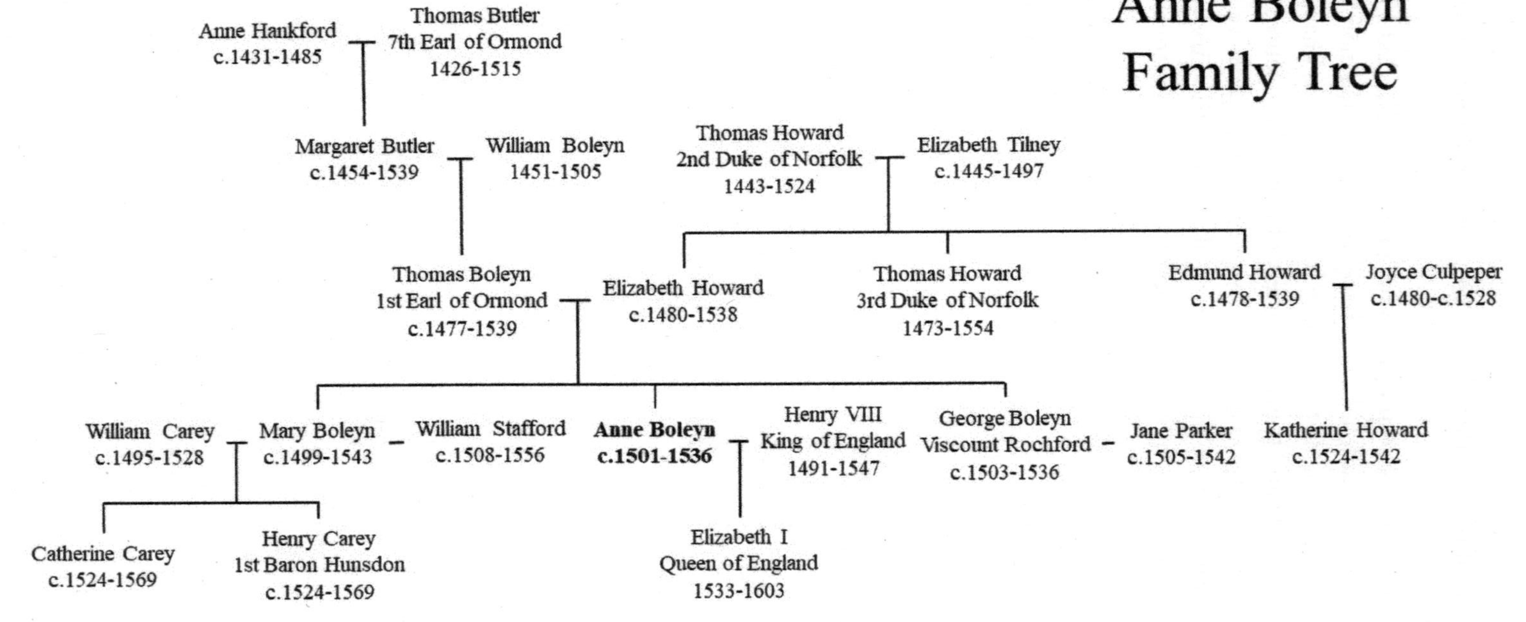

Introduction

Anne Boleyn has fascinated people for over 500 years. The second wife of Henry VIII and England's first executed queen, Anne changed the face of England forever. Perhaps that is why she is so endlessly intriguing. However, there is also a lot of information about Anne's life which is lost. No contemporary portraits of her survive that we know of, and we only have Henry VIII's love letters to her; her responses to him are missing. These omissions leave gaps which people are eager to fill. Plays featuring Anne Boleyn first appeared in the reign of her daughter, Elizabeth I, while novels, television shows and films have been produced throughout the twentieth and twenty-first centuries. Nowadays the incredibly popular *SIX The Musical* is bringing Anne Boleyn to new audiences in an original way.

The historian, Eric Ives, claims that Anne Boleyn was 'the most influential and important queen consort this country has ever had'.[1] The same could be argued of several queen consorts, including Margaret of Anjou, wife of Henry VI, who arguably played a pivotal role in sinking England into the Wars of the Roses. Also, Henrietta Maria, queen to Charles I, who played a key role in the run-up to the English Civil War. However, Anne Boleyn set a precedent for others to follow. She was the catalyst for the Break with Rome and the English Reformation, which began a new stage in English religious and political life. She was also the mother of Elizabeth I who changed the way we see England and queenship. Anne Boleyn was a woman unique in her time, who caught the attention of a king but held out for marriage and would not conform to early modern perceptions of how a wife and queen should be. She promoted her own religious causes and was not afraid to meddle in politics. Dr Owen Emmerson and Claire Ridgway wrote that 'Anne had been [Thomas's] joy and had brought greater wealth and power to the Boleyn family than Thomas could possibly have aspired to', and that 'Anne's rise had been unthinkable and her end unspeakable'.[2] It is difficult to argue with this statement. Anne led an extraordinary life.

There are several different stages in the development of perceptions of Anne Boleyn; the first is during her lifetime and immediately after where she was seen as a whore and homewrecker by the public, then a traitor and adulteress.

Although there is evidence to suggest that immediately after her death, people did doubt the veracity of some of the charges against her. The second stage, in the reign of her daughter, Elizabeth I, and into the Stuart period, Anne was seen as the mother of the reigning queen, and little more. Historian, Tracy Borman's book examines the relationship between Anne and Elizabeth, suggesting that it was a closer relationship than generally imagined, even after Anne's death when Elizabeth kept her mother's memory close to her.[3] Thirdly, the Victorians developed an almost romantic, tragic heroine image of Anne Boleyn, aided by the excavations at the Tower of London in the Chapel of St Peter ad Vincula. Finally, in the present day, Anne is seen as an influential consort and catalyst for the divorce and the Reformation and viewed as being innocent of the adultery and treason charges against her. This may be too simplified a summary but gives an idea of the different versions of Anne we will see in this book.

Stephen Greenblatt, in his book on Renaissance self-fashioning, discusses image and suggests that perception can be altered due to wider circumstances like family, religion, and the state, all of which apply to Anne Boleyn's life.[4] These 'circumstances' like the divorce, the Reformation, and her fall will be explored alongside popular perceptions. Historian, Amy Licence sums it up thus: 'Anne Boleyn's story touches on familiar themes of love, desire, duty, adultery, heartbreak, which transcend her status and time'.[5] The idea of self-fashioning is an interesting one, which promotes the impression that in the sixteenth century particularly, compared to previous centuries, there was a self and a sense that you could fashion it. There was an increased consciousness that you could form and express your own human identity.[6] Greenblatt goes on to say that the people he discusses in his book, including Thomas More, William Shakespeare and Sir Thomas Wyatt, 'embody, in one form or another, a profound mobility' – mobility meaning that they were able to move up from their roots and into a different life.[7] The sixteenth century saw the movement of power away from the nobility and into the hands of 'new men' and thus a new sense of mobility and identity was born. A downside of Greenblatt's study is that he does not devote a single chapter to a woman in the sixteenth century. His subjects are all male. But looking at mobility, Anne Boleyn is certainly a mobile woman in the sixteenth century; she moved from a gentlewoman to the daughter of an earl, a marquess in her own right, then a queen. She is the ultimate upwardly mobile woman. But the greater the rise, the harder the fall.

In a way, Anne Boleyn manipulated her own image in her final words on the scaffold on 19 May 1536, asking 'if any person will meddle of my cause, I require them to judge the best'.[8] Looking at the historiography, as we will in the final chapter of this book, you can see that modern historians tend to judge Anne Boleyn more favourably than she was judged in her own lifetime or across the centuries. There were doubts about the veracity of the charges against Anne early on, but these seem to have solidified as time has progressed. Now it is difficult to find people who believe Anne to be guilty.

This study will take an inter-disciplinary approach to analyse the image and influence of Anne Boleyn by looking at historical sources alongside fictional cultural portrayals. It is politic to study the theories surrounding these often-controversial adaptations. John Grenville speaks specifically with regards to film and television, although his theories could also be applied to novels and plays. He claims that people wanted history to be more accessible, but to make this happen it had to be simplified and was made purely to 'provide entertainment and attract a mass viewing audience'.[9] This could help to explain why academic historians are sometimes scathing of fictional adaptations and why historical novels are occasionally so heavily criticised. However, these adaptations can be insightful. They allow people to see popular perceptions and they also aid our understanding of the wider historical context and introduce history to a wider audience. We just need to be very careful not to treat these fictional portrayals as historical fact. It is often these fictional portrayals which might first draw the attention of the historians of the future.

* * *

This book will not be a biography of Anne Boleyn. However, it will discuss parts of her life in terms of the letters, poetry, written accounts, and fictional portrayals including plays, novels, films, and television shows through the centuries. It is, therefore, appropriate here to do a quick run-through of Anne's life to give some context to what is to come.

Anne Boleyn was probably born around 1501, although this is hotly debated. Some historians believe her birth date could be as late as 1507. However, a letter written in French by Anne Boleyn to her father from Mechelen in the Low Countries in 1513 suggests that Anne was much more than 6 years old when it was written, ruling out the later date. This letter will be discussed in chapter two. The appropriate age for a maid of honour to Margaret of Austria at her court at Mechelen was around aged 12 or 13, meaning that Anne Boleyn must have been born around 1500 or 1501.[10] Her place of birth was probably at Blickling Hall in Norfolk, although much of her childhood was spent at Hever Castle in Kent after her father inherited it in 1505. One of Anne's chaplains who later became Archbishop of Canterbury, Matthew Parker, was quite specific that Anne came from Norfolk, describing himself as her 'poor countryman'; he came from Norwich.[11] Anne's parents were Thomas Boleyn, later 1st Earl of Wiltshire and Ormond, and Elizabeth Boleyn (née Howard), daughter of

Thomas Howard, 2nd Duke of Norfolk. Anne had two surviving siblings, Mary and George. Mary Boleyn is said to have been born around 1499, and George Boleyn around 1503 or 1505, making Anne the middle surviving child. There were two other brothers, Thomas and Henry, who likely died in infancy as they vanish from the records.

Anne joined the court of Margaret of Austria at Mechelen in 1513 before travelling to France the following year to serve Henry VIII's sister, Mary Tudor, when she married Louis XII of France. Anne was able to go to Mechelen as her father had been sent on embassy to Margaret of Austria's court the previous year and built up a rapport with her. He was a notable member of Henry VIII's court, and Henry VII's before that, as well as a talented diplomat. The Boleyns had climbed a good way up the social ladder before either of the Boleyn daughters entered Henry VIII's bed. It was Anne's time at these two Renaissance European courts that would shape her and set her apart from the other ladies on her return to England in 1522. Margaret of Austria wrote to Thomas Boleyn when Anne arrived at her court, to thank him for sending Anne to her. The letter, written in French and translated by historian, Eric Ives, says: 'I find her so bright and pleasant for her young age that I am more beholden to you for sending her to me than you are to me'.[12] This demonstrates just how intelligent and engaging Anne Boleyn seemed to be even at a young age, and how Anne worked with the gifts she was born with to become the alluring woman who held Henry VIII in thrall. Amy Licence writes that Margaret's character and accomplishments, along with the sophistication of her court, would 'provide Anne with a standard that would shape her character and set her aspirations high'.[13] Anne would spend just a year at Margaret's court before moving to France to serve Mary Tudor, the new French queen. When Mary was widowed shortly after her marriage and returned to England, Anne Boleyn did not return with her, but transferred to the service of Queen Claude, wife to Francis I, where she would remain for seven years.

Anne Boleyn was recalled from the French court back to England in late 1521 or early 1522, and records suggest she made her debut at court in the Chateau Vert pageant on 4 March 1522 at York Place, later known as the Palace of Whitehall, allegedly playing the part of 'Perseverance' whilst her sister, Mary, played the part of 'Kindness'; roles which Eric Ives describes as being of 'historic appropriateness'.[14] Mary was certainly kind to Henry VIII and Anne persevered in order to be with the king, and mother his heir. Anne returned to England as the Anglo-French alliance was breaking down. Despite the lavishness of the Field of the Cloth of Gold event in 1520, Henry VIII seemed to favour an Imperial alliance with Emperor Charles V over the French alliance with Francis I. There is also another possible reason why Anne Boleyn was recalled from France in the early 1520s: a marriage was being arranged for her. This marriage was intended to resolve a dispute over the earldom of Ormond. The plan was for Anne to marry James Butler, a cousin on her father's side and the son and heir of Sir Piers Butler. Both Sir Piers and Thomas Boleyn had a claim to the earldom of Ormond, and neither was willing to give in to the other. The marriage of their children, James Butler and Anne Boleyn, would unite the two claims, the plan being that their children would then inherit the earldom, thus resolving the dispute.[15] However, the marriage never happened, although the reasons are unclear as to why. Possibly the Boleyns objected, wanting the earldom for themselves, or the couple themselves would not consent to the match. On 8 December 1529, Sir Thomas Boleyn was created Earl of Wiltshire and Ormond, effectively ending the feud between the Boleyns and the Butlers. By this time, Anne Boleyn was the future queen of England and Piers Butler gave up his claims to Ormond, instead receiving the earldom of Ossory and many Ormond lands in Ireland.[16] Piers Butler would have the earldom of Ormond restored in February 1538. There were two earls of Ormond until Thomas Boleyn's death a year later. This would not be Anne's only relationship, if you can call it that, prior to her entanglement with Henry VIII.

Anne Boleyn is rumoured to have had two other romantic relationships before Henry VIII made his interest clear. They were with Henry Percy, heir to the earldom of Northumberland, and the poet, Sir Thomas Wyatt, the Elder. Neither of these relationships will be discussed in any detail here, as they are discussed in chapter two. Wyatt's relationship with Anne is reflected in the poetry he wrote, and Henry Percy's relationship in the account written by Cardinal Thomas Wolsey's gentleman usher, George Cavendish. The Wyatt poetry gives an insight into Anne's allure to men, and the Percy relationship was later explored in 1536 as a possible reason to annul Anne's marriage to Henry VIII, along with Henry VIII's prior relationship with Anne's sister, Mary Boleyn.

It is unknown exactly when Henry VIII became interested in Anne Boleyn. We cannot accurately date the love letters Henry sent to her, though the earliest is most often thought to be from 1526 or 1527. These love letters are discussed in detail in chapter two. Henry's feelings for Anne seemed to be stronger than those he had for Katherine of Aragon; certainly at least more passionate and all-encompassing, and often described as an obsession. The couple agreed to marry when Anne refused to become the king's mistress; she did not want to end up rejected like her sister, Mary, and married off. The king needed a son, which Katherine of Aragon had failed to provide, and she was, by 1526, past the point of childbearing. Anne Boleyn promised the king that once they were married she would provide the king with a son and heir to follow him onto the throne.

Henry VIII sent envoys to the Pope to request an annulment of his first marriage to Katherine of Aragon and a dispensation to allow him to marry Anne Boleyn, as they were within the forbidden degrees of affinity due to Henry's relationship with Anne's sister, Mary. The Pope sent an envoy, Cardinal Lorenzo Campeggio, to England to act with Cardinal Thomas Wolsey to decide on the case. The trial of the marriage of Henry VIII and Katherine of Aragon would open at Blackfriars on 31 May 1529. There was a delay in Campeggio's arrival in England because of an outbreak of the sweating sickness in 1528. Anne Boleyn, her father, and her brother, George, all fell ill, but survived. Some of the love letters Henry VIII wrote to Anne were written at this time as they refer to 'the illness of my mistress, whom I esteem more than all the world'.[17] Anne's brother-in-law, her sister Mary's husband, William Carey, died in this outbreak. Mary Boleyn was left with two young children, Henry and Catherine Carey. It has been suggested that Henry and Catherine may in fact have been children of Henry VIII from his affair with Mary, though this has never been proven. Henry did not acknowledge them as he did with Henry Fitzroy, his son with his mistress, Bessie Blount. Anne Boleyn was granted the wardship of her nephew, Henry Carey, after his father's death and control over his lands until his majority.[18] This likely happened because of her relationship with Henry VIII and her increasingly powerful position within the Boleyn family as a result.

Chapter six will examine Anne Boleyn's reformist sympathies and portrayals of her in both pro- and anti-reformist texts. Anne is said to have introduced Henry VIII to William Tyndale's *The Obedience of a Christian Man*, first published in 1528, as well as Simon Fish's *A Supplication for the Beggars*.[19] Tyndale asserted the rights of kings and princes over the allegiance, body and soul, of their subjects, and how religion should be based on scripture and reading in the vernacular rather than a dependence on priests and other clergy to read and interpret the Bible for the people. Fish's work was against the indulgences and greed of the clergy, and aimed at Henry VIII directly. It is said that Anne Boleyn brought both of these works to the king's attention and, on reading Tyndale's work, Henry was said to have exclaimed 'this is a book for me and for all kings to read'.[20] It was probably Tyndale's work that influenced Henry VIII to create the Act of Supremacy. In it, Anne is described as a 'virtuous Lady' who opened the king's eyes 'to search the Truth, to advance God's Religion and Glory'.[21] She is often seen as the catalyst for the English Reformation because she introduced Henry VIII to these new and often controversial texts. This chapter will also examine texts by martyrologist John Foxe, Catholic polemicist Nicholas Sander, as well as Reginald Pole and Gilbert Burnet, and some modern historical viewpoints.

Once Henry VIII had established his supremacy over the English Church, he was ready to marry Anne Boleyn. But first he wanted some international recognition from Francis I of France. He could not expect the Emperor, Charles V, Katherine of Aragon's nephew, to approve of the displacement of his aunt. A visit was planned for Henry and Anne to Calais in 1532, but before they left for France, Anne was created Marquess of Pembroke on 1 September 1532 at Windsor Castle. She held the title in her own right and not by right of a husband, which was unusual. The patent also did not specify legitimate heirs, leaving people asking questions about the nature of Henry and Anne's relationship. After the meeting with Francis I, Henry and Anne were held in Calais by poor weather which prevented them sailing back to England. It is widely believed that it was at this time that the couple finally slept together for the first time, and possibly underwent some kind of marriage ceremony as well, which meant that they could sleep together legitimately as husband and wife.[22] Anne quickly fell pregnant and an official marriage ceremony was conducted in England, for either the first or second time, on 25 January 1533 at Whitehall Palace. Henry VIII needed to be absolutely certain that any children born to Anne Boleyn were legitimate and the rightful heirs to the English throne.

Anne Boleyn was crowned queen of England at Westminster Abbey on 1 June 1533, pregnant, and having already been through days of ceremonies and processions. This was the pinnacle of Anne's power. She was crowned with St Edward's Crown, usually reserved for the reigning monarch, rather than a consort.[23] Pageants and plays were designed and performed for Anne and will be discussed in chapter three. At the end of August, Anne Boleyn went into her confinement to await the birth of her child. She did not have long to wait as on 7 September 1533 she gave birth to a healthy infant. But it was a girl, and not the boy she had promised Henry VIII. Both Henry and Anne were disappointed, but there was no reason to believe that a son would not follow. Anne doted on Elizabeth and Elizabeth would remember her mother, attempting a subtle rehabilitation of her memory during her own queenship.

Unfortunately, there would be no son. Anne had at least one miscarriage, possibly two; the first is believed to have occurred in the summer of 1534 and it was rumoured that she also miscarried at some point in 1535.[24] We do know for sure though that Anne Boleyn miscarried for the final time in January 1536. It is traditionally said that Anne miscarried on the day of Katherine of Aragon's funeral, 29 January 1536, almost as if the woman that Anne had forced out and replaced was having her final revenge on her supplanter. Katherine had died on 7 January 1536 from what is now thought to have possibly been cancer, but it was rumoured at the time that she had died from poison. It was even thought that her death had been arranged by Anne Boleyn or one of her supporters. The Imperial ambassador, Eustace Chapuys, reported that Anne was accused of poisoning Katherine, but this charge was not in the indictment in May 1536 when she was arrested.[25] It is possible Anne experienced a long miscarriage in January 1536, beginning not long after Henry VIII's riding accident, which happened on 24 January. Had it been Henry's fall which caused Anne's miscarriage, it probably would have happened earlier, and not taken five days. There is also a discrepancy with the dates from different chroniclers and writers, which could be explained by a sustained miscarriage.[26] Whatever the cause, Anne Boleyn would not conceive again, and she would be dead within four months, on the orders of her husband.

Anne Boleyn was arrested on 2 May 1536 at Greenwich Palace and taken to the Tower of London, accused of adultery and treason with her brother George Boleyn, Henry Norris, Francis Weston, William Brereton, and Mark Smeaton, with the additional charge of incest with her brother. Thomas Wyatt and Richard Page would also be arrested at this time but were never tried and were eventually released. The indictments and trial documents, along with letters from the Constable of the Tower, and a letter supposedly written by Anne herself during her imprisonment, will be examined in detail in chapter four. The charges on her arrest were not necessarily designed to create a watertight case; the will of the king was obvious and would be carried out. However, the charges were intended to 'play into the deepest male fears regarding female misbehaviour', to 'arouse in the minds of Tudor men, their ultimate horror: that of the adulterous wife, who threatened their lineage and made them into a figure of public mockery'.[27] That meant that Henry VIII would be in a position of sympathy rather than vilification, the victim rather than perpetrator.

Norris, Brereton, Weston and Smeaton were tried on 12 May in Westminster Hall; all were found guilty and were condemned to death. Mark Smeaton was the only one who pleaded guilty to charges of adultery. The others pleaded innocent to all charges. Anne and George Boleyn were tried separately on 15 May in the King's Hall in the Tower of London, and pleaded innocent to all charges. They were both found guilty and also condemned to death. The men were executed on 17 May and Anne was executed by a French swordsman two days later, on 19 May 1536. As historian J. J. Scarisbrick says, 'it is difficult to believe that she was ever guilty of adultery with them, or of incest with her brother'.[28] Many historians nowadays believe that Anne did in fact die an innocent woman.

* * *

Eric Ives asserted that Anne Boleyn was 'perhaps a figure to be more admired than liked'.[29] She seems to have divided opinion across the centuries, though people tend to talk about her as a catalyst for the Reformation, or her appalling fall and execution, rather than whether she was likeable or what she was like as a person. But at Anne's execution:

> What stunned the crowd into silence was not what she said, but what she failed to say. She offered no public admission of sin, no confession that she had wronged her husband, not even a hint that she was guilty of the crimes against God and nature of which royal justice had convicted her.[30]

This lack of any admission of wrongdoing was unusual for an execution. Admitting that you were a sinner was traditional and a way of absolving yourself before death in a deeply religious age. That Anne Boleyn failed to do that spoke volumes to the watching crowd. Rumours began fairly quickly that Anne was not actually guilty as charged.

Claire Martin has claimed that there is little to be gained by revisiting Anne's story in the same way unless it is part of a much longer story. As 'despite the passage of centuries, Anne's spirit, her triumph, and her brutal death have lost none of their power to capture hearts and minds', and she still has a huge cultural presence today.[31] This examination of Anne Boleyn from a different perspective aims to examine her cultural influence over half a millennium.

Chapter 1

Portraiture and Image

'A prettying up and a loss of spirit'[1]

There are so many images of Anne Boleyn that exist and that people will recognise, but there is no surviving contemporary portrait from her lifetime. Henry VIII may have had them destroyed when she was executed in May 1536, and replaced by images of his new queen, Jane Seymour, though there is no actual contemporary evidence of such. Those images that remain are largely later copies and interpretations and are 'quite inconsistent with one another'.[2] The only image that we can be sure is from Anne's lifetime is a small lead medal, dated 1534. There is also little agreement over which images show the real Anne Boleyn. Anne stands out among Henry VIII's wives because she appeared to be so different from the others and had such a huge influence on historical events of the sixteenth century. She is often seen as particularly different from the two wives she is sandwiched between, Katherine of Aragon and Jane Seymour, although the three women have more in common than is at first assumed.

Historian, David Loades, claims that people were fascinated by Anne Boleyn because of her variety of accomplishments: she could dance in several styles, play various musical instruments, and hold her own in a conversation, as well as being feisty and independent.[3] It was not her looks that drew people to her. Anne also had a European gloss from her time spent on the continent at the courts of the Low Countries and France, which really set her apart from the English ladies on her return home. She seemed glamorous and exotic. The best-known portraits of Anne Boleyn date from the reign of Elizabeth I, painted to show a strong resemblance between mother and daughter, showcasing Anne's dark eyes, slender neck and pointed chin, similar to Elizabeth's.[4] Both women were said to be striking, and Elizabeth seemed keen to associate herself with her mother, especially in terms of imagery and representation.

It is impossible to discuss Anne Boleyn's image and portraiture without referring to allegations made by Catholic polemicist, Nicholas Sander. He wrote that Anne was 'rather tall of stature, with black hair, and an oval face of sallow complexion, as if troubled with jaundice. She had a projecting tooth under the upper lip, and on her right hand six fingers. There was a large wen under her chin'.[5] None of these appear in any portraits of Anne Boleyn, and Sander's claims are discussed further in chapter six. That she had the beginning of an extra fingernail on one hand is possible, according to George Wyatt. However, even if Anne did have some kind of deformity, it likely would not have appeared in any portraits.[6] It is also unlikely she would have attracted as much favourable attention as she did, had she had as many deformities as Sander described. Historian, Josephine Wilkinson, says that accepted portraits of Anne Boleyn 'do agree with the general descriptions of Anne's looks'.[7] The portraits tend to show a woman with almond-shaped brown eyes, with dark auburn hair and a French hood, with a sallow complexion, long elegant fingers, a thin face with high cheekbones, and a pointed chin. She was not like the traditional idea of beauty at that time with an English rose complexion and blue eyes.

With Anne Boleyn living her life largely in the public spotlight, at least from the mid-1520s, there was a 'calculated distance between the public persona and the inner self'.[8] This in itself poses a problem as Anne did not want to show weakness in the face of her enemies, so it is unlikely that surviving contemporary evidence portrays who Anne Boleyn really was; it more likely shows the face that she wanted the public to see, and any portraits of her probably reflected the same. The queen rather than the woman. With hindsight, Anne's public image is often looked at in comparison with Katherine of Aragon; the two are often seen as rivals, an idea which historians Owen Emmerson and Kate McCaffrey challenge, stating that 'these judgements risk being too simple and reductive' and that history has not 'paid enough attention to the surprising synergies between these two queens' famously disparate lives'.[9] Katherine and Anne had a lot in common: intelligent, well-educated, fiercely protective and stubborn. However, the focus is often put on their differing religious beliefs and their competition over Henry VIII's affections. As mothers to England's first two regnant queens both women deserve more credit, and to be seen as more than just rivals for a capricious king's attention.

Stephen Greenblatt expands on this idea of a separate public persona and private self, and says that there was a widespread idea in sixteenth-century England that the self could be fashioned, but that it was constrained due to family, state, and religious implications; these imposed a rigid and disciplined order on society as a whole.[10] In reference to Anne Boleyn, state implications were particularly important, but also religious implications, as Anne was widely known, or at least was believed, to have reformist tendencies and acted to protect and advance those who shared her beliefs. Anne Boleyn demonstrated that you could try and create your own image, and it would have some success, as today's historians generally see her in a more balanced light – neither entirely good nor entirely bad. Her image has been heavily shaped by Henry VIII, and often discussed alongside him. His possible destruction of images of Anne means that we are missing that elusive contemporary portrait painted from life, which could tell historians much about how Anne wished to be seen. But however much you try to create your own image, it is often out of your control, as people are seen through the eyes of others, and that perception is influenced by our own bias and knowledge. A concept known as 'symbolic iconising' suggests that beliefs or arguments about a person's character can often translate into visual imagery.[11] In Anne's case, images of her seem to show beauty, but she was generally not described as beautiful in contemporary accounts, more like bold or striking.

Josephine Wilkinson, acknowledges that none of the surviving portraits of Anne Boleyn are contemporary but are more likely copies of a lost original.[12] Eric Ives suggests that there was a full-length portrait of Anne owned by Lord Lumley in 1590 and that it even existed as late as 1773.[13] It is unclear what happened to this portrait, though it seems entirely probable and even likely that a full-length portrait could have been painted of Anne while queen, as one was later of Henry VIII's sixth wife, Katherine Parr. It may even have been a lost Hans Holbein portrait, which later images, like the Hever Rose portrait (on display at Hever Castle) and National Portrait Gallery images, are based off. G.W. Bernard asserts that there are 'confusions and uncertainties' over portraits of Anne as, except for the portrait medal, portraits said to be of Anne have all been challenged by one historian or another.[14] There is a lack of agreement over what Anne Boleyn actually looked like, and which are authentic images of her, if any. Several of the most popular will be discussed here, though there is not the space to discuss all potential images.

National Portrait Gallery and Hever Rose Portraits

The Hever Rose portrait is similar to that of the portrait of Anne Boleyn at the National Portrait Gallery,[15] though the Hever Rose portrait sitter is holding a red rose symbolising her connection to the Tudor royal house, hence the common name for the image. These portraits both likely date to the 1590s.[16] It has been said that the National Portrait Gallery image 'provided the model for many later depictions' of Anne, including much of the merchandise that we see today, with Anne appearing on magnets, bookmarks, book covers, mugs, and phone cases, and that it is 'as reliable an indication as we have of what Anne looked like'.[17] The fact that this image, and the Hever Rose one, are said to have been created towards the end of the sixteenth century in the reign of Anne's daughter, Elizabeth, suggests that this was a generally accepted image of the queen's mother. They were likely both based on a portrait painted between

1533 and 1536.[18] It would once have probably been part of a Long Gallery of portraits popular in Elizabethan and Jacobean times.

Historian G.W. Bernard, however, has suggested that both the Hever Rose and National Portrait Gallery paintings are actually of Mary Tudor, Queen of France and Duchess of Suffolk, sister to Henry VIII.[19] However, this does not seem likely. The 'B' pendant that the sitter is wearing was said to represent Brandon (Mary was married to Charles Brandon, 1st Duke of Suffolk), but why would she distinguish herself from the royal house of England to associate herself with a family only newly ennobled and ignore her position as dowager Queen of France? The pendant also looks similar to one Anne was said to own.[20] Anne was fond of initial pendants and known to own an 'A' and an 'AB' pendant, both of which were worn by her daughter, Elizabeth.[21] We do not know what happened to the 'B' pendant as it seems to have just vanished. It is possible it was destroyed and the parts reused in other pieces of jewellery. These portraits we can be fairly certain are supposed to be Anne Boleyn, a copy of an original maybe lost or destroyed after her execution in 1536 on the orders of Henry VIII. The myth of Henry VIII ordering the destruction of the images and possessions of Anne Boleyn is interesting. There is no actual record of an order from Henry being given. The only evidence we do have is in the Records of the Exchequer where it is noted that Henry VIII paid 13s 4d for the removal of the emblems of Anne Boleyn and Thomas Wolsey,[22] and at Hampton Court where Anne's leopard emblems were transformed into Jane Seymour's panther emblem.[23] This is perfectly normal when there is a new queen and did not apply only after Anne's downfall and death. Owen Emmerson and Claire Ridgway suggest that the Hever Rose portrait is 'Anne as her daughter's generation saw her' as no verified contemporary portrait of Anne survives.[24] It was the accepted image of Anne in her daughter's reign. With Elizabeth I as queen, courtiers in particular likely wanted to flatter their queen and gain favour with her, so had paintings of Anne Boleyn recreated and hung in long galleries in their houses, which were fashionable at the time, alongside portraits of Elizabeth I.

Both of these portraits show Anne dressed in the height of fashion in the 1530s, in a black gown with sleeves trimmed in reddish fur. She is wearing a French hood trimmed with pearls situated towards the back of her head and showing a strip of hair at the front, which you would not see with a gable hood. Anne is pictured with multiple pearl necklaces around her neck and her trademark 'B' pendant can be seen hanging from a rope of pearls, with three drop pearls hanging from it. The Hever Castle portrait bears the legend 'Anna Bolina Ang Regina' (Anne Boleyn Queen of England) while the National Portrait Gallery image has the legend 'Anna Bolina Uxor Henri Octx' (Anne Boleyn wife of Henry VIII), both along the top of the image in red lettering on the dark background. The fact that one image has Anne described as queen and the other as a wife is interesting. One has Anne as a woman on her own, but the other in relation to her husband, perhaps suggesting the viewpoints of those who commissioned the different portraits. In addition, the Hever Rose portrait sees Anne holding a red rose in her slender fingers, whereas in the National Portrait Gallery image we do not see Anne's hands, instead seeing more of her furred sleeves. It is interesting that the portraits both date to the 1590s as Nicholas Sander's work *Rise and Growth of the Anglican Schism* was published in 1585. This was the work that said Anne Boleyn had six fingers. Perhaps Anne's hands were so prominently displayed in the Hever Rose portrait because it was a direct answer to Sander's claims. The Hever Rose portrait emphasises the royal connection and describes her as queen rather than wife.

As previously mentioned, the portrait of Anne Boleyn at the National Portrait Gallery is similar to that of the Hever Castle portrait. However, Alison Weir believes that the National Portrait Gallery image shows more of Anne's 'charm and vivacity' than the Hever Castle portrait.[25] This is because she seems to have a bolder gaze, looking directly at the artist. In the Hever portrait, the sitter appears to be looking off to one side rather than at the viewer. The National Portrait Gallery image also shows Anne with auburn hair, similar to other images which are said to be Anne. A black-haired or at least dark-haired Anne is largely a twentieth and twenty-first century invention displayed in the actresses chosen to play Anne: Natalie Portman, Natalie Dormer, Claire Foy, and others.[26] It demonstrates how much influence popular culture has on perceptions of Anne, rather than looking at contemporary or near-contemporary images. Eric Ives describes the progression of Anne Boleyn's image through the 1534 portrait medal and Chequers ring, both of which will go on to be discussed here, to the National Portrait Gallery and Hever Castle portraits, which demonstrate 'a prettying up and a loss of spirit'.[27] The portrait medal, in contrast, shows an almost coquettish tilt to Anne's head which is missing from these later Elizabethan portraits, as she is almost mythologised as the mother of the Virgin Queen, having lost control of her own image which she worked so hard to establish during her reign.

1534 Portrait Medal

The only contemporary image of Anne Boleyn that survives is the portrait medal from 1534, which has recently been reconstructed by sculptor, Lucy Churchill. This contemporary medal, made of lead measuring just 38mm in diameter, survives in the collection of the British Museum in London, though it is seriously damaged. G.W. Bernard describes it as 'not very revealing' as a result of the damage.[28] However, Alison Weir describes Anne's features as being 'faithfully depicted ... the image is clear, in essence the same as the portraits'.[29] Anne Boleyn's image has been much debated, and this medal provides just a tantalising glimpse at the real Anne and her image as queen. The medal could only have been made with royal approval. With the reconstruction work done by Churchill, we can now see more of Anne's image as it may have originally looked.

The medal is generally considered to be the only indisputable image of Anne Boleyn which survives today. It now resides in the British Museum and is dated 'Anno 1534', inscribed 'A.R.' and 'The Moost Happi', which was Anne Boleyn's motto as queen.[30] These inscriptions all tell us that this medal was to celebrate Anne, probably on some kind of occasion. In this vein, Eric Ives suggested that the medal must have been prepared on royal authority and could have been created to celebrate the expected birth of Anne's second child in autumn 1534.[31] There have been some suggestions that the medal was in fact created to celebrate Anne Boleyn's coronation in June 1533, but then the dating of the medal does not make sense. It seems likely, as Ives has suggested, that it was created to celebrate what Henry VIII expected to be the birth of a son and heir. However, Anne's 1534 pregnancy ended in either miscarriage or stillbirth. Anne would not give birth to another child after Elizabeth in September 1533. A miscarriage would also explain why multiple copies of the medal do not survive.[32] The medal would not have gone into full production if the expected son and heir was never born.

Lucy Churchill's brilliant work to reconstruct the portrait medal of Anne Boleyn means that we can see it more clearly through the damage. As Churchill explains, Anne is more often depicted wearing the French hood, but her choice of a gable hood and the crucifix necklace, as in portraits of other of Henry VIII's queens, notably Katherine of Aragon and Jane Seymour, demonstrates how important the style of garments were to the queen's wardrobe.[33] The same items may even have been worn by consecutive queens. Anne Boleyn chose to wear a gable hood at moments in her life when she wanted to declare she was the rightful queen of England, like at this moment in expectation of a male heir being born, and as recorded at her execution in May 1536.[34] It was almost a challenge to those who supported Katherine of Aragon, wearing items from the Queen's Wardrobe. Although the medal may have been made to mark the upcoming birth of a son and heir, Churchill suggests in a reflective post on her blog that the medal was 'a masterstroke of political propaganda', and that Anne's aim was to enforce her child's right to the throne and her own legitimacy as queen.[35] It seems likely that choosing the same style of hood that Katherine of Aragon favoured, rather than what appeared to be her preferred French hood, was designed to demonstrate her role as rightful queen of England and

Katherine's successor – a political statement of her position and legitimacy, and that of her children.

Churchill describes how the reconstruction of the medal came about; after initially being 'appalled by the seeming awfulness' of Anne Boleyn she delved in further to find the evidence on Anne 'tantalisingly contradictory'.[36] She examined the medal close up and made detailed labelled sketches, which can be seen on her website, and it was then made in wax and details added. A mould was made, and the reproduction created. Churchill recognised that elements in the medal were similar to those in portraits of others of Henry VIII's queens, like the Holbein portrait of Jane Seymour, specifically in the woven fabric of the headdress.[37] The care taken with the image suggests skill and attention to detail, and it is likely an accurate view of Anne Boleyn's appearance. Anne, like other royals, wanted to control her appearance so she would likely have approved the image on the medal, as would Henry VIII, to make sure it was how they wanted the public to view her – regal and the legitimate queen and mother of the future king, it was hoped.

Chequers Ring

The Chequers ring gets its name from the manor house known as Chequers in Buckinghamshire, the country residence of the British Prime Minister since 1921, and where the ring is kept. It is mother of pearl and embossed with rubies and diamonds with an entwined 'E' in diamonds and 'R' in blue enamel, standing for 'Elizabeth Regina'. The ring was removed from Elizabeth I's finger when she died in 1603 and was taken by Robert Carey, son of Henry Carey, 1st Baron Hunsdon, and grandson of Mary Boleyn, to Scotland and handed to James VI of Scotland, now James I of England. This was intended to prove that Elizabeth was dead and that James was now king of England as well as Scotland. The ring was given by James to Lord Home, and passed down through the family, hence it ended up in the Chequers collection.[38] The provenance confirms that the ring definitely belonged to Elizabeth I and she obviously kept it close to her and wore it constantly, as a 'poignant symbol of the private reverence in which she held her late mother'.[39] Although Elizabeth does not seem to have often spoken of her mother, presumably recognising potential complications in putting her executed mother back in the public eye, but it does not mean that the esteem was not there; she showed her respect and devotion in other, more private, ways.

The ring hinges open to reveal two miniature portraits; one is certainly Elizabeth I herself, probably from around 1575, and the other is thought to be her mother, Anne Boleyn, though there is no way to know for certain.[40]

G.W. Bernard has suggested that the fact that the ring belonged to Elizabeth does not necessarily mean that the other portrait in the ring was that of Anne Boleyn.[41] Historians John Guy and Julia Fox claim that it is 'surely significant' that the portraits in the ring are of Anne and Elizabeth rather than Henry and Elizabeth.[42] The sitter of the portrait in the ring is wearing a French hood, which Anne was known to have favoured, and appears to be dressed in Henrician court fashions of the 1530s. The image does resemble, as far as we can tell given how tiny it is, the National Portrait Gallery and Hever Rose panel portraits, previously discussed in this chapter. Frankly it is difficult to imagine who else, apart from her mother, Elizabeth would wear in a ring so close to her own image. When the ring was closed the images would be touching.

Katherine Parr, the sixth wife of Henry VIII, has been suggested as an alternative, but this is unconvincing. Katherine was a good stepmother to Elizabeth before her death in 1548, but they did not end on the best terms. Elizabeth had been sent away from Katherine's home for a suspected inappropriate relationship with Katherine's husband, Thomas Seymour, 1st Baron Seymour of Sudeley, before her death. It does not seem like being a good stepmother is enough for it to be Katherine's portrait, especially as there is a lack of other information about their relationship which could potentially explain if there was more to it. The historian Susan Bordo claims that the ring can tell us very little of what Anne Boleyn actually looked like because it was so small.[43] But it is important to examine, as the fact that Elizabeth commissioned the ring and wore it constantly suggests that she accepted it as a good likeness of her mother, and there were people in her court who had known Anne and could have advised on the image.[44] It is at the very least the Elizabethan version of Anne Boleyn.

Tracy Borman opens her book, *Anne Boleyn and Elizabeth I: The Mother and Daughter Who Changed History*, with a brief discussion of the Chequers ring, describing it as Elizabeth's 'most cherished possession' and how she kept it with her until the day she died.[45] Although Elizabeth was not even 3 years old when Anne was executed, she obviously felt a strong connection to her, and images of Anne and Elizabeth show a similar facial structure and look. It seems logical to assume that the portrait in the ring is that of Anne Boleyn. The image is similar to the Hever Castle and National Portrait Gallery images of Anne, both of which show her wearing a French hood, and with what looks like strings of pearls around her neck and the square bodice popular at the time. Eric Ives states that the face in the Chequers ring and that in the 1534 portrait medal of Anne are 'evidently the same'.[46] Different head dresses reflect the different periods in which they lived, but the same oval face, high cheekbones and a strong nose and chin are obvious. Like mother, like daughter, which is nowhere more obvious than in the Chequers ring.

Hans Holbein Sketches

Noted artist and portrait painter, Hans Holbein, seems likely to have painted Anne Boleyn at some point during her tenure as queen. Holbein was Henry VIII's court painter at this time, having returned to England in 1532 from the continent. As queen, Anne would have been a prime candidate for a portrait. If such a painting was commissioned and completed, it no longer exists. Holbein was a hugely respected artist and probably considered the best of the period – today he is certainly one of the best-known – so, surely, Anne would have chosen him to paint her as queen. It is difficult to imagine she would not have, as she commissioned other items from Holbein including gifts for the king. However, some historians suggest that the extant sketches by Holbein said to be Anne are 'supremely unconvincing', suggesting some kind of missing portrait.[47] It is interesting to consider, as many of Holbein's sketches were not labelled until after his death.

There are two sketches in existence by Holbein which are said to be of Anne Boleyn, but these are considered by some to be of doubtful identity.[48] John Rowlands and David Starkey have said that the two sketches 'clearly show different sitters'.[49] Owen Emmerson and Claire Ridgway describe there being 'little solid consensus among art historians' for the identity of the sitters in these sketches.[50] One features a woman in a gable hood looking off to the right, and is kept in the British Museum.[51] The other shows a woman in what appears to be a nightgown or state of undress with a furred robe, and a tight-fitting coif tied under the chin, showing very little hair and looking to the left; this one is kept as part of the Royal Collection at Windsor.[52] The latter is inscribed, 'Anna Bollein Queen', though written in a later hand. The inscription has been described by some as 'meaningless' as it was added a century or more later, based on identifications made in the late 1540s, several of which were mixed up.[53] Alison Weir also describes the portraits as being of 'doubtful authenticity' and the one where the sitter wears a gable hood was not identified as Anne until 1649, which is too late to be proven.[54] The inscribed one, according to the Royal Collection, was not inscribed with Anne Boleyn's name until the eighteenth century.[55] The two portraits do not really look to be of the same woman so, if one was determined to be Anne, it seems unlikely that the other could also be of the executed queen.

Eric Ives claims that the inscribed sketch, which seems to show a woman in a state of undress, has evidence to link it to the Wyatt family, although he does not state what the evidence is.[56] Kate Heard, who works with the Royal Collection, says it is that the Wyatt coat of arms appears on the reverse of the sketch.[57] Sir Thomas Wyatt, the Elder, is said to have been a one-time lover of Anne before the king made his interest clear, and Wyatt was also arrested at the time of Anne's fall, though not convicted of a crime with her. The arms on the reverse of the sketch do not necessarily, however, have to have anything to do with the portrait itself. It is the only one of Holbein's sketches to have anything on the reverse, which suggests this particular portrait has a different status to the others. It is possible that it was used as a piece of scrap after Anne Boleyn's fall and execution, then returned to the collection when the sheets of Holbein's sketches were assembled for the book which then passed into royal hands on Holbein's death in 1543.[58] There is a suggestion that the sketch of the Wyatt arms on the reverse could have been from the death of Henry Wyatt in November 1536, after Anne's death when the paper may have been used as scrap.[59] Another suggestion is that the Wyatt coat of arms on the reverse of the portrait suggests that the sitter is not Anne Boleyn, but actually Jane Haute, who in 1536 was preparing to marry Thomas Wyatt's son, Sir Thomas Wyatt, the Younger.[60] G.W. Bernard suggests that the sketch could be unfinished, and so the sitter could have been Anne, and that Holbein was adapting it for finishing later.[61] It does not seem like it would be unusual for an artist to do some preparatory sketches for a larger complete portrait, or even a miniature which was supposed to be looked at in private, and could explain the state of undress of the sitter.

The other Holbein sketch which has been suggested to be Anne, shows a woman in a gable hood with a square neckline dress; it is the less popular of the two and often glossed over. The dress and neckline do echo other portraits of Anne Boleyn's tenure as queen but the sitter lacks Anne's slender neck. Alison Weir describes this sketch as being of 'doubtful authenticity' as Anne's face is fuller than in other accepted portraits. But, at the same time, it is difficult to tell as the sitter is painted from a different angle.[62] It does seems unlikely that this is Anne Boleyn, as the face is perhaps too different to other images of Anne and actually echoes some of Holbein's sketches of some of the other ladies of the court. Anne probably would have wanted to differentiate herself from the other court ladies, in order to stand out. Her image would be designed to portray her difference in status, to show her as a queen; a display of her legitimate right to be on the throne and her daughter's right to be the heir.

Returning to the Royal Collection portrait of a women in deshabille, the caption was likely the result of the work of Sir John Cheke, tutor to Edward VI, who had known Anne Boleyn. He identified the drawings in a book acquired by Henry VIII after Holbein's death. That the names were written on the portraits throughout the book suggests that there was already some uncertainty about the identities.[63] Some labelling of sketches, including those of Thomas More's family, have proven to be incorrect, so we cannot necessarily take this at face value. However, John Cheke had been introduced by Dr William Butts to Henry VIII because of his interest in reform. Cheke 'must have known Anne' and 'of all the identifications he made it seems inconceivable that he could have been mistaken about this one'.[64] We will likely never know for sure, though, the true identity of the sitter.

These two sketches by Holbein may well have been preparation for either a head and shoulders portrait, a full-length portrait, or a miniature portrait of Anne Boleyn. Ives points out that compared to the image of Anne on the 1534 portrait medal, it would seem that she sat for neither of the Holbein drawings as there are no real similarities.[65] However, the facial shape does seem similar between the portrait medal and the Holbein deshabille sketch. Joanna Denny writes that it was 'nonsense' to believe that the queen would have sat for a portrait dressed like this.[66] If it was a preparatory sketch for a full portrait, it does make a certain amount of sense to get the contours of the face more easily, perhaps, and a sense of the movement of the person, without the restrictions of court clothing. The clothing could have been changed in the completed image. It was not unheard of for an artist to draw or paint the clothing separately, to be able to examine the cloth more closely without the sitter having to be there. Several of Holbein's male subjects appear in a state of undress, including Henry VIII's illegitimate son, Henry Fitzroy, but Anne Boleyn seems to be the only woman to do so.[67] Perhaps the chemise or nightgown that the sitter wears is one that was gifted to her by Henry VIII, listed in his privy purse accounts. On 17 June 1532 there is an entry for '13 yds. of black satin for a nightgown for lady Anne, at 8s., and taffeta, velvet and buckram for lining'.[68] It could be that Henry VIII commissioned a miniature of Anne wearing this intimate piece of clothing to be looked at privately. It certainly cannot be ruled out that this was the case.

Personally, it is difficult to believe that both of these sketches which have been said to be Anne are of the same woman. One, perhaps, could be Anne, though neither seems to echo the face shape we see in the National Portrait Gallery or Hever Castle portraits. Given these portraits were both painted decades after Anne's death, though, they are not conclusively accurate images of the queen. Both faces seem too rounded and not angular enough. It is more difficult to compare the sketches to the 1534 medal which is very damaged, though the rounded facial shape of the portrait medal and the Holbein deshabille sketch do look similar. The identification of the Royal Collection portrait was made by Sir John Cheke, who had known Anne. It seems possible, and even likely, that it was Anne and probably a preparation for a more complete portrait of the queen which is now lost.

Other Possible Images of Anne Boleyn

Many other portraits said to be of Anne Boleyn are different in style and the sitter looks like a different person in most of them. There is a miniature by Lucas Horenbout, now kept in the Royal Ontario Museum in Canada, along with a similar image in the collection of the Duke of Buccleuch and Queensberry from the Horenbout workshop. These are similar to the portrait known as the Nidd Hall portrait, held at the Bradford Art Galleries. In these, it is easy to see more of a resemblance to Henry VIII's third wife, Jane Seymour, or his first wife, Katherine of Aragon, than we can to Anne. This is because the sitters wear gable hoods rather than the French hood generally associated with Anne, and appear to lack the pointed chin, defined cheekbones and oval face that we can see in both the National Portrait Gallery and Hever Castle portraits, as well as the Chequers ring, which are the most accepted images of Anne aside from the portrait medal. However, as can be seen with the 1534 medal, Anne did wear a gable hood occasionally, possibly when she wanted to emphasise her position as rightful queen of England.

Joanna Denny, agrees with the interpretation that they are unlikely to be Anne, adding that the Horenbout miniature has been dated to between 1528 and 1532, too early for Anne as queen.[69] Antonia Fraser dates it even earlier, to around 1526.[70] However, one or both of them could perhaps have been commissioned by Henry VIII as images of his future wife and queen, and the woman he loved. By the logic of dating, however, it also rules out Jane Seymour as the sitter. Fraser identifies the Horenbout miniature as 'plausibly' the 'only contemporary likeness' of Anne Boleyn.[71] It does resemble both the National Portrait Gallery and Hever Castle portraits, though her eyes seem less hooded and her face more rounded, similar to the portrait medal and deshabille Holbein sketch, which features the French hood and the B pendant which marks the figure out as Anne.

In the Nidd Hall portrait, the sitter wears a brooch of a single pearl drop hanging from an AB initial. Historians have taken this as evidence that the sitter is Anne. However, Denny says that the AB initial was changed in copies of the portrait after 1618 to a square-cut jewel.[72] This was possibly because the portrait resembles what we know of Jane Seymour more than it does Anne Boleyn, though there does not seem to be a real explanation for why the change took place. This does not necessarily rule out the sitter as Anne Boleyn, however. It is always going to be difficult to know for sure, as with much information surrounding Anne Boleyn. The miniature is dated 'ano xxv' suggesting that the sitter was aged 25 when the painting was completed. If we take Anne's birth date as 1501 it would have been painted around 1526, which G.W. Bernard believes is too early for it to have been commissioned when Henry VIII fell in love with her.[73] Given that we cannot date the love letters or the beginning of the relationship, it is possible that Henry VIII could have had the image commissioned in 1526, right at the start of his infatuation with Anne. The same logic of dating could again be applied to Jane Seymour as the sitter, as she is believed to have been born around 1508/1509, meaning it would have been painted around 1533/1534, also placing it too early for it to have been painted when Henry VIII fell in love with her. The evidence is not particularly strong for either woman to be the sitter, though the AB initial is compelling evidence of it being a representation of Anne Boleyn.

The John Hoskins miniature, in the collection of the Duke of Buccleuch and Queensberry, echoes the Anne Boleyn seen in the National Portrait Gallery and Hever Castle portraits, though on a much smaller scale. It was likely made in the seventeenth century, slightly later than the National Portrait Gallery and Hever Rose panel portraits.[74] On the back of the miniature someone has written 'from an ancient original'. It seems likely that Hoskins had access to an earlier portrait of Anne, perhaps that from which the National Portrait Gallery and Hever Castle portraits originated, or the Lumley portrait said to be in existence as late as 1773.[75] The similarities are too many to be ignored, despite the Hoskins being a miniature and the other two being panel portraits. But where is the Lumley portrait now? Was it destroyed or could it be somewhere in a private collection, unrecognised for what it is?

* * *

The portraits, sketches, and other images and likenesses can give us a clue to Anne Boleyn's appearance and what might have made her so attractive to Henry VIII. Comparing portraits of Anne to those of Katherine of Aragon and Jane Seymour, Anne comes across as unusual, helping to popularise the French hood in England and standing out after an adolescence spent in the Low Countries and France, with European exoticism. The portraits we can probably be the surest of are the National Portrait Gallery and Hever Castle portrait as accepted Elizabethan representations of the queen's mother, the Chequers ring, likely from the same image as the Hever and National Portrait Gallery portraits, and the 1534 portrait medal. The medal is the only contemporary image we can conclusively date to Anne's reign as queen. The others are certainly later, with the ring from the reign of Anne's daughter, Elizabeth, and the two panel portraits are copies of a lost original, also probably Elizabethan, but accepted images of the queen's mother. Given the similarities to the Chequers ring and the panel portraits, the Hoskins miniature also seems likely to be Anne. The others are more contentious. Personally, it seems likely that the Holbein sketch of a woman in a coif and a nightgown or chemise is quite possibly Anne, a preparation for a more complete portrait that was maybe halted when she was arrested and executed. This could explain why the reverse of the sketch was possibly used as scrap, and could explain the Wyatt arms. It seems that only a queen might have the audacity and permission from her husband to sit for a portrait in such a state of deshabille before a trusted royal portrait painter like Hans Holbein.

Even today there is still ongoing debate over what Anne Boleyn looked like and there has been some discussion around trying to date the surviving images more accurately. Dr Owen Emmerson has suggested that there is some new research to be revealed, so we may yet have new information and discoveries to uncover. It is possible we may gain more certainty and information over what Anne actually looked like.

Chapter 2

Anne as Mistress

'*Noli me tangere* for Caesar's I am'[1]

The difficult thing in writing about Anne Boleyn is the paucity of surviving sources, particularly in her own hand, or that are unbiased. She provoked such strong opinions in her lifetime that many of the sources are very obviously biased against her. However, there are some works that survive that paint Anne in a very positive light, largely from before her tenure as queen of England and before she was better known across England and Europe. These come from her future husband, Henry VIII, and a rumoured lover, Sir Thomas Wyatt. We also have a letter written by Anne Boleyn to her father, Sir Thomas Boleyn, in 1513 from the court of Margaret of Austria at Mechelen in the Low Countries, when she was likely only around aged 12 or 13.

It is also important to examine the work of George Cavendish, a gentleman usher to Cardinal Thomas Wolsey, who wrote a biography of his master. He was in service to Wolsey from 1522 until Wolsey's death in 1530. Cavendish's account covers an important part of Anne's life when it was rumoured that she would marry Henry Percy, heir to the Earl of Northumberland, and the beginning of her relationship with Henry VIII. Legend says that it was the Cardinal who put a stop to Anne's relationship with Percy, and Anne declared that 'if it lay ever in her power, she would work the Cardinal as much displeasure' as he had done to her.[2] As indeed she would in the fullness of time. Cavendish had first-hand knowledge of many of the events of the period, though he is biased in favour of Wolsey and against Anne Boleyn, so we need to take his account with a pinch of salt.

In many ways, Anne's greatest power lay in her role as emotional mistress to Henry VIII. He confided in her and she had intimate knowledge of the king's thoughts and feelings as probably no one else at the time did, not Wolsey, or Suffolk, or later, Cromwell. That power ebbed once Anne gave herself physically to the king and they married. He expected a more demure and less demanding woman as a wife. Anne bridled against this expectation, not changing as the king expected from the role of mistress to that of wife. This was her major failure, aside from not giving birth to a son.

This chapter will examine the earliest known letter to survive written by Anne Boleyn to her father in 1513 from the Low Countries, the account of Cardinal Wolsey's gentleman usher, George Cavendish, the poetry of Sir Thomas Wyatt, and the love letters from Henry VIII to Anne Boleyn, along with the letter supposedly written from Anne to the king around the same time as the love letters he wrote to her. These sources show Anne's development from a girl to a desirable woman, to a future queen of England.

Letter from Anne Boleyn to Her Father from Mechelen

This is the earliest surviving letter from Anne Boleyn, written to her father, Thomas Boleyn, from the court of Margaret of Austria at Mechelen in the Low Countries. It is currently held at Corpus Christi College in Cambridge. The letter was written in French, which Anne was learning at the time and she was demonstrating her new knowledge to her father. Anne Boleyn probably left England in summer 1513 for the court of Margaret of Austria. She remained in the Low Countries only for around a year until mid-1514 when she travelled to France to serve the new French queen, Mary Tudor, sister to Henry VIII, who married Louis XII. At Margaret's court, Anne learnt French and was exposed to Renaissance ideas, even some early religious reformist ideas which would be further developed in France.

The letter demonstrates Anne's determination to please and honour her father, and to make a good impression when she returned to England, whenever that would be, as she talked about how her father desired her to be:

> …a worthy woman when I come to the Court and you inform me that the Queen will take the trouble to converse with me, which rejoices me much to think of talking with a person so wise and worthy.[3]

Being 'worthy' probably meant well-educated, versed in etiquette, dancing, singing, and embroidery. It meant that she would have the skills required to gain a good husband and bring benefits to her family. Anne hoped that the queen, Katherine of Aragon, would converse with her when she returned to England and took up a place at court. This would probably be in the queen's household, as her father was in a respected position in order to make this happen. Anne and Katherine are often considered to be rivals because of their later relationship, but here we can see that Anne looks up to Katherine and hopes to impress her. Anne wanted to make her father proud and bring benefits to her family. She could not have imagined when she wrote this letter the trajectory her life would take.

The letter is written in 'poor, scattered French for which the young Anne apologises'.[4] She says that the potential of speaking with Katherine of Aragon on her return to England would 'make me have greater desire to continue to speak French well and also spell, especially because you have so enjoined it on me' and that 'I beg you to excuse me if my letter is badly written, for I assure you that the orthography is from my own understanding alone, while the others were only written by my hand'.[5] This suggests that Anne had previously written to her father, but that her tutor, Symmonet, had drafted the letters for Anne in correct French and she had copied them out. This letter, as Anne explains, she wrote wholly by herself, so the French may not be entirely correct.

Anne must have been aware of how privileged she was to be at Margaret of Austria's court. She would be educated alongside Margaret's nieces and nephews, including the future Charles V. Anne had ended up at Mechelen because her father had been on embassy to Margaret's court in 1512 to broker negotiations for an alliance against France between Henry VIII and Margaret's father, Maximilian I, the Holy Roman Emperor. Thomas Boleyn's ability to cultivate important relationships is what led to Anne's appointment to Margaret's court.[6] It was this appointment which would give Anne her later flair, elegance, and allure, which would set her apart at the English court.

Few of Anne's letters survive today and the ones that do are from later in her life when she was at the English court. The existence of this letter today demonstrates that Thomas Boleyn kept this letter and shows 'just how proud he was of his daughter and of the impression she made in Brussels'.[7] She seemed to learn French quickly and this letter is evidence of her developing knowledge of the language, and that she was able to write a letter in slightly broken French by herself to her father.

George Cavendish's *The Life of Cardinal Wolsey*

George Cavendish was a gentleman usher to Cardinal Thomas Wolsey, and he wrote a biography of his master, which included several events involving Anne Boleyn. He is the main source for Anne's relationship with Henry Percy, later 6th Earl of Northumberland. Cavendish was there at the time serving Wolsey, though his work was not written in its final form until the reign of Mary I (1553–1558), as there is a reference in the manuscript to 'King Philip, now our sovereign lord', meaning Philip II of Spain, husband of Mary I, who she married in 1554.[8] So there was around a thirty-year gap between the events themselves and the writing of the manuscript. It is more than possible that Cavendish had made notes and part-written it much earlier, cementing it in its final form in the 1550s. Writing the book under Mary I, it would have been politic to write disparagingly of Anne Boleyn, as she was the woman who had been the catalyst for the divorce of Mary's parents, Henry VIII and Katherine of Aragon, as well as the English Reformation, which Mary tried to reverse.

The only thing we have from either Anne or Percy themselves regarding their relationship seems to be a brief letter from Percy in May 1536 when Anne was imprisoned in the Tower of London on charges of adultery and treason. Percy had been approached regarding the accusation that he and Anne had been betrothed, as that would give grounds for an annulment of the marriage between Henry VIII and Anne Boleyn. Percy denied it, writing to Cromwell on 13 May 1536 that, 'assuring you, Mr. Secretary, by the said oath and blessed body, which afore I received and hereafter intend to receive, that the same may be to my damnation if ever there were any contract or promise of marriage between her and me'.[9] Percy emphatically denied any long-lasting connection between himself and Anne, meaning that it probably was not the reason why Anne's marriage to Henry VIII was annulled. An alternative reason for the annulment was Henry's former relationship with Anne's sister, Mary. Cavendish's account offers valuable insight into perceptions of Anne before her marriage.

Cavendish says that Henry began to 'kindle the brand of amours' for Anne on her return from France, though in the beginning Anne did not know of it because she was involved with Henry Percy.[10] Any betrothal would need the king's permission, but this did not seem to occur to the young couple when Percy fell:

> … in dalliance among the queen's maidens, being at the last more conversant with Mistress Anne Boleyn than with any other; so that there grew such a secret love between them that, at length, they were ensured together, intending to marry.[11]

George Cavendish was present around court with Cardinal Wolsey at the time when this was happening, so he would likely have been aware of any kind of friendship or relationship within the bounds of the court and reported back to Wolsey. Whether we can be sure that the pair had reached the stage of a betrothal is unclear, or what kind of betrothal that was. However, Cavendish's reports of what followed suggests that there was some kind of intention for Henry Percy and Anne Boleyn to marry.

According to Cavendish's account, Henry VIII told Cardinal Wolsey of his feelings for Anne and asked him to break off the relationship and betrothal.[12] What is difficult to understand here is that Anne and Percy's relationship probably took place in the early 1520s, while we have no evidence for any kind of relationship between Henry and Anne Boleyn until around 1526 or 1527; so why the delay if Henry had feelings for her much earlier? Wolsey was said to have called Henry Percy to him and said, 'I marvel not a little ... of thy peevish folly, that thou wouldest tangle and ensure thyself with a foolish girl yonder in the court, I mean Anne Boleyn'.[13] In this scenario, Wolsey's opinion of the Boleyns is clear: they are not good enough to marry into the top echelons of the nobility, and Percy should aim higher, and listen to the wants of his king and father when choosing a bride. However, Percy declared that 'in this matter I have gone so far, before many so worthy witnesses, that I know not how to avoid myself nor to discharge my conscience'.[14] This suggests some kind of official betrothal between Percy and Anne that he believed it would not be easy to disentangle himself from. Henry Percy would marry Mary Talbot, the daughter of George Talbot, 4th Earl of Shrewsbury, soon after the dissolution of his relationship with Anne, who was considered to be a better match for the future earl of Northumberland. But the marriage would disintegrate, with no children born from it. Percy would become Earl of Northumberland in 1527 but die just a decade later, leaving everything to the king.

We also need to bear in mind that Cavendish's account was being written in the 1550s, over twenty years after the events it describes, so some recollections may be hazy or written with the benefit of hindsight. It is important not to necessarily take it at face value. Eric Ives writes of Cavendish's intent to portray Anne Boleyn as the agent of Venus, called in to humble Wolsey.[15] Thus his account may have been manipulated to suit his agenda. Ives also describes Anne's reaction in Cavendish's account as 'improbable', as making threats against the cardinal in around 1522 or 1523 was 'both unwise and childish, and Anne was neither'.[16] This was probably something Cavendish added with the benefit of hindsight, knowing that Anne would go on, almost inexplicably, to be in a position to do harm to the cardinal; it is a foreshadowing of what is to come.

Cavendish's account goes past Percy and Anne's relationship, to when Anne returned to court after a brief banishment and that the 'grudge, how it began, that in process of time burst out to the utter undoing of the cardinal'.[17] Anne soon came to know the king's feelings and 'the great love that he bare her in the bottom of his stomach', beginning to 'look very hault and stout, having all manner of jewels and rich apparel'.[18] There are no timings given in Cavendish's work, no years or months or any sense of how much time had passed so we cannot be sure when Anne and Percy's relationship took place, or when Anne came to know of the king's feelings, or when Wolsey was told either.

There were people around Anne, like her father and uncle, the Duke of Norfolk, who allegedly wanted to bring Wolsey down 'perceiving the great affection that the king bare lovingly unto Mistress Anne Boleyn, fantasying in their heads that she should be for them a sufficient and an apt instrument to bring their malicious purpose to pass'.[19] Anne did speak out against the cardinal to the king over time, asking 'what things hath he wrought within this realm to your great slander and dishonour' and 'is it not a marvellous thing to consider what debt and danger the cardinal hath brought you in with all your subjects?'.[20] However involved Anne was or was not with Wolsey's fall from power, after the disaster of the Blackfriars trial in 1529 and the case being recalled to Rome, he had failed the king, and Henry was not known for his forgiveness. On 9 October 1529 Wolsey was indicted for praemunire, which was the assertion of foreign authority in England against the will of the monarch, in this case the authority of the Pope.

Thomas Wyatt's Poetry

There is little evidence of just what Anne Boleyn's relationship was with either of the men she was linked to prior to her relationship with Henry VIII; Henry Percy, the future 6th Earl of Northumberland, and Sir Thomas Wyatt. Anne's relationships with both Percy and Wyatt affected her relationship with the king because of his suspicious nature but 'she touched their lives, as they did hers', and each left a lasting impression on the other.[21] Anne's romantic entanglements would affect her life more than she could have known. Percy would be asked about a precontract between him and Anne in order to annul her marriage to the king, and Wyatt would be arrested in 1536 alongside Anne's other 'lovers'. Anne's relationships with men would be used as an excuse to execute her.

Anne Boleyn's relationship with Thomas Wyatt has attracted more popular attention than her relationship with Henry Percy. This is probably due to poetry written by Wyatt supposedly about Anne, although there is no definitive evidence within them to prove the identity of the subject. Wyatt was nearly executed alongside Anne in 1536, although he was released after a short period in the Tower of London.[22] Because of this connection, many have assumed that Wyatt and Anne were very much in love and that their relationship may have been sexual. This is not helped by television shows like Showtime's *The Tudors* where Thomas Wyatt, played by Jamie Thomas King, says to Thomas Tallis, played by Joe van Moyland, 'for what it's worth I did fuck her'.[23] There is no evidence of a sexual relationship between them, or more than friendship given their family seats were relatively close – the Boleyns at Hever Castle and the Wyatts at Allington Castle. There is no indication of Anne's feelings for Wyatt and the only evidence of his feelings for her can be found in his poetry, much of which cannot definitively be attributed to being about Anne.

There are three shorter poems written by Thomas Wyatt which are certainly thought to be about Anne Boleyn, which perhaps offer more insight into his feelings for her. These will be examined as if they are definitely about Anne in this section. The poems are: *Whoso List to Hunt*, *Sometime I Fled the Fire*, and *If Waker Care*. The first, *Whoso List to Hunt*, outlines Wyatt's early feelings for Anne and how he backed off when Henry VIII made his interest in her clear. Wyatt could not compete with the king of England for a woman's affections. When Anne made it clear that she was choosing Henry VIII over him, Wyatt writes: '*noli me tangere*; for Caesar's I am'.[24] 'Noli me tangere' translates as 'do not touch me'. Anne was declaring that Wyatt could not touch her because she now belonged to someone higher and more powerful than he, stronger and more desirable than anyone else in England. Wyatt acknowledged that he did not have a chance with Anne as he 'farthest come behind' once Anne knew she had the interest of Henry VIII.[25] She would not choose a poet over a king. Wyatt knew Anne was ambitious so retired from the competition, admitting defeat.

Wyatt accepted the folly of trying to compete with a king – 'the vain travail hath wearied me so sore'.[26] Vain because he knew he would lose, but travail suggested it was hard work and Anne Boleyn was not a woman easily won. Henry VIII would also discover this. Although Anne agreed to marry him, it would take six years before the pair would marry and Henry would have Anne physically. Wyatt implied that his mind would not let go of Anne 'by no means my wearied mind draw from the deer'.[27] He maintained the metaphor of he and Henry as the hunters and Anne the prey by having her as the deer. Even though Wyatt relinquished the hunt, the prey was still on his mind. The last line of *Whoso List to Hunt* seems to sum Anne Boleyn up and although we cannot be sure the poem is about her, it is still apt: 'wild for to hold though I seem tame'.[28] Anne was difficult to trap or keep engaged, though she was good at projecting an image. However, under stress, the image would crack which happened as she began to lose the king in early 1536. Anne used her position as the prey to hold the king almost at arm's length, making Henry think he was hunting her, but it was Anne who refused to be the king's mistress.

Sometime I Fled the Fire is a metaphor for Wyatt's fiery feelings for Anne Boleyn. Wyatt says that he was burnt by his powerful feelings for her and fled the court to avoid them when she was being courted in earnest by Henry VIII.[29] He recognised that he may have overreached himself in his pursuit of Anne and that his efforts to curry favour could all have been in vain, as he was entangled in Henry and Anne's relationship at its most volatile 'and all his labour laughs he now to scorn'.[30] His efforts were futile with no chance of victory. The poem suggests that the relationship with Anne was 'of vital importance' to Wyatt and that it continued to affect his thoughts and actions.[31] This reflects what Wyatt had written in *Whoso List to Hunt* when he said, 'by no means my wearied mind draw from the deer'.[32] Wyatt could not stop thinking about Anne.

The poem must have been written around September or October 1532 as Wyatt refers to 'the coals I follow that be quent, from Dover to Calais, with willing mind'.[33] This is a reference to Henry and Anne's trip to Calais to meet with Francis I of France and gain his support for their upcoming marriage. Wyatt had previously been sent to the Vatican as part of a diplomatic mission to persuade the Pope to grant the king an annulment of his marriage to Katherine of Aragon to enable him to marry Anne. This was probably quite surreal for Wyatt; possibly even painful if we believe he really loved her. There is also a suggestion in the poem that Wyatt's love for Anne Boleyn was in the past rather than the present. He writes of 'how desire is both forth sprung and spent'.[34] Wyatt had gone past the point of believing he could ever have Anne and claimed his desire was now 'spent'. Whether his desire or love really had gone, or if he was trying to persuade himself or the king, if the poem came to his notice, is unclear.

The third poem is one which begins *If Waker care; if sudden pale colour*. This is a poem which has a very obvious change of wording. The line reads 'Brunet, that set my wealth in such a roar', but the line originally read 'Brunet, her that did set our country in a rore'.[35] This change of line may have been made after Anne Boleyn's execution to avoid it being so controversial, about a woman accused of treason, who Henry VIII was determined to wipe out any remaining signs of. It is difficult to think what other woman set a country 'in such a rore', and not just appealed to a man's heart. The poem begins on a note of longing or yearning 'if many sighs with little speech to plain'.[36] It suggests that Wyatt could only watch from afar as Henry VIII wooed and won Anne Boleyn. It gives a sense that Wyatt was pining after what he had lost. But after the 'Brunet' line, the tone changes and Wyatt focused more on his present and what had changed. The 'unfeigned cheer of Phyllis hath the place that Brunet had'.[37] Wyatt had another lady in his life who helped him to move on from Anne Boleyn. 'Phyllis' is possibly a reference to Elizabeth Darrell, Wyatt's long-term mistress who gave him three sons.

Whatever the relationship was, it continued to have implications for both Wyatt and Anne despite them both seeming to have moved on from it. There was danger even in continuing to reflect on the relationship with the woman who was queen of England from 1533. This is probably why none of Wyatt's poetry is explicitly about Anne and why the 'Brunet' line in *If Waker care* was later altered. This danger would be proven in Wyatt's arrest in May 1536, alongside the other men, though Wyatt did escape execution. In this way, Anne Boleyn's public image was shaped by something she could not control. Anne's image was affected by Thomas Wyatt's poems, and she could not counteract the implied feelings in them. There is no evidence of Anne speaking out against anything

Wyatt had said in his poetry either. We have no confirmation of how the poems were received at court, though Wyatt's inclusion as a possible lover in May 1536 suggests that the king or Cromwell may have used their relationship against him. Today, the poems are sometimes seen as evidence of a romantic relationship between the pair, or unrequited feelings from Wyatt towards Anne Boleyn.

Thomas Wyatt was very much embroiled in court life, as was Anne Boleyn. It was possibly this which drew them together, and they had known each other for most of their lives, with their childhood homes being fairly close to each other in Kent.[38] David Loades, however, says that their relationship was 'anti-Boleyn propaganda' of later years and calls it 'infatuation' written in 'cryptic verse' on the part of Wyatt, but fails to mention Anne's possible emotional involvement.[39] Josephine Wilkinson does suggest that historians need not look at Wyatt's poetry for evidence of a connection. She relates a story where Wyatt visited Anne and found her in bed. Allegedly, Wyatt then told Anne that he loved her then kissed her, and she did not stop him.[40] This story came from Martin Hume who was a Victorian writer, and author of the *Chronicle of King Henry VIII*.[41] Wyatt was 'honest and indiscreet' in his writing about Thomas Cromwell posthumously, so we can assume he may well have been the same after Anne Boleyn's execution, although we cannot confirm this.[42] Retha Warnicke has claimed that the love triangle between Anne, Wyatt and Henry VIII is 'another of the myths obscuring her role in Reformation politics' and should be abandoned, seeing that Anne's religion was more important than her relationships.[43] But this opinion should be discarded as Anne Boleyn's early relationships affected her marriage and, although it is not known for certain, her relationship with Henry Percy was possibly used as a reason to annul Anne's marriage to Henry. It was Henry VIII's suspicions and paranoia over Anne's associations with men at the English court that caused her fall and execution, so it is important not to underestimate the significance of Anne and Wyatt's relationship.

Love Letters from Henry VIII to Anne Boleyn

Henry VIII's love letters to Anne Boleyn are a window into the mind of a king having fallen hopelessly in love with a woman at his court, a lady serving in the household of his wife and queen. The letters survive supposedly because they were secretly taken from England by Cardinal Campeggio and now reside in the Vatican Archives.[44] The letters are available to view online since the Vatican Archives have digitised them.[45] It gives a frisson of excitement to see Henry's writing and the little hearts he draws around Anne's initials in the signatures of the letters. He was madly in love. David Starkey wrote that the letters were a testament to Henry VIII's grand passion for Anne Boleyn which pulled England apart.[46] Henry's signatures certainly demonstrate his love and devotion. It was Henry's love for Anne and his determination to marry her that was the catalyst for the Break with Rome and the English Reformation. However, Anne's exact involvement in these events remains clouded and unclear. We do not even know exactly when Anne agreed to marry Henry but once the agreement was made, they believed they would be able to marry within months. The many years of political wrangling that would follow were unexpected and frustrating. Henry's love and desire for Anne was seemingly the most intense of his life. We do not see the same level of passion and devotion to any of his other wives or mistresses.

The sequence and timing of the love letters Henry VIII wrote to Anne Boleyn in the 1520s can be problematic as none of them are dated, so we can only work on inferences from comments made in the letters themselves. There have been a variety of suggestions from historians, although none seem to fully concur. Retha Warnicke claims that the earliest letters from Henry must have been written in around 1528.[47] She rejects an earlier date that other historians have suggested, such as David Starkey, who dates the letters to the winter of 1524.[48] Karen Lindsey also dates the letters to around 1524, at about the time of the end of Anne's liaison with Henry Percy.[49] Lindsey assumes that Henry's interest in Anne was the reason for the end of her relationship with Percy. If this is the case, it seems unusual that Henry would have waited so long to have instigated divorce proceedings to make Anne his. This earlier date is largely rejected because there is no evidence of a relationship between Henry and Anne prior to 1527 and one of what is assumed to be from the earliest batch of letters claims that Henry had 'been for the whole year stricken with the dart of love'.[50] Hence, according to Warnicke, this has to date the earliest letters to 1528. However, although Henry appears to have been in love for a year, this does not denote any kind of a relationship or agreement between them, though Henry's character suggests that he would just go after what he wanted. Contrary to Warnicke, Joanna Denny has asserted that Henry's interest in Anne began in 1525.[51] She uses the same logic as Warnicke – 'struck with the dart of love' for over a year – but uses it in a different way to date the earliest letters to 1526. David Loades appears to agree with Denny's logic, 'tentatively dating' the first letter to autumn 1526.[52] Also in agreement with autumn 1526 as the date of Henry's first letter to Anne is Eric Ives.[53] This reasoning places Henry's first interest in Anne to early 1526.

Backing up this reasoning, G.W. Bernard suggests that, as Henry VIII first explored an annulment of his marriage to Katherine of Aragon in May 1527, the latest that he and Anne could have committed to each other was August of that year.[54] Bernard asserts that the reason for this date was that August 1527 was when Henry drafted the dispensation for the Pope to allow him to marry

Anne once free of Katherine, despite a prior relationship within the forbidden degrees of affinity. This does make sense and means that Warnicke's reasoning is faulty. The arguments of Loades, Denny and Bernard, therefore, seem to be the most likely. The dating of these letters is essential to understanding more about Anne Boleyn's role in the divorce proceedings. If Henry and Anne had not committed to each other prior to summer 1527 then Anne was not the primary reason for the Great Matter.

What is frustrating for historians looking at Anne Boleyn's life is that we only have Henry VIII's letters to Anne and not hers to him. We supposedly have one of Anne's letters to Henry, probably from early on in their courtship given the content, but we cannot glean much from it compared to the wealth of information we can get from Henry's letters. Henry was open about how he was feeling and his frustration that Anne seemed to have held herself back from him. Elizabeth Norton says that there is 'considerable doubt over the authenticity' of the letter attributed to Anne, and it must 'be viewed with a great deal of suspicion'.[55] In the letter, Anne is almost overly appreciative of Henry, perhaps playing to his ego, almost further than the bounds of courtly love. She claims that she feels joy 'in being loved by a king whom I adore' and says she would willingly sacrifice her heart 'if fortune had rendered it worthy of being offered to him'.[56] The implication is clear – that she sees herself as unworthy to have his attentions bestowed upon her. She may have considered herself even more unworthy to be queen of England, given that Henry's first wife was Katherine of Aragon: a Spanish princess, and aunt to the Holy Roman Emperor, Charles V.

This early letter, if genuine, could merely be a part of the ritual of courtly love, which was essential to the royal court. It meant that people could flirt without any obligation, and it kept the court alive and exciting. Anne's professed modesty in the letter was also in line with the expectations of a subject's deference towards her king. If this is an early letter, dating possibly from the beginning of 1527 or even 1526 at a push, then there was not yet a suggestion that Anne could be queen. At first, it seems as though Henry VIII was not considering marriage to Anne, but more some kind of sexual liaison like that he enjoyed with Anne's sister, Mary Boleyn. There seems relatively little written on this surviving letter of Anne's, though it does fall at a pivotal point in her life. Perhaps because it tells us so little compared to Henry's letters, and the authenticity is in doubt, it is often disregarded.

Henry VIII's surviving love letters to Anne Boleyn are genuine. There is no doubt over their authenticity. Nine of the seventeen surviving letters are written in French and eight in English. As discussed, the dating of the letters is unclear, as is the sequence. Elizabeth Norton in her book *Anne Boleyn in Her Own Words and the Words of Those Who Knew Her* sets out a 'probable order' of the letters and quotes them in full, putting the one which begins 'my mistress and friend' and speaks of the king gifting Anne 'my picture set in bracelets' as the first in the series.[57] However, reading Eric Ives's analysis of the letters, he places this letter seventh in the sequence. The letter that Ives places first, Norton places tenth; Henry sent Anne a 'buck, killed late last night by my own hand'.[58] There is little discussion on why the letters are placed in the orders they are by historians, though some are easier to place in a particular year or even month as they discuss the sweating sickness outbreak in 1528, or the arrival of Cardinal Campeggio in England also in 1528 for the Blackfriars trial in 1529. These letters logically probably come towards the end of the sequence as Anne then returned to court so there was no need for any more letters between them.

The main point which comes across from Henry VIII's letters to Anne Boleyn is that he wanted her more, precisely because she would not let him have her. Henry was so used to women falling at his feet and being able to have what he wanted that, when someone said no, he wanted them more. There are parallels with Adam and Eve and the forbidden fruit. In one letter to Anne, Henry complained that she kept him at a distance 'both from speech and the person of the woman that I esteem most in the world' and that 'absence from you grieves me sorely'.[59] What this suggests is that Henry accepted that he could not possess Anne physically, but that he wanted all of her affection and love for himself, and he wanted her to be near him. The letters tended to be written when Anne was away from court at Hever Castle in Kent, which was her family's home. She retreated there when things got difficult, like during the Blackfriars trial in 1529 when it was better that she stayed out of sight. Possibly the compliments and esteem that Henry endowed Anne with were his attempt to wear her down and convince her that she was all he wanted. Seth Lerer, in his book on courtly letters, suggests that 'if the king's hand is the instrument of love, it is also the tool of violence'.[60] This view is enhanced by one particular gift the king sent to Anne at Hever: – a buck he killed with his own hand. According to Denny, this gift demonstrated 'barely suppressed sexual violence'.[61] Courtly love usually sees women being gifted with small jewels or material for dresses, or ribbons and other trinkets, so this appears to be outside the norm. A buck is a strong-willed animal with survival instincts, but also prey to humans. It puts an audience in mind of Anne herself; the prey being hunted by a king, ultimately captured, echoing sentiments from Wyatt's poetry.

Henry VIII sent Anne Boleyn gifts which we know about through the letters, including a picture of himself in addition to the buck killed by the king's own hand. However, the only record remaining of a gift Anne sent to Henry during their early courtship exists in the love letters:

> For a present so beautiful that nothing could be more so (considering the whole of it), I thank you most cordially, not only on account of the fine diamond and the ship in which the solitary damsel is tossed about, but chiefly for the fine interpretation and the too humble submission which your goodness hath used towards me in this case.[62]

Anne appeared to be fond of symbolism and chose to submit to Henry in the form of a visual image. Most historians appear to accept the connotations of the different elements, but it is the meaning which encourages debate. The ship means protection, like the ark that protected Noah in the Bible. The woman supposedly represented Anne herself, while the diamond demonstrated her faithful and unwavering relationship with Henry. She wanted Henry to protect her, knowing that their relationship would make waves and there would be dissenters. Henry writes '*Aut illic, aut nullibi*' meaning 'either there or nowhere'.[63] Henry was determined to be with Anne, body and soul, or not to live, is the undertone. This is probably an exaggeration but demonstrates the king's obsession with and devotion to Anne. This seeming obsession may have led to a later accusation that he had been bewitched by her.[64] Geoffrey Chaucer's *The Romaunt of the Rose* describes a 'herte as hard as Diamaunt, Stedfast, and naught pliaunt' meaning 'heart as hard as a diamond, steadfast and never-changing'.[65] Carolly Erickson suggests that the ship was an 'allegory of Anne's own tempest-tossed life'.[66] Anne's life had certainly not been straightforward, even up to her controversial relationship with Henry VIII. There was the question in the early 1520s over her potentially inappropriate relationship with Thomas Wyatt, and the possible broken engagement with Henry Percy. There was also her proposed marriage to James Butler which fell through. The gift was a clever way for Anne to acquiesce to Henry, and he was delighted that she agreed to marry him. It is an early example of Anne's witticism and command of imagery which would also be demonstrated in her badge as queen: a crowned white falcon holding a sceptre rising out of a bed of Tudor roses.

Many of the love letters highlight Henry VIII's sexual passion for Anne, based around the lure of her body, rather than the emotions she raises in him. Possibly the most memorable line of the letters is that Henry wished himself '(especially in the evening) in my sweetheart's arms, who pretty dukkys I trust shortly to cusse'.[67] The word 'dukkys' is used to refer to Anne's breasts, and 'cusse' is to kiss. Although it seems unlikely that their relationship went as far as consummation, at least before autumn 1532, this line in particular suggests that there was at least some kind of physical element to the relationship. Possibly Anne allowed Henry some access to her body to keep him attracted to her over the seven years of their courtship, as otherwise perhaps it is difficult to imagine how she managed to keep his interest piqued for so long. Gradually granting the king more access to her body would keep him wanting more. Seth Lerer claims that the intimacy within the relationship, as demonstrated in some of the letters, was a literary ploy as Henry needed some love and comfort to contrast with the pain and hardship of the divorce.[68] This would make sense; Henry consoled himself with thoughts of what he and Anne could have when his divorce from Katherine of Aragon was eventually granted. It would make it easier to face Katherine and deal with the problems arising from her stubbornness, believing that it would end, and he would be happy with Anne.

In summer 1528, an outbreak of the sweating sickness spread through England. We can date a couple of Henry's love letters to this period. One letter which Norton places third in the sequence says that:

> For when we were at Walton, two ushers, two valets de chambre, and your brother, fell ill, but are now quite well; and since we have returned to your house at Hunsdon, we have been perfectly well, and have not, at present, one sick person, God be praised; and I think, if you would retire from Surrey, as we did, you would escape all danger. There is another thing that may comfort you, which is, that, in truth, in this distemper few or no women have been taken ill, and, what is more, no person of our court, and few elsewhere, have died of it.[69]

Henry obviously cared deeply about Anne and was trying to calm and reassure her, and no doubt himself, about the sickness that was spreading. The letter clearly says that Anne's brother, George, had been taken ill but recovered. Another letter then says that Henry had received 'afflicting news' of 'the illness of my mistress, whom I esteem more than all the world, and whose health I desire as I do my own, so that I would gladly bear half your illness to make you well'.[70] This is quite a substantial thing for Henry to say. Henry was notoriously scared of any kind of illness, 'petrified' and fled at the first sign of it.[71] So the fact that he would say he would bear half of Anne's illness to make her well, is a sign of the level of his devotion to her and love for her.

Anne appears to have told Henry of her fears that he would abandon her and put her aside, but Henry attempted to allay these fears, calling her 'entirely beloved' and asking her not to be 'uneasy' at his absence.[72] Anne knew that Henry was at Hunsdon when she was at Hever, spending time with Katherine of Aragon and Princess Mary. She was obviously worried that, in her absence, Katherine would persuade Henry to abandon his divorce and return to her.[73] However, Henry was well aware that, should he die, the realm may have fallen back into civil war, a repeat of the Wars of the Roses, as there was no male heir of his body to succeed him, and several potential claimants. Henry's daughter, Princess Mary, could have been competing with Henry's Scottish nephew, James V, and Henry Pole, 1st Baron Montagu, the great-nephew of both Edward IV and Richard III.

What complicates the implications from the love letters is that we only have half of the conversation. Anne's letters are missing and so we have to infer from Henry's letters what Anne said to him and what she thought. Her answers would add so much to our knowledge of both Anne's character and the development of her relationship with Henry VIII. However, it seems almost certain that Anne's letters were destroyed, quite possibly by Henry VIII himself, and we will never know what was in them. It is possible that Henry wanted to remove any trace of Anne after her execution in 1536 and it is likely that her letters to him were destroyed as part of this purge.

The historian Lacey Baldwin Smith claims that the love letters tell us nothing important, except that Henry was 'head over heels in love' with Anne.[74] This is inaccurate, as the letters reveal so much about the development of the relationship in a personal rather than political context. This is important as the relationship between Henry and Anne was so essential to the changing political landscape in the late 1520s and 1530s. Seeing the passion and love in Henry's letters to Anne makes you wonder how he could pursue her for six or seven years, break with the Church in England to marry her, and then execute her just three years later. That is what is difficult to understand. But the letters do give us a sense of how Henry viewed Anne at the beginning of their relationship.

* * *

Anne Boleyn was the focus of Henry VIII's devotion and passion for the seven years of their courtship. We can see the level of his love for her in his surviving letters. But it was not just the king who appears to have had some kind of a relationship with Anne; also the poet Sir Thomas Wyatt and Henry Percy, later 6th Earl of Northumberland. Wyatt wrote cryptic poetry which we cannot be sure is even about Anne, while the evidence for Percy's relationship comes from Wolsey's gentleman usher, George Cavendish, not his own words. It is difficult to figure out the exact nature of these early relationships as there are missing documents and cryptic references, and we will, in all likelihood, never know the truth.

The letter written in Anne's own hand to her father is an insight into her own mind. Very little survives from Anne herself, and those few documents we do have are very controversial and often disputed, so this is a tantalising glimpse into what she thought her life would be and how she envisioned herself. Anne was already fashioning her own image of herself.

With hindsight, we know that Anne captured Henry's heart and, in all likelihood, he hers. Anne was at the height of happiness and power, then crashed into the depths of despair. Anne's ambition was her death, and her relationship with Henry VIII helped her to the pinnacle of her ambition. Then he crushed her and forgot his love for her because she failed to fulfil her main role as a wife and consort and give the king a son. The king broke with the Roman Catholic Church, abandoned his first wife, and destroyed his relationship with his eldest daughter all because he believed Anne would give him a son. She failed and this had a huge effect on her public image for centuries. Anne's role as a mistress put her at the centre of the king's world, but a pedestal is not a safe place to be when you cannot achieve what is expected of you, especially when that expectation comes from a king.

Chapter 3

Anne as Queen and Mother

'Behold and see the Falcon White'[1]

Henry VIII spent seven years endeavouring to marry Anne Boleyn. Their marriage lasted just over three years, or only a thousand days (to be precise 1,083 days from coronation to execution), before Henry had Anne beheaded on charges of adultery, incest and treason. However, Anne's period as queen of England was revolutionary. Not only had Henry broken with the Roman Catholic Church in order to marry her, but new acts were introduced during her reign, including the Treason Act 1534 and the Act of Succession 1534. These were intended to cement Henry and Anne's marriage and the rights of their children to succeed to the throne above all others. Anne and her children were to displace Katherine of Aragon and her daughter, Princess Mary. This was likely the basis, along with their religious differences, for the difficult relationship Mary and Elizabeth had in later life after their father's death. Anne's queenship had far-reaching consequences into the lives of her daughter, and the English people.

Anne's queenship was legitimised by her coronation on 1 June 1533, when she was already pregnant with the future Elizabeth I. There is then evidence of Anne's relationship with her daughter, Elizabeth, born on 7 September 1533, along with the many acts and official documents which were used to support Henry and Anne's marriage, and Anne's position as queen. Tracy Borman's recent research on the relationship between Anne and Elizabeth has been invaluable. She suggests that our focus on the six wives, or whether Elizabeth I really was a virgin queen, means that, 'along the way, we have missed the most fascinating relationship of all: that between a mother and daughter who changed the course of British history'.[2] It is often assumed that, as Elizabeth was not yet 3 years old when her mother was executed, Anne cannot have had much influence over Elizabeth and her life, but it is far more complex. Elizabeth's relationships were complex with many of the people in her own life and throughout her reign, and her relationship with her mother often seems hidden. A shining example of Elizabeth's dedication to her mother's memory was taking her white falcon badge as her own when she became queen in 1558.

Anne Boleyn as Henry VIII's mistress was a very different role to that she played as a queen and mother. Anne as a mistress had a lot more agency and authority, as she could, in theory at least, walk away at any time, so the king was dancing around her in order to keep her. Once she was married, crowned, and had a child, all of which took place in under a year, Anne could not just walk away. She was in the relationship for the long haul. She had given up a lot of the power she had as a mistress, and was now completely answerable to her husband and king. So, when Henry decided to end her queenship, and her life, she was powerless to do anything about it. But Anne had done her best to be a good queen and mother to her daughter, and did her best to provide the king with a son. When Henry and Anne worked together for his divorce they shared the same goal, and their joint resolve went into achieving that. When they were married, 'they were no longer hunting the same quarry'.[3] This divided them, leaving them with the only common goal of a son, which Anne failed to deliver on for Henry.

It was not enough for Henry VIII that she failed to give him a son, despite him pursuing her for seven years in order for them to marry. In this chapter, however, we will not focus on how the marriage ended, but we will instead examine the triumphs of Anne's queenship including the verses and pageants composed for her coronation, her relationship with her daughter, Elizabeth, and the account written later by George Wyatt, the grandson of Anne's rumoured lover, Sir Thomas Wyatt the Elder. These will help us to understand a little better the position Anne was in as queen and how she did her best to meet the challenges and expectations put upon her.

Coronation Pageants and Verses

Anne Boleyn was crowned at Westminster Abbey on 1 June 1533, already visibly pregnant with the future Queen Elizabeth I who would be born just three months later. It would have been exhausting for her to go through days of pageants and long ceremonies at six months pregnant. This coronation was a 'dramatic statement that Henry VIII was 100 percent committed to his new queen and their child, whatever Catholic Europe or many of his subjects and nobility might think'.[4] Henry was declaring before the world that Anne Boleyn was his rightful queen, and their children were the future heirs. Failure to recognise this would soon be made treason by the 1534 Treason Act. The verses and pageants which were written and performed in Anne's coronation pageant reflected these ideas: her rightful place on the throne and the legitimacy of her heirs. This was as opposed to the claims of Katherine of Aragon to be the rightful queen and her daughter, Princess Mary (soon to be demoted by her father to Lady Mary), to be the rightful heir to the English throne.

At the coronations of all the Tudor monarchs, and those before and after as well, pageants were a key part of the coronation procession, enacted throughout the streets of London, from the Tower of London to Westminster, prior to the crowning itself. They were used as propaganda to promote certain ideas and assert the monarch's divine right to the throne. It was also a way for the monarch to show themselves to the people and gain their trust and support. Typically, in the Tudor period, pageants were put on at Gracechurch Street, Cornhill, and Cheapside, among others.[5] Anne Boleyn's coronation, though that of a consort rather than a regnant monarch, was no different. Verses were written in her honour by loyal reformers like Nicholas Udall and John Leland.[6] Even in the writing of the verses the religious element was of paramount importance to both Henry and Anne, to show her as devout and a fitting woman to be queen. In order to understand some of the allusions in the verses, it is important to understand what the pageants were representing, and why and how they related to the new Queen Anne.

An anonymous text written in 1533 gives us some insight into Anne's coronation from a person who was actually there and was relatively unbiased.[7] It appears unbiased because it mainly reports precisely what happened rather than relying on opinions or gossip, though it is possible it was a government report of the coronation to be spread across the country to validate Anne's queenship. Conversely, Eustace Chapuys, as a servant of the Emperor Charles V, was biased against Anne, and there are many letters and reports from him which survive. One describes the coronation as a 'cold, poor, and most unpleasing sight'.[8] But it is important to take Chapuys' assertions with a pinch of salt, not forgetting that he always refused to call Anne queen, or her daughter a princess, instead referring to them as 'the lady' or 'the concubine', and 'the bastard' respectively.

What is particularly intriguing about the coronation verse is just how often Anne Boleyn's badge of the falcon is used, particularly at Leadenhall in a pageant about St Anne. St Anne was said to be the mother of the Virgin Mary, and thus the grandmother of Jesus Christ, and was venerated as such. Making a connection from St Anne to Anne Boleyn as she was about to be crowned was symbolic of the hope of her producing such prodigal offspring:

> Behold and see the Falcon White!
> How she beginneth her wings to spread,
> And for our comfort take her flight.
> But where will she cease, as you do read?
> A rare sight! And yet to be joyed.

On the Rose; chief flower that ever was,
This bird to 'light, that all birds doth pass!
Honour and grace be to our Queen Anne!
For whose cause an Angel celestial
Descendeth, the Falcon white as swan,
To crown with a Diadem Imperial!
In her honour rejoice we all.
For it Cometh from God, and not of man.[9]

The description of a 'Falcon White' being crowned with an Imperial crown 'cometh from God' was designed to demonstrate Anne's fitness for the throne and almost that it was meant to be, as she was chosen by God and the king to be queen of England. Henry VIII was determined that the people would accept Anne Boleyn as queen, over Katherine of Aragon, and their children over Princess Mary. There was no reason to think that the child in Anne's belly during her coronation was not the son and heir they both wanted and hoped for. Anne knew that her position depended upon a son.

The falcon itself appears to be a metaphor for Anne, with the colour white said to represent chastity and virginity. The idea of an Imperial crown suggests that Henry was growing into his power, more of an emperor than a king, ruling over multiple territories. A falcon is a bird of prey, beautiful but ruthless, perhaps a symbol that Anne would not give up her hard-won position easily and would take down anyone she needed to. Eric Ives points out that the white falcon was also representative of Anne's links to the Butler family and the earls of Ormond, a title which Anne's father, Thomas Boleyn, had held since 1529.[10] These multiple meanings suggest that Henry was trying to counteract assertions that Anne's ancestry was not good enough for her to be worthy of being queen, and the mother of the heir to the throne.

All of the language used in the verses is positive and hints at not only an acceptance of Anne as queen, but also the joy that the future will have with her as queen for the whole country. Descriptions like 'excellent Queen', 'bounteous lady', 'Queen most excellent' and 'Dear Lady' are used possibly to try and endear Anne to the people.[11] However, it was also about more than that. It was about ensuring that no one would try to unseat her or speak against the marriage or their future children. If the marriage was not accepted, then their offspring would not be considered legitimate. These ideas were enshrined in the 1534 Act of Succession. Some accounts of the coronation suggests that these positive images of Anne Boleyn do not appear to have worked. Chapuys called Anne the 'Concubine' and reported back to Charles V on the coronation. In a letter dated 16 June 1533 to the Emperor, Chapuys described the coronation as 'a cold, poor, and most unpleasing sight to the great regret, annoyance, and disappointment not only of the common people but likewise of all the rest, so much so that public indignation has apparently increased by one half since the said coronation'.[12] Chapuys was naturally biased against Anne, so may have exaggerated some of the hostility towards Anne, though Charles V would still expect Chapuys to report the truth of what he had seen and experienced, but it is worth considering that he may have interpreted things in his own way, as with any source either for or against. Anne Boleyn was, and still is today, a polarising figure.

At Cornhill, there was a pageant of the Three Graces: Aglaia, Thaleia, and Euphrosyne, who praised the new queen and wished her well. Each Grace stood for a different characteristic: 'hearty gladness', 'stable honour', and 'continual success', respectively. It was written in three verses, the opening lines of each below:

> Aglaia. Hearty gladness.
> Queen Anne! Whom to see, this City doth rejoice;
> We three Graces, Ladies of all pleasance,
> Clasped hand in hand, as of one mind and voice …
>
> Thaleia. Stable honour.
> And I, Stable Honour, gracious Queen Anne!
> In honour and dignity, all that I can,
> Shall you advance! As your Grace is most worthy …
>
> Euphrosyne. Continual success.
> And for the great virtues, which I perceive
> To be in your Grace, so high and excellent![13]

Anne was officially queen after the ceremony on 1 June 1533; it was the pinnacle of her power. She was imbued with divine acceptance and anointed with the holy oil. She hoped and prayed that she would give birth to a son to carry on the Tudor dynasty. Anne was honoured by the king, and, in return, she was expected to provide him with a son and make the country stable with respect to the succession. She hoped to be successful, not just in birthing a live son, but in promoting Church reform, poor relief, and the new monarchy. She had large ambitions. It is a great unanswered question of what kind of queen Anne Boleyn would and could have been, had she given the king a son and kept her head.

In particular, the verses composed for Anne Boleyn's coronation demonstrate that Henry VIII was worried about what the people would think of his new queen, and so he was determined to make every effort to endear Anne to them. Alison Weir claimed that Henry VIII had spared no expense on the event, but that the people were still cold towards their new queen and the event intended to celebrate her.[14] Anne had replaced a very popular and pious queen who was languishing in the countryside, having been banished from the royal court. Katherine of Aragon would remain popular and favoured, after her death, their loyalty would move to Katherine's daughter, Mary. Anne Boleyn would not be popular during her lifetime with the English populace, but her daughter, Elizabeth, would be the ultimate queen: popular and powerful.

Treason Act and Act of Succession 1534

New acts were introduced through parliament in 1533 and 1534 in order to secure the rights of Anne Boleyn as queen and her children as heirs to the crown, as well as to cement the Break with Rome and the king as Head of the Church in England. Henry VIII was determined to ensure that Katherine of Aragon and Princess Mary would be supplanted by Anne Boleyn and her children. The Act of Succession embodied in law that the succession lay with the children of Henry VIII and Anne Boleyn, declaring Princess Mary illegitimate. The Treason Act meant that it would be treason to deny Anne Boleyn as queen or her children as heirs, or to call Katherine of Aragon queen or her daughter, Mary, princess.

Beginning with the Act of Succession, the act itself starts by asking the king to 'foresee and provide for the perfect surety of both you, and of your most lawful succession and heirs'.[15] With this act made law in 1534, just a year after Henry VIII's marriage to Anne Boleyn, it is obvious that it is intended that the lawful heirs be their children, and not those of Henry and Katherine of Aragon. The act harks back to the Wars of the Roses, reminding people of the 'great divisions which in times past have been in this realm, by reason for several titles pretended to the imperial crown of the same'.[16] The wording is invoking a sense of fear that England could return to the same uncertainty if this act is not passed, where both Mary and Elizabeth could make a claim on the throne if Anne failed to have a son. However, the hope at the beginning of 1534 is that Anne will have a son, and the Act of Succession is intended to ensure that he is seen as legitimate and the legal heir to the throne. But that acceptance begins with an acknowledgement of Princess Elizabeth as legitimate and the now Lady Mary as not.

There is some potentially inflammatory speech at the beginning of the act about the 'Bishop of Rome and see apostolic' and how they have 'presumed, in times past' to 'invest who should please them' as monarch in England which the king's English subjects 'abhor and detest'.[17] The implication is that the Pope has no such power in England any longer. He may want Katherine of Aragon to be restored as queen, and Princess Mary as the heir, but that is not what will happen. There is also a distinct sense that those who drafted the act are demonstrating their absolute loyalty to the king in declaring their distaste for the Pope and the papal see in the introduction to the act, and a tacit approval of the measures Henry VIII implemented in order to marry Anne Boleyn.

The act quickly goes on to establish that the marriage between Henry VIII and his first wife, Katherine of Aragon, was declared null and void, 'absolutely declared, deemed, and adjudged to be against the laws of Almighty God, and also, accepted, reputed, and taken of no value or effect, but utterly void and annulled'.[18] The assumption is therefore that their issue is illegitimate. Following immediately on the heels of this declaration is the acknowledgment of the validity of the subsequent marriage of Henry VIII and his second wife, Anne Boleyn:

> That the lawful matrimony had and solemnised between your highness and your most dear and entirely beloved wife Queen Anne, shall be established, and taken for undoubtful, true, sincere and perfect ever hereafter, according to the just judgment of the said Thomas, archbishop of Canterbury, metropolitan and primate of all this realm, whose grounds of judgment have been confirmed, as well by the whole clergy of this realm in both the Convocations, and by both the universities hereof.[19]

Of course, Henry VIII considered Anne Boleyn to be his first wife at this time, as he would also later consider Jane Seymour. Henry believed he had never been married to Katherine of Aragon and so his first marriage took place in 1533 in his mind. The wording of the act establishes the basis of the marriage as love in the description of Anne as the king's 'dear and entirely beloved wife'. With hindsight, it is ironic that the marriage is declared 'perfect ever hereafter' by Archbishop Thomas Cranmer, when that same man would declare the marriage null and void less than three years later at the king's request, as his wife was imprisoned in the Tower of London awaiting execution. The Succession Act came into being alongside the Treason Act which made it treason to support the Pope's attempts to stand against Henry's second marriage; the act intended to set out clearly that the second marriage to Anne Boleyn was the legal one. There are notes in Cromwell's hand as the bill was drafted, as Cromwell wanted to make it treason not just to attack the marriage overtly in deeds or writing, but also in word only, and advisers shied away from this.[20] However, it seems Cromwell got his way, as the Succession Act states that it would be treason 'if any person or persons … by any words, without writing, or any exterior deed or act, maliciously and obstinately shall publish, divulge, or utter any things' against the king's life, his marriage to Anne Boleyn, or their issue.[21] Anne Boleyn, in May 1536, could have been condemned under this act which was designed to protect her and her children, because she made a comment to Sir Henry Norris that, 'you look for dead men's shoes, for if aught come to the king but good, you would look to have me'.[22] In having this conversation with Norris, Anne 'had unwittingly handed her enemies the means with which to destroy her'.[23] Under the terms of the act, speaking against the king's life was treason, and Anne had done just that.

What is interesting about the act is that it states that papal dispensations for marriages within the forbidden degrees of affinity, for instance, to allow a man to marry his dead brother's wife, like in the case of Henry VIII and Katherine of Aragon, 'of right ought not to be granted, admitted, nor allowed; for no man ... has power to dispense with God's laws'.[24] If this was true, then Henry should not have married Anne Boleyn as their marriage would be null and void as they were connected within the forbidden degrees of affinity. This was because of Henry's prior relationship with Anne's sister, Mary Boleyn. Although we do not know what reason was used to annul Henry and Anne's marriage in May 1536, it is possible it was in fact that prior relationship. Thus, the Act of Succession itself, which was designed to protect Anne and her children, had been used to end her marriage and make her daughter illegitimate.

The other key passage in the Act of Succession is the one which declares that it is the children of Henry VIII and Anne Boleyn who will succeed to the English crown. Anne's position as queen has already been asserted previously in the act, but this is to specifically cover the rights of her children, and disinherit the rights of Princess Mary:

> All the issue had and procreated, or hereafter to be had and procreated, between your highness and your said most dear and entirely beloved wife Queen Anne, shall be your lawful children, and be inheritable, and inherit, according to the course of inheritance and laws of this realm, the imperial crown of the same, with all dignities, honours, pre-eminences, prerogatives, authorities, and jurisdictions to the same.[25]

The interesting thing about this section is that it does not specify that the children have to be legitimate or conceived within wedlock. Princess Elizabeth was conceived, in all likelihood, before Henry and Anne were married. It is possible that they went through 'some sort of formal commitment' ceremony in November 1532 after which they slept together for the first time.[26] But the official wedding does not seem to have been held until January 1533 when

Anne was certainly already pregnant. The act declares that children born to Henry VIII and Anne Boleyn are 'lawful' and that they will inherit the crown and everything which goes with it. It specifically covers issue already born, meaning Princess Elizabeth, and any to follow, referring to the sons which the couple hoped would follow the birth of their daughter. This hope for sons is set out, declaring that the first heir will be the first son born to Henry and Anne, and his heirs, then to the second son born to the couple, and his heirs, and 'so to every son of your body and of the body of the said Queen Anne'.[27] It goes on to say that, if Anne died without sons, then the crown would go to any legitimate sons of a future marriage, and only if there are no further sons, or if they have no heirs, would the crown then pass to the Princess Elizabeth.

The 1534 Treason Act attempts to shame all those with 'cankered and traitorous hearts' who might make 'shameful slanders, perils, or imminent danger or dangers' against Henry VIII, Anne Boleyn, or their heirs.[28] The intention is to ensure that everyone knows the penalties for failing to accept the king's new marriage. This is also enshrined in the Act of Succession, but the Treason Act goes further, setting in stone the religious division with Rome which allowed Henry to marry Anne in the first place, stating that it would be treason to call the king 'heretic, schismatic, tyrant, infidel, or usurper of the crown'.[29] The Treason Act has a much wider reach.

The Treason Act of 1534 came from a draft bill prepared in the parliament of 1530 to 1531 when it became clear that the people would not just accept the annulment of Henry VIII's marriage to Katherine of Aragon and recognise Anne Boleyn as queen. It was raised again during the parliament of 1531–1532 but was again abandoned before finally being passed in 1534.[30] Perhaps there was a reluctance to tighten the existing definitions of treason and turn the people more against the monarch. The King's Great Matter was already hugely divisive without adding the additional threat of execution for treason if you did not accept it. The Act also required every person in England to take an oath in support of the Boleyn marriage and the rights of Henry and Anne's heirs to succeed to the throne, and there was a huge drive to swear all adult males in the country.[31] Sir Thomas More and Cardinal Bishop John Fisher were both beheaded in mid-1535 for refusing to take this oath recognising Anne Boleyn as queen and the king as Head of the Church in England.

The Act of Succession was primarily about setting out the rights of succession to the children of Henry VIII and Anne Boleyn and establishing Anne as the rightful queen over Katherine of Aragon. It sets out that to deny this would be treason, but the Treason Act goes further in setting out all cases where the act could be applied to secure a conviction of treason, and the death penalty:

> That if any person or persons ... do maliciously wish, will or desire, by words or writing, or by craft imagine, invent, practise, or attempt any bodily harm to be done or committed to the king's most royal person, the queen's, or their heirs apparent, or to deprive them or any of them of their dignity, title, or name of their royal estates.[32]

This passage covers treason in deed, writing, word, or even a wish or desire, in terms of denying Henry, Anne and their children royal titles or estates. It suggests that even people's thoughts were not their own, and their own heads were not a safe place to be. The atmosphere at court for those who opposed Henry and Anne must have been intolerable, full of fear that at any moment they could be arrested and put to death.

Anne Boleyn and Elizabeth I

It has often been thought that Elizabeth I must not have known or appreciated her mother, as Anne Boleyn died when Elizabeth was not quite 3 years old. But Anne doted on her daughter, buying her an extensive wardrobe. There is also evidence that Elizabeth, after her mother's death, did remember her and wanted to try and rehabilitate her memory. One of the most poignant things is the Chequers ring discussed in chapter one. The ring opens to reveal two portraits, one of Elizabeth I, and one said to be of Anne Boleyn. Tracy Borman describes the ring as 'a poignant symbol of the private reverence in which [Elizabeth] held her late mother throughout her long life'.[33] It is a beautiful object and a reminder that, even though Anne was executed on charges of adultery and treason before Elizabeth could really get to know her, Elizabeth still loved and cherished her memory.

Tracy Borman says that Elizabeth I learnt from Anne Boleyn and both women had defied convention: 'Elizabeth had been the living embodiment of her mother's legacy and, as queen, she had constantly striven to avenge Anne's death – and, more positively, to celebrate her achievements'.[34] Without Elizabeth's reign, would Anne Boleyn's image have gone through the rehabilitation it did, and would we have the same understanding of Anne and her position as we do today? Later historians built on Elizabeth's own position towards her mother and brought Anne further into the light. The pageant on Gracechurch Street during Elizabeth I's coronation procession in January 1559 showed Henry VII and Elizabeth of York on the lowest tier as her grandparents, and herself on the topmost tier as the queen. But the middle tier had statues of Henry VIII and Anne Boleyn.[35] This was probably the first time that Anne had been publicly seen or acknowledged since her execution twenty-three years earlier.

If we only had Henry VIII's vision of Anne as an adulteress and traitor, and not Elizabeth's as a mother and trailblazing queen, today we might have a very different view of her.

A letter from the Imperial ambassador, Eustace Chapuys, to Emperor Charles V, written on 15 September 1533, reports that the child born to Anne Boleyn was named Elizabeth not Mary, and that the christening was like Anne's coronation, 'very cold and disagreeable, both to the Court and to the city, and there has been no thought of having the bonfires and rejoicings usual in such cases'.[36] The planned jousts were cancelled, but this had been the same after the birth of Princess Mary in 1516, so was not unusual for the birth of a princess rather than a prince.[37] Henry VIII was disappointed at the birth of a daughter rather than the son he wanted and expected. The chronicler Edward Hall wrote that 'the seventh day of September, being Sunday, between three and four of the clock after noon, the Queen was delivered of a fair lady, which day the duke of Norfolk came home to the christening and for the Queen's good deliverance, *Te Deum* was sung in continently and great preparation was made for the christening'.[38] Hall goes on to say that, at the christening, the Duchess of Norfolk held Elizabeth, who was dressed in a mantle of purple velvet with a long train furred with ermine and as the ceremony ended, the Garter King of Arms declared, 'God of his infinite goodness, send prosperous life and long to the high and mighty Princess of England, Elizabeth!'.[39] Although Elizabeth was not the son and heir Henry and Anne had wanted, she was very obviously being declared and treated as the legitimate offspring of the king and queen, and in line for the throne. There is no public suggestion that she was not loved or wanted by her parents at this time. But, no doubt, Henry must have felt humiliated and disappointed that it was a girl and not the son he needed to silence his critics, after all he had gone through to marry Anne.[40] Anne knew she needed to produce a son, but Elizabeth would be her only surviving child.

Sir William Kingston wrote to Lord Lisle on 18 April 1534 that 'the King and Queen were at Eltham, and saw my lady Princess, as goodly a child as hath been sent, and her grace is much in the King's favour as goodly child should be'.[41] Anne was aware that the English people did not necessarily see Elizabeth as the rightful heir to the throne and was determined to dress her in a fashion befitting her royal station. Tracy Borman has examined the accounts of materials purchased for the use of Anne Boleyn and Princess Elizabeth, including the collar of a dress made of russet velvet, to purple sarsenet to line a sleeve of purple satin, and a purple satin cap.[42] Anne was spending around £40 a month on clothes and accessories for herself and her daughter, which is around £18,000 today, and the total annual bill for Elizabeth's household was around £2,000 – much higher than that of her half-sister, Mary, when she was a princess.[43] Perhaps Anne was making a statement that Elizabeth was more important than Mary, the rightful and legitimate princess and heir to the throne of England, where Mary was illegitimate and fit only to serve her half-sister.

In summer 1534, Anne Boleyn tried to promote a marriage between the baby Princess Elizabeth and Charles, third son of Francis I of France. There was talk of a marriage between Mary, daughter of Henry and Katherine of Aragon, to the French Dauphin, which angered Anne, so she did her utmost to promote the claims of her own daughter. She knew that allying her daughter to France through marriage would enhance Elizabeth's legitimacy and her own position as queen.[44] However, the negotiations failed. Although Anne had been made queen by Henry, and crowned, it was more difficult to gain international recognition and acceptance, especially when the Pope would not recognise her as queen.

It can be argued that one of Anne Boleyn's greatest achievements was in her daughter, Elizabeth. Elizabeth I would go on to be a very successful queen, fighting off multiple rebellions and attempts on her life and throne, defeating the Spanish Armada, and trying to find a unifying religious settlement, but how much of an influence did Anne Boleyn have on these achievements? Because Elizabeth did not really talk much about her mother, it is difficult to know her exact feelings, but the little glimpses we get demonstrate that Anne Boleyn seemed to dote upon her daughter, showering her with clothes and visiting when she could. Elizabeth also showed her respect for her mother's memory by taking her falcon emblem as her own, and making sure she had a public role to play in her coronation procession. Probably two of the most famous women in Tudor history, quite possibly in all of English and British history, and they were mother and daughter.

George Wyatt's *Life of Queen Anne Boleigne*

George Wyatt was the grandson of the poet Sir Thomas Wyatt the Elder. Thomas Wyatt was a rumoured lover of Anne Boleyn as was discussed in chapter two. It is thought that perhaps George Wyatt got some of the information contained in his biography of Anne Boleyn from his grandfather, who was also arrested alongside Anne in May 1536, but released without charge after Anne's execution. Wyatt's work was intended to refute the work of Nicholas Sander (discussed in chapter six), who had attacked Anne, and gave rise to the sixth finger myth. Historian Retha Warnicke describes Wyatt as having a 'somewhat naïve approach' and being 'not a great scholar'.[45] Warnicke does not specify why she believes George Wyatt to be naïve, or not a good scholar, but the implication is that it is due to his grandfather's relationship with Anne and some sense of favouritism towards her. It is worth considering when reading Wyatt's work.

Wyatt believed he was defending Anne from 'malice and venomous untruths', not accusations of witchcraft.[46] He thought that Sander was accusing Anne of heresy and not witchcraft, as many later historians have suggested. His work is the earliest and most complete account we have of Anne's life, with evidence from people who knew her.[47] But he was also trying to ingratiate himself with Elizabeth I as his father had been executed for treason under Mary I, and his grandfather had been imprisoned several times under Henry VIII.[48] However, it did not have the wide reach of Sander's publication and was not widely published until the nineteenth century alongside George Cavendish's *The Life of Cardinal Wolsey*.[49] Nevertheless, 'many of the most repeated stories in twentieth and twenty-first century historical fiction about Anne have their origins in George Wyatt's biography'.[50] Wyatt's work could have been included in several chapters in this book, as it covers her first appearance at the English court, her relationship with Thomas Wyatt, religious beliefs, and her dramatic fall. However, there are some very interesting observations on Anne's conduct as queen which is why this text is being discussed here.

Wyatt's account of Anne's life is entirely favourable to her, declaring that 'neither also were her virtues only enclosed in her own breast or shut up in her own person'.[51] She shared what she had with others, including her beliefs. He wrote about how she 'had procured to her chaplains, men of great learning and no less honest conversing', and 'to be attending on her, ladies of great honour, and yet of greater choice for reputation of virtue undoubted witnesses of her spousal integrity'.[52] Wyatt was determined to present Anne as innocent of the crimes of which she was accused, using her religious beliefs and the ladies with whom she surrounded herself as witnesses to the fact. As would be seen in 1541 to 1542 with Katherine Howard, Anne's cousin and fifth wife to Henry VIII, a female accomplice was needed in order for a queen to commit adultery. None of Anne's ladies or female attendants were ever arrested, accused, or seemingly even suspected of aiding and abetting her in the adultery she was accused of. But when Katherine Howard's conduct was being investigated, her ladies were all questioned and Jane Boleyn, Viscountess Rochford, was arrested and imprisoned, and executed alongside Katherine in February 1542. Jane Boleyn had also been Anne Boleyn's sister-in-law and was 'involved up to the hilt' in Katherine Howard's actions.[53] These complicit women were not seen in Anne's arrest and execution. Those executed alongside her were exclusively men. Wyatt uses Anne's conduct as queen to evidence why she was not guilty of the crimes she was later accused of.

Wyatt goes on to discuss how Anne was determined to help the poor and needy, along with her ladies and her household. She wanted to set a good example to others. She did:

> Those works in the sight of God, which she caused her maids and those about her daily to work in shirts and smocks for the poor. But not staying here her eye for charity, her hand of bounty passed through the whole land, each place felt that heavenly flame burning in her, all times will remember it, no place leaving for vain flames, no times for idle thoughts.[54]

It is quite possibly an exaggeration that her 'hand of bounty passed through the whole land', as the king, queen, and court were largely based around London. Even their progresses did not venture too far north or west, remaining largely in the southeast of the country. This was also the area where the reformed faith was strongest. The idea of Anne burning with a 'heavenly flame' suggests some kind of divine intervention, like it was God's plan for Anne to be queen and to be able to help those less well off than she was and instil in them the reformed faith.

Eric Ives wrote that Wyatt had 'access to some genuine family traditions of his own about Anne'.[55] What these were we will never know, but it gives a sense of credence to the events he relates. Writing about the years 1535 into 1536 when Anne was again pregnant, Wyatt writes that 'the time was taken to steal the king's affection from her, when most of all she was to have been cherished'.[56] Wyatt does not mention Jane Seymour by name at this point, choosing instead to focus on Anne and her increasingly difficult position. With Anne pregnant again by the end of 1535 and into January 1536, there would not have been any real hope in displacing Anne as queen. Henry VIII still hoped for a son, and one would hope that he would try and limit any upset to his pregnant wife. However, once Anne miscarried at the end of January 1536, it may have put hope into her enemies that she could be replaced. Wyatt goes on to report that, 'unkindness grew, and she was brought a bed before her time with much peril of her life, and of a male child dead born, to her greater and most extreme grief'.[57] This was Anne Boleyn's final pregnancy. She would not provide the king with a son.

It has been suggested that it was this miscarriage which led directly to Anne's downfall, but it is more complex than that. Anne, however, did know that her miscarriage would further imperil her relationship with the king. Her entire position rested on his love, and she had probably lost it by the beginning of 1536, though he kept supporting her, at least in public. Until Katherine of Aragon's death on 7 January 1536, Anne was safe. This was because, if Henry repudiated Anne, he would have been expected to reunite with Katherine. Henry would never do that as it would mean admitting he was wrong to have annulled the marriage in the first place. So, Katherine's life protected Anne.

But when Katherine died and Anne miscarried, she was in the most vulnerable position of her life.

* * *

Anne Boleyn's time as queen was short, only three years compared to the twenty-four years Katherine of Aragon was officially queen (though by her own reckoning that would have lasted until her death, making it twenty-seven years). However, her successors would struggle to reach three years as queen with Jane Seymour not quite surviving a year and a half before dying in childbed, Anne of Cleves lasting only just six months, Katherine Howard around a year and a half, and Katherine Parr being successful in lasting nearly four years as queen and surviving Henry VIII to remarry. But it has been argued that despite her short reign, Anne was 'the most influential and important queen consort this country has ever had'.[58] She was queen at a time when momentous changes were taking place in England, and she had been the catalyst for many of them.

Anne Boleyn's just over a thousand days as queen demonstrated how a marriage based on love and passion, combined with a suspicious and paranoid king, made for a difficult and tempestuous time. It sowed the seeds for the religious disorder which would plague the lives of Henry VIII's heirs, culminating in the reign of Anne and Henry's daughter, Elizabeth. Anne's period as queen was a turning point in Henry VIII's reign – dramatic religious changes, a marriage borne out of passion, and the brutal acknowledgement that queens of England were just as vulnerable to the whims of a tyrannical king as anyone else.

Chapter 4

Anne as Traitor

'These bloody days have broken my heart'[1]

Anne Boleyn's fall from power and favour is probably the most written about part of her life and story. It is certainly one of the most shocking and controversial events of the whole Tudor period. Lacey Baldwin Smith has said that 'the closer the proximity to the crown, the greater the danger' and this definitely proved true in the case of Anne Boleyn.[2] Anne was executed in May 1536 for adultery, incest, and treason:

> …following daily her frail and carnal lust, did falsely and traitorously procure by base conversations and kisses, touchings, gifts, and other infamous incitations, divers of the King's daily and familiar servants to be her adulterers and concubines.[3]

The trial documents are interesting and will be further discussed later in this chapter, but the wording of the above section places the blame firmly at Anne's door, saying that she did 'procure' by 'incitations' the men to have sex with her. There appears to be little blame attached to the men in the sense that they are also portrayed as victims of Anne, but that they still needed to be punished for their violations. Anne is portrayed as the scheming and ambitious harlot who manipulated men to satisfy her own wants and needs. This was the image that Henry VIII wanted to portray of his once loved wife and queen, just three years into their marriage. He was willing to wear the cuckold's horns to be rid of her.

Anne Boleyn was arrested on 2 May 1536 while at Greenwich Palace and was taken down river to the Tower of London. A court musician, Mark Smeaton, had already been arrested, questioned, and confessed to adultery with Anne. Henry Norris, the king's Groom of the Stool, was also under arrest. Anne's brother, George Boleyn, along with Francis Weston, William Brereton, Thomas Wyatt, and Richard Page would follow. Wyatt and Page alone would escape the executioner's axe. Alison Weir claims that Thomas Cromwell had always intended that Wyatt and Page would be released in order to 'prove' the guilt of the rest.[4] A letter survives from Thomas Wyatt's father, Henry Wyatt, which seems to support the supposition that Cromwell at least intended Wyatt to go free, where he thanks Cromwell for the 'comfortable articles therein touching his son Thomas' and asks 'when it shall be the King's pleasure to deliver him … and to admonish him to fly vice and serve God better'.[5] The implication is that Wyatt will be released, and his father was not concerned about his fate after receiving a letter from Cromwell. It may well be that Wyatt was arrested because of his prior known connection to Anne, to make the charges against her seem more believable.

Thomas Cranmer, Archbishop of Canterbury, wrote to Henry VIII on 3 May 1536 having heard of Anne Boleyn's arrest and imprisonment the day before, saying that the king had 'great causes of heaviness' and that his honour was 'highly touched'.[6] Cranmer made sure that he was seen to be supporting the king and agreeing with his point of view, even if he did not believe it himself. It was too much of a risk in an atmosphere of suspicion and fear to come out in Anne's favour. Those known to be close to her were in the Tower already or trying to distance themselves from her. However, Cranmer said more in Anne's favour than we have evidence of anyone else at court saying:

> If the reports of the Queen be true, they are only to her dishonour, not yours. I am clean amazed, for I had never better opinion of woman; but I think your Highness would not have gone so far if she had not been culpable. I was most bound to her of all creatures living, and therefore beg that I may, with your Grace's favour, wish and pray that she may declare herself innocent. Yet if she be found guilty, I repute him not a faithful subject who would not wish her punished without mercy.[7]

It is a very interesting letter, as Cranmer is making sure that the king knows he is on his side and will support him, but Cranmer is also attempting to speak up for Anne in his own way. He was close to the Boleyn family and had been their chaplain before he came to court, proclaiming he was 'most bound to her of all creatures living', possibly because she had assisted Cranmer in his rise to power, though the exact relationship between them is unclear. Anne must have been beholden to Cranmer for assisting the king to obtain the annulment of his marriage from Katherine of Aragon in order to marry her. Cranmer's letter certainly suggests that he was close to Anne in religious terms and thought highly of her, declaring that 'I loved her not a little for the love which I judged her to bear towards God and His Gospel'.[8] It is undoubtedly more than just a passing acquaintanceship that Anne and Cranmer shared, and it seems likely that they discussed religion, the Gospels, and quite possibly the course of the Reformation in England as well. Cranmer worried that the pace of Reformation could slow, or stop, with Anne's death. He underestimated Henry VIII's determination to remain without the Pope in England, though the king would keep many Catholic doctrines in his Church of England.

On 12 May 1536, Henry Norris, Francis Weston, William Brereton, and Mark Smeaton were tried and found guilty of adultery and treason. Anne and her brother, George, were tried on 15 May and found guilty of the same charges, but with incest as an addition. The men were executed on 17 May and Anne followed them just two days later on 19 May 1536. Henry VIII became betrothed to his third wife, Jane Seymour, a day later, and they were married on 30 May 1536, just eleven days after Anne Boleyn's execution. There are surviving documents and poems that reflect the shock, grief, and sadness of the events of less than three weeks in May 1536. They demonstrate the general belief today in Anne's innocence of the charges against her. She and five men, including her brother, went to their deaths knowing that they were innocent, but unable to save themselves, at the mercy of an increasingly tyrannical king.

William Kingston's Letters to Thomas Cromwell

Sir William Kingston was Constable of the Tower of London from 1524 to 1540, overseeing the imprisonment and execution of Anne Boleyn and the men imprisoned alongside her. He wrote a series of letters to Thomas Cromwell during May 1536, reporting on what Anne was saying and her state of mind. They give an interesting insight into what happened within the Tower during those crucial weeks. The Kingston letters were damaged by fire in 1731 but can be reconstructed from the work of John Strype who had already made use of them.[9] Parts of some of the letters are completely unreadable and we only have odd words. But, because of Strype's work we can still read most of these letters today, which offer so much insight and understanding of Anne's mindset in May 1536 under threat of execution.

The first letter we have is dated 3 May 1536, written the day after Anne Boleyn was arrested at Greenwich Palace and taken to the Tower. Kingston wrote of what happened on arrival at the Tower – that Anne asked, 'Mr Kingston, shall I go into a dungeon?' to which Kingston replied, 'No, Madam. You shall go into the lodging you lay in at your coronation' and Anne answered, 'It is too good for me, Jesu have mercy on me'.[10] The lodgings Anne occupied before her coronation were the royal apartments, which no longer exist at the Tower today having been destroyed. This happened during the Commonwealth and Restoration periods when they fell into decay.[11] The fact that Anne stayed in the royal apartments suggests that she was still being treated as a queen on her imprisonment, her rank not yet having been demoted or her marriage to the king annulled. Alison Weir observes that the conditions of her confinement may have been reason for optimism in Anne's eyes, and a hope for mercy.[12] Her comment about it not being good enough for her is interesting, given that she would maintain her innocence to the end of the crimes of which she was accused. Had she done something else that she believed she should be punished for? Kingston then related that Anne wept, then laughed 'as she has done many times since'.[13] This suggests a hugely volatile emotional state, understandable given that she was being imprisoned on suspicion of adultery with, at this time, three men. There are two key things to come out of this first letter that Kingston sends to Cromwell. The first is the report of a comment made by Anne about Francis Weston where she told him that he loved her kinswoman, Madge Shelton, and said he did not love his wife. He was reported to have responded to her that 'he loved one in her house better than them both. And the Queen said, who is that? It is yourself'.[14] This would lead to Weston's arrest on 4 May, just a day after this letter was sent to Cromwell. The net was widening.

The other key part of this letter is a report in Anne Boleyn's own words of a conversation that she had with Sir Henry Norris on either 29 or 30 April 1536. News of the conversation spread around the court, and it was probably this which prompted the arrest of Norris on 2 May. However, it is one thing to hear second or third-hand news of a conversation which may have been embroidered with each retelling, but to have it directly from Anne's mouth is critical evidence:

> For I asked him why he did not go through with his marriage, and he made answer he would tarry a time. Then I said, You look for dead men's shoes, for if aught come to the king but good, you would look to have me. And he said if he should have any such thought, he would his head were off.[15]

This may have seemed just an innocent jest, part of the game of courtly love, but it had sinister undertones which Cromwell would take full advantage of. Even just speaking of the king's death was treason, as per the 1534 Treason Act. Anne and Norris's conversation was thus treason under this act, an act which had been designed to protect Anne Boleyn and her issue as heirs to the throne.

There are a couple of letters which cannot be precisely dated. In one of these letters, Kingston reports that 'one hour she is determined to die and the next hour much contrary to that'.[16] No doubt, Anne hoped for mercy from the husband who had turned his country upside down for her, but at the same time, she must have realised the seriousness of her situation and probably came to the conclusion that she would die and that it was better to do it well. Anne also reflected on her arrest at Greenwich, saying that she was 'cruelly handled' and that Thomas Howard, 3rd Duke of Norfolk, tutted and shook his head at her, whilst making the arrest.[17] Norfolk was Anne's uncle and, no doubt, was doing his part in Anne's arrest in order to distance himself from her and save himself. Norfolk had an uncanny ability to survive. Anne also spoke about 'my bishops', meaning the reforming bishops she had helped to promote, like Thomas Cranmer, Archbishop of Canterbury, and Nicholas Shaxton, Bishop of Salisbury.[18] As we have already seen, Cranmer had written to the king but in the end had to accept what was happening to maintain his own position.

In a letter written on 16 May, the day after Anne Boleyn was tried, found guilty and condemned to death, Kingston wrote again to Cromwell regarding 'preparation of scaffolds' and reported that Cranmer had been to see Anne to take her confession that very day.[19] He does not recount how Anne was or what was said in her confession, so we only get a tiny glimpse of what was going on in her day-to-day life during her imprisonment. Much of her time must have been taken up with thinking about death once her trial was concluded. However, Kingston did record that he had told George Boleyn 'to be ready to suffer tomorrow, and so he accepts it very well'.[20] The other men would also have been informed. George Boleyn, Henry Norris, Francis Weston, William Brereton and Mark Smeaton were all executed on 17 May 1536.

Preparations were underway for Anne's own execution. Kingston wrote to Cromwell that he was 'very glad to hear of the executioner of Calais, for he can handle that matter' and how carpenters were making 'a scaffold of such height that all present may see it'.[21] In a different letter Kingston wrote of Cromwell's instruction to 'have strangers conveyed out of the Tower'.[22] No foreigners would be permitted to hear Anne Boleyn's final words or see her last moments. They would have to rely on the reports of others. Cromwell probably wanted what was told abroad to be approved by himself and the king, to make sure that the official story was what people heard and believed. He did not know what Anne would say on the scaffold, whether she would make a big pronouncement of her innocence. He could not let that happen. He did not need to worry. As will be seen later in the chapter, Anne Boleyn's final speech was eloquent and non-confrontational, asking us only to 'judge the best'.[23] She did not make any waves.

As the time for her execution drew closer, Kingston wrote of Anne's state of mind that, 'to my knowledge this lady has much joy and pleasure in death'.[24] This is borne out by a conversation Kingston reported back to Cromwell in a letter tentatively dated 19 May 1536 where Kingston told her that there should be no pain as the blow was so subtle, and Anne replied, 'I heard say the executioner was very good, and I have a little neck' and she put her hands round her neck laughing.[25] This was likely a response to the stress she was under, of the execution having been postponed, and her desire that it was over and done with so she did not have to wait any longer.

Anne Boleyn's Letter From the Tower, 6 May 1536

There is a letter purporting to be written by Anne Boleyn while she was imprisoned in the Tower of London before her trial in May 1536. This is of doubtful authenticity to some historians and was discovered in the possessions of Thomas Cromwell after his execution in July 1540, found with the words 'To the King from the Lady in the Tower' written on it.[26] It is the tone of the letter that many believe makes it questionable that it was indeed written by Anne to the king, as it is doubtful she would have dared to write to him in that tone with her own life, and that of her daughter and other family members, under threat. The letter was almost destroyed in a fire at Ashburnam House in London where it was stored along with many other documents, including the Kingston letters.[27] Luckily, copies had already been made of Anne's letter, so we are still able to read the complete document, whereas some of the Kingston letters are now hard to decipher.

In the letter, Anne Boleyn blamed 'such an one whom you know to be my ancient professed enemy' and begged the king not to let it ruin her.[28] Joanna Denny suggests that Anne realised Cromwell had sacrificed her in order to save himself.[29] This does make a certain amount of sense, since Anne and Cromwell seemed to have conflicting views on policy, and were moving in different directions on religious issues as well, particularly on what to do with funds from the dissolved monasteries. Anne had begun to attack Cromwell publicly.[30] He would not let this pass. Perhaps he had realised that it was him or Anne, and he struck. Cromwell orchestrated the charges against Anne, but it is debated over how involved Henry VIII was. Talking to the king in such a bold and provocative tone would certainly have rubbed him up the wrong way. It may even have destroyed any chance of survival for Anne, or of her going to a nunnery, which she seemed to have some hope of as late as 16 May. However, in this same letter, William Kingston, the Constable of the Tower, also consulted Cromwell regarding the preparation of scaffolds, so although Anne hoped for life it seems that her fate had already been decided.[31] When Anne supposedly wrote the letter to the king, she had not yet been put on trial, so her fate was not yet sealed in her mind. Consequently, it would have been foolish to irritate him.

In the letter, Anne professed her loyalty to the king, declaring that 'never Prince had wife more Loyal in all Duty, and in all true Affection', and she realised that her position was based on 'no surer Foundation than your Grace's Fancy'.[32] Anne's position as queen had always been based on his affection for her. That affection was the catalyst for the Break with Rome and pushed Henry through his divorce from Katherine of Aragon. That affection now also led the king to love another, which Anne alludes to 'your Affection already settled on that Party, for whose sake I am now as I am'.[33] There is blame attributed to Jane Seymour for the position Anne found herself in. Anne asked Henry to look back on that affection he once felt for her and remember how he had raised her higher than any other woman. He had chosen her 'from a Low Estate, to be your Queen and Companion, far beyond my Desert or Desire'.[34] Harking back to the love letters we have surviving from Henry VIII to Anne Boleyn, the emphasis is on how undeserving Anne believed herself to be queen, but Henry's love and affection won out. Even right at the end of the letter, Anne signs off 'Your most Loyal and ever Faithful Wife', putting the emphasis very much on her position as the king's wife, rather than his queen.[35] The importance is placed on the personal rather than the political at the end. Anne hopes Henry will remember how he once felt about her.

Historian Sandra Vasoli argues for the letter being genuine, describing it as 'poignant, courageous, noble and masterfully composed' revealing a 'fervent proclamation of guiltlessness from a wife to her husband, along with her concern for his immortal soul, expressed in a language both intimate and assertive'.[36] Anne expresses her worry about Henry's soul, but also talks about her belief that God knows her innocence and when facing Him, she will be cleared:

> But if you have already determined of me, and that only my Death, but an Infamous Slander must bring you the enjoying of your desired Happiness; then I desire of God, that he will pardon your great Sin therein … and that he will not call you to a strict Account for your unprincely and cruel usage of me, at his General Judgment-Seat, where both you and my self must shortly appear, and in whose Judgment, I doubt not (whatsoever the World may think of me) mine Innocence shall be openly known, and sufficiently cleared.[37]

Describing the charges against her as 'Infamous Slander' is a certain way of declaring her innocence and putting the slander back to Henry as the perpetrator. Anne hoped that God would forgive the king for his slander against her, and executing an innocent woman as she is sure that He will clear her of the charges when she faces him. She acknowledges that the living world does not look kindly on her, though even those who dislike her doubt the veracity of the charges against her, including Eustace Chapuys, whose opinions will be examined further in chapter five.

So, who wrote the letter said to be from the 'Lady in the Tower'? It is quite possible that it was a scribe or secretary who actually wrote down Anne's words. Scribes were common in the sixteenth century though perhaps we would expect Anne herself to have signed at the bottom and it does not appear to match other examples of her signature which survive. Anne would also have expected any letter which she wrote to the king to go through the hands of Thomas Cromwell, hence perhaps her reference to 'one whom you know to be my ancient professed enemy' – did she know that Cromwell would read it and know who she blamed for her predicament?[38] It is very likely. Many different people have been suggested as the writer of the letter from Cromwell to Thomas Wriothesley, to William Kingston, to Stephen Gardiner, and even Anne's uncle, the Duke of Norfolk. Norfolk is actually a plausible writer, or the hand of one of his secretaries at least. Perhaps Cromwell or Henry VIII thought that Anne would speak more openly to her uncle, though they were known to have argued on several occasions and Norfolk was trying to distance himself from his disgraced niece. It is also possible that Norfolk was sent as a way of him proving his loyalty to the king. If we had the writing of one of Norfolk's secretaries then we could compare it to the Tower letter and possibly have an answer.[39] New discoveries are happening all the time, so this is not outside of the realms of possibility.

Sandra Vasoli says that to read the letter 'is to gain a private glimpse into the spirit of a brave, articulate woman who well knew she faced death'.[40] The tone certainly seems to match up with some of the comments we have about Anne Boleyn, in that she said what she thought, and was spirited, witty, and religious. It is easy to believe Anne wrote that letter, but what is perhaps less easy to believe is that she sent it to her husband. Perhaps she really did believe she had no hope of life and would die, so she may as well say what was on her mind. The difficulty with that, however, is Elizabeth. Would Anne have potentially jeopardised the position of her daughter to have the last word?

Trial Documents, 15 May 1536

In some ways it is interesting and quite amazing that the trial documents survive, as so much other evidence relating to the life of Anne Boleyn has been lost. Perhaps the trial documents remained because they were official government documents and Henry VIII wanted a record of how right he was to condemn and execute his second wife. Anne's initials, badges and symbols were removed from royal palaces, and it seems possible that portraits of her were also destroyed, though there is no evidence of such destruction. Sir Henry Norris, Sir Francis Weston, Sir William Brereton and Mark Smeaton were tried on 12 May 1536 in Westminster Hall, part of Westminster Palace, where the law courts were based at the time. Anne Boleyn and her brother, George, Lord Rochford, were tried separately on 15 May 1536 in the King's Hall at the Tower of London.

All were found guilty of adultery and treason and sentenced to death. Anne and George Boleyn were also found guilty of the additional crime of incest.

The document which survives for the trial of Norris, Weston, Brereton, and Smeaton is less complete than the one for the Boleyn siblings. Commissions of oyer and terminer were convened in Middlesex and Kent and among those listed and called to judge were the king's chief minister, Thomas Cromwell, the king's former brother-in-law, Charles Brandon, 1st Duke of Suffolk, and Thomas Howard, 3rd Duke of Norfolk.[41] Even though Norfolk was Anne and George Boleyn's uncle, he would act as Steward of England during the trials. Their father, Thomas Boleyn, 1st Earl of Wiltshire and Ormond, is only named in the commission for Middlesex and not that of Kent, possibly because Kent was his home county. There is also an erasure under the description for Middlesex where it seems Smeaton's name has been erased for some reason, and he only appears in the commission for Kent. There is not the same amount of detail in this document as there is in the surviving indictment for the trials of Anne and George Boleyn. The document states that 'Smeaton pleaded guilty of violation and carnal knowledge of the Queen' and put himself at the king's mercy.[42] Henry Norris, William Brereton and Francis Weston pleaded not guilty to all charges, but were found guilty, sentenced to death, and their goods forfeit to the crown. The document also asserts that, 'judgment against all four as in cases of treason; execution to be at Tyburn'.[43] Tyburn is often where common criminals were hanged, or hung, drawn, and quartered in more serious cases. The death sentences for Norris, Brereton, Weston, and even Smeaton, who was a commoner, would be commuted from hanging, drawing, and quartering at Tyburn to beheading on Tower Hill.

The document which survives for the trial of Anne and George Boleyn gives a lot more detail of the exact nature of the charges than the document for the trial of Norris, Weston, Brereton and Smeaton. Anne and George's father, Thomas Boleyn, is not named in this commission, unlike the one for the other men. It was probably thought to be too controversial and insensitive for a father to sit in judgement on his own children, though apparently not for an uncle to judge his own niece and nephew and condemn them to death. Thomas Howard would once again be Lord High Steward for Anne and George's trial. Other names listed in the document as judges include the likes of Charles Brandon, 1st Duke of Suffolk, along with Anne's rumoured once-betrothed, Henry Percy, now 6th Earl of Northumberland, and George Boleyn's father-in-law, Henry Parker, Lord Morley. A familial or friendly relationship with one of the accused was no excuse. Refusing to sit in judgement when called upon to do so could have repercussions for them, their position, wealth and lands, and even their freedom.

Looking at the charges in the indictment, the overview of the charges against Anne are outlined in detail, less is given about George Boleyn, and initially the men are not named at all, but only appear later in this section, almost as an afterthought to substantiate the accusations made against Anne. The focus is very much on Anne as the accused with the men almost as a means to an end:

> … whereas queen Anne has been the wife of Henry VIII for three years and more, she, despising her marriage, and entertaining malice against the King, and following daily her frail and carnal lust, did falsely and traitorously procure by base conversations and kisses, touchings, gifts, and other infamous incitations, divers of the King's daily and familiar servants to be her adulterers and concubines.[44]

The descriptions clearly refer to Anne as queen and the wife of the king, though Henry VIII was already looking into annulling the marriage and bastardising their daughter, Elizabeth. However, the king could not annul the marriage before the trial, otherwise Anne could not be guilty of adultery if she was never married. Anne is also painted as the one who incited the others – she was the one who did 'procure' them to touch her and act against their king. The blame is very much on her, and the men are almost seen as victims but will pay the same price as their queen. If the king did not execute the men as well, it would have been obvious that they were actually innocent and, by extension, Anne as well. That could not happen.

There are several dates given in the document for when Anne Boleyn was with one or other of the men. However, most of these dates can be dismissed when you consider that either Anne or the men were not in the place stated, or Anne herself was recovering from childbirth or a miscarriage so would have been in seclusion. For example, it was said that Anne Boleyn had sexual relations with Sir Henry Norris at Westminster on 12 October 1533.[45] However, at the time the court was at Greenwich, and Anne Boleyn was still in seclusion having only given birth a month earlier to Princess Elizabeth.[46] Anne was also said to have had sexual relations with Sir Francis Weston on 20 May 1534 at Westminster.[47] But, Anne Boleyn was at Richmond on this date, and said to have been heavily pregnant, though the child would not survive.[48] These potential discrepancies with dates could explain why the document also says 'and divers days before and after'.[49] This would have been difficult to disprove, unlike the specific dates.

There is an implication that Anne Boleyn encouraged the jealousy of the men giving her 'secret gifts and pledges' because they were 'inflamed with carnal love of the Queen', but also that Anne got jealous when the men conversed with others 'showing great displeasure'.[50] Anne is placed at the centre of this sexual circle, keeping the men in line with sex and gifts, and her displeasure if they did anything she did not approve of. It is difficult to believe these accusations were true as Anne, as queen, would have been surrounded by her ladies, day and night, and she could not have carried on sexual affairs without the involvement of at least one, if not more, of her women, and none were arrested and condemned, as we see later with Katherine Howard.

The most damaging accusation in the indictment, however, is that the queen and the five men plotted against the king, wanting his death in order to rule through the infant Elizabeth. It was treason to even discuss the death of the king, and it was said that Anne, George, Norris, Weston, Brereton and Smeaton:

> … conspired the death and destruction of the King, the Queen often saying she would marry one of them as soon as the King died, and affirming that she would never love the King in her heart.[51]

For Henry VIII, this must have been the worst blow, assuming that he really believed it. He had been so in love with Anne at the beginning of their relationship, barely able to leave her side, that to hear that she never loved him would have been devastating. This accusation against Anne that she would marry one of her supposed lovers may have come from Henry Norris's conversation with Anne on either 29 or 30 April 1536, discussed earlier in this chapter. It was an allusion to the king's death, so would have been treason according to the Treason Act 1534. It was likely just an overstep of the bounds of courtly love, probably brought about by Anne's fear of a net closing around her, knowing she had lost the king's love and failed to give him a son. Anne would be condemned under an act designed to protect her and her children. It was said that due to finding out about Anne's adultery, 'certain harms and perils' befell the king's body.[52] This could be the ulcer on his leg getting worse, which had reopened after his jousting accident in January 1536 and would only get worse towards the end of his life, or that he was temporarily impotent.

Anne Boleyn pleaded not guilty to all of the charges against her, but given that Sir Henry Norris, Sir Francis Weston, Sir William Brereton and Mark Smeaton had already been found guilty of the same crimes, including adultery with her, her fate was sealed. She was sentenced to be taken 'to the green within the Tower, and there to be burned or beheaded as shall please the King'.[53] Anne was removed from the courtroom before the trial of her brother began. His trial had a more uncertain outcome, as he had not necessarily been condemned by the trials that had gone before. The Imperial ambassador, Eustace Chapuys, reported to Charles V that, 'to all he replied so well that several of those present wagered 10 to 1 that he would be acquitted'.[54] Little is said in the trial documents about the trial of George Boleyn, Lord Rochford, but that the peers were asked for judgement, except the Earl of Northumberland who was 'suddenly taken ill'.[55] Northumberland was Anne's alleged former betrothed and perhaps it took a toll on him, having to find his former love guilty of treason and sentence her to death. Northumberland would die just a year after Anne, in June 1537. George Boleyn was also found guilty and sentenced to death at Tyburn, as with the other men, but his sentence would be commuted to beheading on Tower Hill, also like the others. Henry VIII would choose the kinder death of beheading for Anne Boleyn and choose a French swordsman to do the deed.

The day before the trial, Thomas Cromwell wrote to the English ambassadors in France, Stephen Gardiner and John Wallop, to tell them what was going on in England, describing it as 'a most detestable scheme', and describing Anne Boleyn's 'incontinent living' as 'so rank and common that the ladies of her privy chamber could not conceal it'.[56] It is almost like Cromwell was determined to make sure that the official story was disseminated as far and wide as possible, though Anne had not even been tried yet. He wanted to portray the king as a victim rather than a man who put his innocent wife to death. It is also made clear that Anne's ladies were co-operative and revealed what they knew, explaining why none of them were put to death alongside their mistress for concealing treason. Emphasis is put on the plot against the king's life, describing it as 'a certain conspiracy of the King's death, which extended so far that all we that had the examination of it quaked at the danger his Grace was in'.[57] This echoes the statements found in the trial documents which stressed that Anne Boleyn was at the centre of a web which posed huge danger to the king and the government of England, but that they were discovered in time.

These surviving trial documents give an insight into exactly what Anne Boleyn was accused, found guilty of, and executed for. There is no mention of witchcraft, which seems to be a common misconception around her execution. She was found guilty of adultery, incest, and treason, though never admitted any guilt, and indeed would subtly remind the watching crowds at her execution of her innocence, asking 'if any person will meddle of my cause, I require them to judge the best'.[58] She went to her death innocent of the crimes of which she had been found guilty, but unable to speak out or save herself.

Thomas Wyatt's *Circa Regna Tonat*

The full title of *Circa Regna Tonat* is *Innocentia Veritas Viat Fides Circumdederunt me inimici mei*, and is a poem written by Sir Thomas Wyatt, the rumoured former lover of Anne Boleyn, in May 1536. Wyatt was arrested and imprisoned in the Bell Tower in the Tower of London alongside Anne herself and her other suspected lovers. It was here that Wyatt wrote about the events of that month and the tragic ending.[59] It is probably Wyatt's best-known and certainly most haunting poem. 'Circa Regna Tonat' aptly translates from the Latin as 'thunder rolls around the throne'.[60] However, Greg Walker who examines English writing in the period, reflects that 'around the throne *he* thunders' is a more apt translation.[61] The 'he' is likely a reference to Henry VIII. The title is probably a reference to Anne and Henry's relationship and how it irrevocably changed England, her tumultuous three years on the throne, and how low she had been brought by rumour. Stephanie Russo explains that 'around the throne the thunder rolls' comes from Seneca's *Phaedra* where the peace of the country is contrasted with the danger of court.[62] It is an interesting consideration, but the only times we know that Anne Boleyn was in the country was before she went to the Low Countries in 1513 and when she was at Hever after her broken engagement with Henry Percy and at times during Henry's courtship of her. She probably yearned for the court when she was in the country.

Walker's translation puts the emphasis on Henry and how he had complete control of the fate of the people within his court. Regarding the translation of 'Innocentia Veritas Viat Fides Circumdederunt me inimici mei', it translates as 'Innocence, truth, Wyatt, faith, my enemies surrounded me'. Wyatt describes May 1536 as 'these bloody days' where eight were arrested and six executed, and he acknowledged that 'the fall is grievous from aloft', meaning that the higher you rise, the further you have to fall, as in Anne's case.[63] Anne had begun life as Mistress Boleyn, rose to become Lady, then Marquess, and then Queen of England, before ending as a traitor at the sharp end of a sword.

Probably the most famous verse of this poem is worth dissecting in more detail as it comes to the heart of what Wyatt was thinking and feeling at this critical time. It is also the middle verse of the poem, so not only is it making the critical point but is literally at the centre:

> These bloody days have broken my heart.
> My lust, my youth did them depart,
> And blind desire of estate.
> Who hastes to climb seeks to revert.
> Of truth, *circa Regna tonat.*[64]

Wyatt attributes this moment in the Tower of London in May 1536 to his loss of youth. He is thought to have been born around 1503 so would have been about 33 years old in 1536. It is certainly a life-changing moment being under threat of trial and execution for treason. However, Wyatt was never tried and was released after Anne Boleyn and her so-called 'lovers' were executed.

Greg Walker sums up this poem in the best way, saying that 'Wyatt forges poetry from the raw emotions of personal experience, or rather uses verse as a means of reflecting upon and containing emotion that might otherwise prove uncontrollable'.[65] For Wyatt this is not a political execution but a very personal one. It is easy to believe that Wyatt was in love with Anne when reading his early poetry and that this is not just the death of his queen, but of the love of his life. That certainly seems to be the implication in the raw emotion and his regret that Anne chose her ambition over him.

Stephanie Russo in her book *The Afterlife of Anne Boleyn* notes that Wyatt did not seem willing to name what he was describing, saying 'The bell tower showed me such a sight, that in my head sticks day and night'.[66] The reader is left to imagine for themselves what that sight might be, but it must be horrendous if Wyatt is unwilling to even name it. In the final verse of the poem, Wyatt outlined what people could do to avoid the situation he found himself in; that ambition and wit will not help you and are more likely to bring you down low, and his current position was the proof of it.

> By proof, I say, there did I learn:
> Wit helpeth not defence too yerne,
> Of innocency to plead or prate.
> Bear low, therefore, give God the stern,
> For sire, *circa Regna tonat*.[67]

Wit does not help in declaring innocence, but if you stay out of the limelight and do not climb higher than your birth position, then you will not fall, but by all means leave it to God and the fates. Ambition was a large part of court life, so those within the court were largely aiming higher for wealth, titles, and power. Court was a dangerous place, particularly as Henry VIII became increasingly suspicious as he aged, probably due to what happened to Anne Boleyn and the rumours that brought her down.

Wyatt's attempts to describe what happened at the end of Anne's life have been dissected over and over by historians, who try to establish some kind of relationship between him and Anne, based on this poem. However, *Circa Regna Tonat* is not written about Anne, but about the events surrounding her, of which Wyatt was a part. This affected Anne Boleyn's public image because Wyatt uncovered the philosophical truth behind her rise and fall – she was ambitious and reached above her station. She created enemies who brought her down. Although Wyatt does not condemn her for her ambition, he implies that she could have avoided it yet knowing that she would not have. Anne's fall was not her fault. She was a victim of a mean, capricious, egotistical and all-powerful king, and her public image has suffered because of this. This outlines literature's importance in examining image and perception because it tells us what was thought about a person or event, even if it was not true.

Anne Boleyn's Execution Speech on 19 May 1536

There are several versions of Anne Boleyn's execution speech which survive, but all seem to be fairly similar in nature, with some differences in the grammar and syntax but with the same essence. The below is as reported by John Foxe in his *Actes and Monuments*, better known as the *Book of Martyrs*:

> Good Christian people! I am come hither to die, for according to the law, and by the law, I am judged to death; and therefore I will speak nothing against it. I come hither to accuse no man, not to speak any thing of that whereof I am accused and condemned to die; but I pray God save the king, and send him long to reign over you, for a gentler, or a more merciful prince was there never; and to me he was ever a good, a gentle, and a sovereign lord. And if any person will meddle of my cause, I require them to judge the best. And thus I take my leave of the world, and of you all, and I heartily desire you all to pray for me. O Lord have mercy on me! To God I commend my soul.[68]

In terms of last words, Anne's seemed to be fairly conventional, non-confrontational, and accepting of her fate. However, saying that she required people 'to judge the best' seems to be a subtle way of proclaiming that the charges against her were not all they appeared to be, and that she was not the monster she was portrayed as at her trial. She praised the king, recognising that he put her in the exalted position she held, describing him as 'a good, a gentle, and a sovereign lord' and that 'a gentler or a more merciful prince was there never'.[69] There has been debate over the years about whether Anne truly loved Henry, or whether she married him for the power and prestige of a crown. It seems that Anne did love Henry, maybe not right at the beginning, but she grew to. Anne did not have to be quite so effusive in her praise of the king. Many execution speeches which survive seem to accept the justness of the sentence under the law and ask forgiveness, perhaps admitting sins, and praying for the king. Anne's seems more positive, perhaps her way of showing her love, even though it is his wish that she died and leave their daughter motherless.

Tracy Borman writes that Anne's 'act of calm acquiescence was deliberate', hoping to soften Henry's heart towards her and, more importantly, their daughter, Elizabeth.[70] Elizabeth's prospects were bleak at this point: motherless, illegitimate, and likely without anyone to speak up for her. It would not have been lost on the people who gathered to watch the execution that Anne confessed to no sin and had not admitted to deserving the punishment about to be meted out.[71] Perhaps her refusal to admit to any wrongdoing and have people believe it would soften the public's attitude towards the young daughter she was leaving behind.

Tradition says that Anne's lifeless body was buried in an arrow chest as no one had thought to provide a coffin.[72] However, Natalie Grueninger questions this as the main source is a lost diary, and a contemporary Italian account records that the remains were placed in a coffin at the side of the scaffold.[73] So it is possible that Tower officials did provide a simple coffin for Anne to beburied in the Chapel of St Peter ad Vincula within the Tower of London.

* * *

What we learn from portrayals of Anne Boleyn as a traitor is that things are not always necessarily as they seem. There are some very different portrayals. The trial documents paint Anne in the blackest way, designed to condemn her utterly under the law and in the eyes of the people. However, we see grief and even anger in Wyatt's poetry, and the defiant attitude in the letter allegedly written to Henry VIII by Anne while she was imprisoned in the Tower awaiting trial. William Kingston's letters are probably the most accurate documents we have from May 1536. Kingston was told to report everything Anne said and did to Thomas Cromwell and, although there was a purpose to this, it does not make sense for him to report things that did not happen or were not said. Kingston could not control what Cromwell did with the information but there is no reason to think that what he reports in his letters was not what really happened, and it gives a sense of Anne's chaotic, confused, and scared mindset at the time.

May 1536 was the most turbulent time in Anne's life. She had been at the pinnacle of power in England and had held the love of a king for seven years before her marriage, producing an heir to the throne, though a daughter not a son. That marriage lasted just three years and would end on 19 May 1536 under the blade of an executioner's sword in the Tower of London. Anne could not have known that her greatest achievement would be her daughter, Elizabeth. Her death as a traitor is probably what most people remember about her. She was the first 'beheaded' in 'divorced, beheaded, died, divorced, beheaded, survived'. But as Katherine Howard states in *SIX The Musical*, there is so much more to all of Henry's queens than being just one word in a rhyme.[74] Anne Boleyn was so much more than 'beheaded', and she deserves to be remembered for more than her death and the charges against her.

Chapter 5

Anne Through Foreign Eyes

'It was in his power to humble her again in a moment more than he had exalted her'[1]

Anne Boleyn was an important figure in England in the late 1520s and 1530s so, naturally, foreign ambassadors in England wrote about her and reported back to their masters and mistresses. There were many comments made about this alluring woman who prompted the king of England to attempt to annul his marriage to his first wife, Katherine of Aragon, and then was often blamed for the Break with Rome. Anne quickly became well known across Europe, and generally not favourably. Letters from ambassadors tended to include Anne from around 1529, once the annulment case was common knowledge. It is harder to find letters referencing her prior to this period.

The most notable foreign ambassador to write about Anne Boleyn was Eustace Chapuys, ambassador to the Holy Roman Emperor, Charles V, from 1529 to 1545, which covers the key period of Anne's rise and queenship, if not the courtship phase. We have to acknowledge that Chapuys was loyal above all to Katherine of Aragon and Princess Mary, and this does colour his opinions on some of the events he related in his letters, but he is not 'rabidly catholic, misogynistic, blinded by personal hatred and driven by personal agenda' as we see in some popular culture.[2] David Starkey says that Chapuys 'despite his evident bias, was careful about his sources. He usually gives the names of his informants, and, on inspection, they turn out to be an impressive bunch. They include leading councillors and courtiers, as well as intimate hangers-on about the great, such as doctors and priests'.[3] Stephanie Russo declares that the dispatches of Eustace Chapuys 'helped to shape many of our conceptions of Anne as a woman of dangerous and disruptive sexuality'.[4] We cannot just dismiss Chapuys' accounts because he was hostile to Anne Boleyn, because his letters are a hugely valuable source in studying her life. He relates events truthfully as he understands them, though often adds his own opinions as well.

Antoine de Castelnau, Bishop of Tarbes, was the French ambassador to the English court during the pivotal period of 1535 to 1537, covering Anne Boleyn's queenship, fall from power, and execution. When he was recalled to

France in 1537, Castelnau then became French ambassador to Spain for a short period before his death in 1539. It was under Castelnau's roof that his secretary, Lancelot de Carles, wrote a poem about Anne Boleyn, her life, and eventual fate.

Lancelot de Carles was a member of a French embassy in London at the time of Anne Boleyn's fall and execution, and he wrote a poem about the events less than a month after Anne's death. But the veracity of his account, like many of the accounts from foreign ambassadors and visitors, has been questioned. We cannot be sure how much Carles knew as he was not an integral part of the court, or close to those involved. Much of his information would have come second-hand, or from rumours which swirled around London at the time. There has not been a full English translation until recently, completed by Joann DellaNeva, but Elizabeth Norton has reproduced an English summary created in the nineteenth century.[5] This will be examined more closely as part of this chapter.

We cannot discount foreign accounts of the events in England. Although they may not have had all of the information, few people did. Ambassadors would have been fed the information that the host country, in this case England, wanted them to know. But they would also report on any rumours and reports they had been able to glean from elsewhere. It is quite possible that they paid informants to give them information from the inner circles at court. This may be why Eustace Chapuys seemed to be so well informed. Ambassadorial accounts are interesting to read, as they contrast events that we know happened with some more controversial accounts, so it can be difficult to know what is truth, and what is a rumour or fabrication. But it is important to examine the accounts as they can give a sense of how Anne Boleyn was viewed abroad and what the rulers of Europe were being told about events in England at the time.

Eustace Chapuys, Imperial Ambassador to Charles V

Eustace Chapuys was the English ambassador to the Holy Roman Emperor and king of Spain, Charles V. Charles V was the nephew of Katherine of Aragon and stood against the divorce of Henry VIII from his aunt, and his remarriage to Anne Boleyn. Chapuys was in England through the annulment of Henry VIII's marriage to Katherine of Aragon, his marriage to Anne Boleyn, the birth of Elizabeth I, Anne's fall from power and execution. Chapuys would also see the king marry Jane Seymour, Anne of Cleves, Katherine Howard, and Katherine Parr. Historian Lauren Mackay has written an interesting study called *Inside the Tudor Court: Henry VIII and his Six Wives through the eyes of the Spanish Ambassador* and she opens the study by describing Chapuys' importance in providing observations on the Henrician Tudor court:

> From Chapuys we learn about Henry the man, his matrimonial woes, his six wives, and other colourful personalities. Historians have provided us with sketches of these individuals, but Chapuys provides us with invaluable letters and despatches, which give them their colour and texture. His reports transcend politic because he focuses on personalities rather than just diplomatic process. Eustace Chapuys has for too long remained in the shadow of other Tudor personalities.[6]

Mackay opens Chapuys up as a person rather than just an ambassador in England. Chapuys is dismissed by some historians as being overly biased and thus diminishes the value of his letters and accounts. However, Chapuys' accounts are incredibly important in the history of the reign of Henry VIII as he sees so much during his sixteen-year tenure, through all six of Henry VIII's wives, and the Break with Rome. His 'ambassadorial correspondence provides historians with a rich and detailed narrative of the players and proceedings' at the Henrician court.[7] It is a pivotal time and Chapuys is trusted to report the truth back to his master, Charles V. So as much as he refuses to refer to Anne Boleyn by her name, or as queen, we cannot merely dismiss his letters out of hand as there is a lot of valuable information within them. We just need to be aware of his biases towards Anne Boleyn and the reformed faith. The events he reports, though, are more than likely to be true.

Not long after Chapuys arrived in England as ambassador, he reported to Charles V in a letter dated 4 September 1529 that 'the dukes of Suffolk and Norfolk, and Milord Rochfort, the father of Lady Anne Boleyn, are the King's most favourite courtiers' and that 'if the said Lady Anne chooses, the Cardinal will be soon dismissed, and his affair settled; for she happens to be the person in all this kingdom who hates him most, and has spoken and acted the most openly against him'.[8] Chapuys seemed to immediately grasp what was going on, and the power that Anne had in England. The Duke of Norfolk was her uncle, and Lord Rochford was, at this time, her father, though the Rochford title would go to Anne's brother, George, when her father was created Earl of Wiltshire and Ormond in December 1529. Wolsey would soon after this letter be toppled and would die in disgrace on 29 November 1530 on his way back to London from York to be tried for treason.

Chapuys records an event in a letter dated 15 June 1530, which demonstrated Anne Boleyn's frustration at the length of time the annulment was taking to achieve, and how Henry VIII still seemed reluctant to break with his first wife, Katherine of Aragon. Chapuys had written that if Anne could be kept away from the court for a while, then Katherine might regain her influence over the king, as Henry had sent Katherine some fabric and asked her to make it into shirts for him. Anne Boleyn heard about the request and sent for the gentleman who had delivered the fabric to Katherine on the king's orders, and 'abused the bearer in the King's very presence, threatening that she would have him punished severely'.[9] There was talk after this event of dismissing some members of the royal household to please Anne. Henry VIII was bending over backwards to do whatever he could to make things easier for her, but he was not yet willing to break with Katherine completely.

Anne Boleyn was created Marquess of Pembroke in her own right on 1 September 1532 and Chapuys recorded the event in a letter to Charles V on 5 September. He wrote that the 'appointment was publicly made with much ceremonious pomp' and Anne was granted a 'fine revenue of 4,000 ducats a year' with a 'most solemn mass' then being celebrated to mark Anne's elevation.[10] Chapuys then wrote of the plan for Henry VIII and Anne Boleyn to visit Calais together in October 1532, and that Henry would journey out from Calais to meet Francis I, but that Anne would remain behind at Calais. There is then a comment that repairs have been made both inside and outside the Tower of London, refitting the royal apartments 'which circumstance makes some people believe that it is the King's intention to send the Queen thither, whilst he himself is out of the country. This, however, is highly improbable, unless the King wants to exasperate his subjects and drive them to rebellion'.[11] The queen referred to is, of course, Katherine of Aragon. That Chapuys believes Henry would do this to his wife is telling of what he thinks of the king. However, that was never the king's intention. The apartments at the Tower were being refurbished in anticipation of Anne Boleyn's coronation, which would take place less than a year after this letter, on 1 June 1533. It was tradition for a monarch to reside in the Tower before their coronation.

Eustace Chapuys reported on 3 September 1533, just days before the birth of Princess Elizabeth, that Henry VIII and Anne Boleyn had quarrelled and that Henry had 'told her that she must shut her eyes, and endure as well as more worthy persons, and that she ought to know that it was in his power to humble her again in a moment more than he had exalted her'.[12] Anne would have been in seclusion, but she still had her ladies around her, who were in and out of her rooms and could have passed information on, or spread rumours. Chapuys claimed that Henry had not spoken to Anne in two or three days, but that 'no doubt these things are lovers' quarrels, to which we must not attach too great importance'.[13] Chapuys must have known that Henry and Anne's relationship had been stormy from the beginning, and that it was made up of tempestuous arguments and passionate reunions. It is difficult to understand why an argument such as this would have happened at this point, with Anne days away from giving birth to what both believed would be a son and heir. Henry would not want to threaten to lower Anne at a time when she was expected to give birth to an heir, and which could be seen at this time to threaten her health and that of her unborn child. Perhaps it was merely a rumour which Chapuys reported, hoping that it would be true, and that the marriage was already rocky.

Chapuys was always opposed to Henry VIII's marriage to Anne Boleyn, and devoted to Katherine of Aragon and her daughter, Princess Mary. Katherine was also the aunt of Charles V, so Chapuys felt a huge amount of loyalty to her. It has been suggested that Chapuys always referred to Anne as 'the Concubine' and it is true that he never referred to her as 'Queen' in his letters, but he actually usually referred to her as 'the Lady'. This idea that he called her a concubine all of the time has been largely debunked by Lauren Mackay. The original letters only have him call her a concubine in a single letter in 1531, and again in 1535 through to her execution.[14] It is possible that this was a confusion or deliberate change in the process of translation. Chapuys refers to Anne as 'the Concubine' and revels in her fall from power and imprisonment in the Tower of London in a letter dated 2 May 1536. He opens his letter referring to the conversation he had with Cromwell 'about the divorce of this King from the Concubine'.[15] It seems word had already got out that Henry wanted out of his second marriage before Anne was arrested. The matter was raised with the council who, Chapuys reports, advised the king, 'that he could not separate from the Concubine without tacitly confirming, not only the first marriage, but also, what he most fears, the authority of the Pope'.[16] Henry had broken with Rome in order to annul his marriage to Katherine of Aragon and marry Anne Boleyn. He would not go back on either of those things, and he certainly was not willing to accept that he could be wrong. Henry was stubborn and convinced of his divine right.

The letter written on 2 May, the day of Anne's arrest, demonstrates Chapuys' knowledge that three men had already been arrested alongside Anne: Mark Smeaton, 'a player on the spinnet', Henry Norris, 'for not having revealed the matter', and Anne's brother, George Boleyn.[17] Chapuys did not seem to know that Norris was also arrested for adultery and not just misprision, although there would have been a lot of rumours flying around London and the court and it would have been unclear which ones were true. Chapuys also noted that the marriage between Henry VIII and Anne Boleyn could be annulled, as witnesses had testified that a marriage had been made and consummated nine years earlier between Anne and Henry Percy, now Earl of Northumberland.[18] Henry VIII would not now be expected to return to Katherine of Aragon, which he would have been prior to January 1536 when Katherine died. Katherine of Aragon had been Anne Boleyn's safety net. Chapuys seems to have been very well informed, possibly getting his information directly from Thomas Cromwell, who allegedly had orchestrated Anne's fall. In a letter on 6 June 1536 from

Chapuys to Charles V, he reports that Cromwell had told him that 'he, himself, had been authorised and commissioned by the King to prosecute and bring to an end the mistress's trial, to do which he had taken considerable trouble' and had 'planned and brought about the whole affair'.[19] When Charles V replied to Chapuys' letter of 2 May, his focus was on arranging another marriage for Henry VIII, 'as we suppose that the King will put her and her accomplices to death and take another wife, as he is of amorous complexion and always desires to have a male child'.[20] Charles understood Henry. He proposed the Infanta of Portugal or the dowager Duchess of Milan as a third wife for the English king, unaware that he had already chosen to marry Jane Seymour, his second wife's lady-in-waiting.

Chapuys did not just write to Charles V, but also to one of his most trusted advisers, Nicolas Perrenot de Granvelle. In a letter to Granvelle dated 18 May, Chapuys described Anne Boleyn as 'the English Messalina, or Agrippina'.[21] Messalina was the third wife of the Roman Emperor, Claudius, and was said to be sexually promiscuous. Agrippina was the fourth wife of that same Roman Emperor, Claudius, and she had huge influence, but fell out of favour and was killed. Chapuys was placing Anne Boleyn in history as a sexually promiscuous woman with undue power and influence, foreshadowing her death the day before her actual execution. In that same letter, Chapuys reported that Anne blamed him for her predicament, and said that, 'I confess that I was rather flattered by the compliment and consider myself very lucky at having escaped her vengeance'.[22] The idea that Anne Boleyn was vengeful is not new. She was thought to have been involved in the fall from power of Cardinal Thomas Wolsey in 1529, and his death the following year. According to George Cavendish, Wolsey's gentleman usher, she had sworn 'that if it lay ever in her power, she would work the cardinal as much displeasure'.[23] Chapuys never supported Anne's marriage to the king and wanted her out of the way. He had hoped to restore Katherine of Aragon to the throne but after her death in January 1536, he hoped instead to restore Princess Mary, Katherine and Henry's daughter, to the succession. Mary would eventually be returned to the succession in 1544, along with Elizabeth, though neither daughter was legitimised.

One of the key takeaways from this letter is that Chapuys reported on the annulment of Henry VIII and Anne Boleyn's marriage, and the bastardisation of Princess Elizabeth, hoping that Princess Mary would now be declared legitimate as a result. He assumed that the fall of Anne and Elizabeth would mean the restoration of Katherine and Mary. Chapuys at this point, however, underestimated Henry VIII and his inability to admit he was wrong. Regarding the annulment of Henry and Anne's marriage, Chapuys reported that Thomas Cranmer, Archbishop of Canterbury:

> …had pronounced the marriage of the King and of his mistress to have been unlawful and nul in consequence of the King himself having had connexion with Anne's sister, and that both he and she being aware and well acquainted with such an impediment, the good faith of the parents could not possibly legitimize the daughter.[24]

Chapuys sounded gleeful that the marriage was annulled, as he never accepted it was valid anyway, hopeful for Princess Mary's legitimisation. Chapuys was convinced that the reason for the annulment was Henry VIII's previous relationship with Anne's sister, Mary, rather than Anne's own previous relationship with Henry Percy. Perhaps Percy's letter to Cromwell stating that 'the same may be to my damnation if ever there were any contract or promise of marriage between her and me' had convinced the king and Cromwell that it could not be used as a reason for annulment.[25] However, Henry VIII's relationship with Mary Boleyn was well known so that was an easy alternative reason. It is one of Henry's only extra marital sexual relationships that we can be certain of, along with that with Elizabeth 'Bessie' Blount, who was the mother of the king's illegitimate son, Henry Fitzroy. Henry probably would have favoured using Anne's relationship with Henry Percy as then it would be Anne's fault, where his relationship with Mary Boleyn was his fault. Henry did not like to accept blame, even if it was in his interests. Chapuys commented in a letter, dated 19 May 1536 to Charles V, that the joy at the 'ruin of the Concubine' is 'inconceivable' and that Henry VIII had told his illegitimate son, Henry Fitzroy, that he and Princess Mary were 'greatly bound to God for having escaped the hands of that accursed whore' who had intended to poison them both.[26] The insinuation is that Anne Boleyn could not stand the thought of any other children of the king being placed above her own, and that she would do whatever she needed to in order to stop that happening.

In this same letter, Chapuys reported on the mood of the people, saying that although people rejoice at Anne's execution, 'there are some who murmur at the mode of procedure against her and the others' and that 'already it sounds ill in the ears of the people'.[27] Even before Anne's execution, there seems to have been some questions over whether Anne was really guilty of the crimes of which she was accused, and how it was all done. Chapuys believed that the king had shown himself happy since Anne's arrest and was banqueting with ladies, accompanied by music. He thought it would not 'pacify the world when it is known what has passed and is passing' between the king and Jane Seymour.[28] Even at the time, there was some doubt over whether the charges were true, and whether there was another reason why Henry wanted so desperately to be rid of Anne that he would kill her. Henry would be betrothed to Jane Seymour the day after Anne Boleyn's execution, and they would marry just ten days after that, on 30 May 1536.

Chapuys also commented on Anne Boleyn's reformist beliefs, saying that he believed 'most of the newly created bishops will soon have their desert', meaning that they will soon be out of their positions when the Reformation was undone on Anne's fall, and that he believed that the reformist bishops had encouraged Anne to seek sexual favours elsewhere, even within her own family, when her husband was unable to perform.[29] This makes no sense in terms of the bishops, as any child Anne bore needed to be unquestionably legitimate. As would be proven as well, the Reformation would not be undone with Anne's disgrace and execution in 1536. Chapuys believed that Anne Boleyn was the catalyst and creator of the Reformation in England and the destruction of the religious houses, and he thought that Henry VIII would undo the reforms and correct the succession once Anne was gone. However, Henry would never again make the Pope head of the Church in England or legitimise Princess Mary.

Eustace Chapuys, as a staunch supporter of Katherine of Aragon and her daughter, was also a strong devotee of the Catholic faith, making him a natural enemy of Anne Boleyn and Protestantism. He would never refer to Anne Boleyn as queen or acknowledge her as such and he blamed Anne for the annulment of the marriage of Katherine of Aragon and Henry VIII and the bastardisation of their daughter, Mary. However, there are possible complications with the translation of Chapuys' letters as he spoke very little English and spoke and wrote largely in French or occasionally Latin, and his early reports on Anne and the Boleyns were 'positive, without the malice or hostility that he has often been accused of'.[30] This is an interesting insight which comes from reading the letters directly, and not relying on the opinions of others. His hostility developed as it became clear to him how far Henry VIII and Anne Boleyn were willing to go, but even he, in the end, recognised Anne's courage and bravery.

French Ambassadors to England

Francis I of France was considered to be Henry VIII's great rival. The two met at the Field of the Cloth of Gold event in 1520, 'both in their prime' with Henry VIII aged 28, and Francis I aged 25 – 'the two men were known for their charisma vitality, athleticism and their love of pleasure'.[31] The pair were determined to outdo each other, and this vein of competition and rivalry continued throughout their reigns. Francis I would outlive Henry VIII by just two months, so their reigns run parallel to each other. Jean de Dinteville, Bailly of Troyes, was sent to England on several occasions during the years of Anne's rise to power and during her queenship and his letters give some information about Anne. Antoine de Castelnau, Bishop of Tarbes, was the French ambassador in England for just two years from 1535 to 1537. France and the Empire were constantly at each other's throats in this period and turned to England for support. With Katherine of Aragon having a familial tie to Emperor Charles V, France looked like a natural ally for England in this period with Anne Boleyn on the throne. Castelnau wrote to Jean de Dinteville, who had been a former French ambassador to the English court, and Dinteville was sent back to England to support Castelnau in September 1535. Castelnau had received a 'chilly' reception on his arrival in England when he was denied access to Bridewell Palace, a semi-official residence for the French ambassadors.[32] This was not a good start to his ambassadorship, and probably made him more hostile towards Henry VIII. When Dinteville arrived, he was received by Henry VIII and Anne Boleyn at Winchester, but there is no record of Antoine de Castelnau being present.[33] The reason for this snub is unclear. Castelnau does not talk about Anne Boleyn so much in his letters, unlike Chapuys. There are occasional references to the queen and the old queen, but he does not seem to have the fascination and almost revulsion for Anne that we find in the Imperial correspondence; even during Anne's fall from power, there is little written. Dinteville is a more reliable author in terms of correspondence and one of his periods in England covers the birth of the future Elizabeth I.

In March 1533 there is a tantalising glimpse of the relationship between Anne Boleyn and the French. In a letter from Anne de Montmorency, 1st Duke of Montmorency to Jean de Dinteville, he wrote that he 'sends a letter in the King's hand to Madame la Marquise', meaning Anne Boleyn.[34] Although Anne Boleyn and Henry VIII had been married for nearly two months at this time, the news had not been made public yet. That happened at Easter 1533. Anne had been created Marquess of Pembroke in her own right on 1 September 1532, to prepare her to travel with Henry VIII to France. Her title was marquess up until the announcement of her marriage and queenship. This letter from Francis I to Anne Boleyn does not seem to survive and was likely destroyed. It would be interesting to read it and to see what the French king was saying to Anne at this pivotal time; was he declaring his support for her and the king following their meeting at Calais in October 1532? Like so many things about Anne Boleyn, we will never know. In June 1533 Marguerite of Navarre, sister to Francis I, also wrote a letter to the Bailly of Troyes, enclosing a friendly message to Anne.[35] Again, we do not know what was in the letter, but Marguerite had known Anne when she was growing up at the French court, serving Francis's first wife, Claude, from 1515 onwards. It has been suggested that it was Marguerite who informed Anne's passion for religious reform, but 'the evidence for a close relationship is inconsistent at best'.[36] Even if they did not have a close relationship, it is possible that Anne was influenced by Marguerite, and that Marguerite sought to use this connection with Anne Boleyn to form stronger religious ties between prominent reformers.

On 3 September 1533, just four days before Anne Boleyn gave birth to her first child, Dinteville wrote to Francis I that the Duke of Norfolk had asked him 'whether the Bailly has orders to hold at the font the child of which the Queen is pregnant, if it is a boy … the King said the Queen would probably be delivered before an answer could be had … the King means the child, if a boy, to be named Edward or Henry'.[37] The inference of the constant refrain 'if it is a boy' suggests that the child was not to be offered the honour of being held by the French ambassador if it was a girl, as indeed it would be. This child would not be named Edward or Henry, but Henry VIII's later son with Jane Seymour would be christened Edward. Perhaps as Henry VIII's first son, Henry, Duke of Cornwall, had died within weeks of his birth, it was considered a bad omen, though many children were given the same names as dead siblings in this period. In response to this letter, Francis I wrote that he 'would be glad to send some notable personage to be present at the baptism of the expected prince … will send a ring to be presented to the Queen'.[38] The French sending an envoy to be at the christening of Henry VIII and Anne Boleyn's child, which would not turn out to be a prince but a princess, was a tacit confirmation from France that their marriage was valid and their children the legitimate heirs to the English throne.

In a letter written shortly after his arrival in England in 1535, Castelnau wrote that 'all the people is marvellously discontented; most of them, excepting the relations of the present Queen, because of the old Queen and her daughter, others because of the subversion of religion', and that 'the lower people, in consequence of these things, are greatly exasperated against the Queen, saying concerning her a thousand ill and improper things'.[39] Castelnau's tone is a lot less blunt than Chapuys and almost confrontational, though Castelnau did not have the history with Katherine of Aragon and Princess Mary that would make him such a staunch partisan of their cause. The people of England were seemingly upset at the fate of Katherine of Aragon and her daughter, and their displacement by Anne Boleyn and Princess Elizabeth. Katherine had been banished to Kimbolton Castle as she had refused to accept the annulment, and people blamed Anne for this, and for the religious changes sweeping across England. We know now, with hindsight, that these religious changes would not stop with Anne's death and in fact would gather pace. So perhaps blaming Anne was not entirely accurate. 'Ill and improper things' probably include an assertion by one Suffolk woman that Anne was a 'goggle-eyed whore'.[40] Women in particular could not stomach the fact that their king had abandoned his wife and child for a younger woman.

Eustace Chapuys, the Imperial ambassador, wrote in a letter dated 19 May 1536 that the men accused with Anne Boleyn were beheaded, 'notwithstanding the intercession of the bishop of Tarbes, the French ambassador resident, and the sieur de Dinteville, who arrived the day before yesterday on behalf of one named Weston'.[41] John Husee wrote to Lord Lisle on 13 May that 'if any escape, it will be young Weston, for whom importunate suit is made'.[42] Could this have been because the French were trying to intervene? It is not clear, nor why the French would want to protect Weston above the others.

The ambassadors from the French court to the English court in the 1530s were far less forthcoming on their opinions of Anne Boleyn than the Imperial ambassador, Eustace Chapuys. There is a further complication in that Chapuys was consistently in England throughout Anne's tenure, both before and after her wedding, whereas the French ambassadors changed more often, and so they probably had less knowledge of the English court, and fewer connections through which to glean information. The various French ambassadors also had less of a personal interest in Anne – Emperor Charles V was Katherine of Aragon's nephew, so her replacement was a personal slight to him. Francis I had no personal connection to the annulment case. This places his ambassadors at more of a remove, and with less interest in Anne Boleyn herself.

Lancelot de Carles

Lancelot de Carles was a young Catholic cleric serving as a secretary to the French ambassador, Antoine de Castelnau, Bishop of Tarbes, in England. Carles would later be made a bishop himself when he became Bishop of Riez in 1550. Carles arrived in England in 1535 with Castelnau and makes some interesting comments on Anne Boleyn's fall, but any comments on her earlier life would have been based on hearsay and rumour, or earlier accounts, as he was not then present in England.[43] Carles is 'remarkably balanced' in his portrayal of the reformist Anne Boleyn in his poem *The Story of the Death of Anne Boleyn*, as he believed Anne presided over a flirtatious court, but that her courage and religious fortitude took centre stage as she came to the end of her life.[44] The portrait of Anne that Carles produced suggests that he believed she was innocent of the charges against her, even at the time of her death. It often seems to be assumed that everyone at the time thought her guilty, but this was not the case. Even those you would not take to be her supporters doubted the veracity of the charges.

A big part of Carles' account is the relating of a conversation between siblings Sir Anthony Browne and Elizabeth Somerset, Countess of Worcester. Lady Worcester responded to her brother's accusations of her own loose conduct by accusing Anne Boleyn of worse, including incest with her brother. If the Lady Worcester conversation did actually happen, she would have been dependent on interpreting things in the queen's chamber, not witnessing the adultery or incest herself.[45] It is possible that this is where the accusation of incest against George and Anne Boleyn originated, rather than with George's wife, Jane, Lady Rochford. However, there is not enough solid evidence against either woman to say which, if either, gave evidence against Anne and George. In a modern court, this would not have been enough to convict, as it is circumstantial and interpretative. Susan Bordo describes Worcester's comments as a 'desperate attempt to deflect attention from her own guilt, as a child will do when accused'.[46] Siblings even when grown can quarrel like children. Eric Ives says that it is 'highly plausible' to say that the woman and her 'strait-laced' brother were Anthony Browne and Lady Worcester.[47] Carles specified a single woman as the source of the story, in comparison to Thomas Cromwell's official version of events which says that ladies of the queen's chamber told councillors about her behaviour, not naming Lady Worcester or any other specific lady. Cromwell's words were that 'the queen's incontinent living was so rank and common that the ladies of her privy chamber could not conceal it'.[48] But if the first instance, as in the indictment, happened just after Elizabeth's birth in September or October 1533 then her ladies had concealed it for several years already before it came out. We cannot, therefore, say for certain that Lady Worcester did in fact speak against Anne Boleyn, though she appeared to be linked to the events of May 1536 fairly quickly, so it seems likely she was at least questioned. Carles probably heard rumours at the court and in London of what was going on during this time.

Given that Carles' poem is the first real suggestion and the earliest implication we have of Lady Worcester's involvement in Anne Boleyn's fall and execution, it is worth examining this section of his work in more detail. Joann DellaNeva has written a detailed translation of the poem, from a previously unstudied manuscript. The nineteenth-century English summary of Carles' poem, however, describes it thus:

> A lord of the Privy Council seeing clear evidence that his sister loved certain persons with a dishonourable love, admonished her fraternally. She acknowledged her offence, but said it was little in her case in comparison with that of the Queen, as he might ascertain from Mark [Smeaton], declaring that she was guilty of incest with her own brother. The brother did not know what to do on this intelligence, and took counsel with two friends of the king, with whom he went to the king himself and one reported it in the name of all three.[49]

Elizabeth Norton states that the lord of the Privy Council was Anthony Browne, or possibly his half-brother, William Fitzwilliam, and the sister was Elizabeth Somerset, Countess of Worcester.[50] If this conversation did happen and it was reported to the king, which is heavily debated by historians, then a spat between siblings turned into something with much wider ranging political consequences, and deadly ones at that. There is a lack of names in this description altogether, not even naming Browne and Lady Worcester, let alone the two friends Browne confided in. It feels very elusive and unclear. This means that we cannot altogether trust the account with the lack of important details. It does not mean that it did not happen, but at a distance of 500 years we cannot take it at face value as fact.

Carles, when writing about Anne Boleyn's trial, said that she entered the court 'not as one who had to defend her cause but with the bearing of one coming to great honour'.[51] Perhaps Anne knew that this would be her one and only time to speak and shape how history would see her on the record. Unfortunately, if Anne got the chance to speak at the trial, her words do not survive. We are left with her words on the scaffold as her testament to history. As much as Carles does not share Anne's religious convictions and asserts that she was at the centre of a flirtatious court, he does put emphasis on her strength and bravery at the end in various ways. He reports that she 'defended herself soberly against the charges, her face saying more for her than her words; for she said little, but no one to look at her would have thought her guilty'.[52] It seems Anne Boleyn's guilt was immediately in doubt before it had even been declared.

When compared with the Catholic polemicist Nicholas Sander, Lancelot de Carles comes across as much more accepting and believable, despite his account being written as a poem rather than a historical account. When Anne Boleyn was declared guilty of adultery, incest and treason and sentenced to be burned or beheaded at the king's pleasure, Carles has Anne appealing to God. According to Carles, she says, 'whether the sentence was deserved; then turning to the judges, said she would not dispute with them, but believed there was some other reason for which she was condemned than the cause alleged, of which her conscience acquitted her, as she had always been faithful to the king'.[53] Once again, Anne's courage and strength shine through in Carles' account, that she maintained her innocence to the end, even knowing that she would certainly die and would have to face her God. That she died proclaiming her innocence says a lot for such a pious woman. In such a religious time, going to your death without admitting such a big sin would mean you would not be allowed into heaven. Anne would not have risked that, as her immortal soul was the most important thing to consider at the time of death in the sixteenth century.

Stephanie Russo explains that Carles' work is a 'rather odd generic hybrid that sits in a liminal space between fact and fiction'; fundamentally a literary text, a forerunner of modern historical fiction, but based on historical fact as he knew it.[54] Susan Bordo says Carles' work is 'rightly regarded as not much more than a description of a chain of gossip and accusation'.[55] It was written in the weeks immediately following Anne Boleyn's death, so it does not have the hindsight that we have in the twentieth century, or even that which the likes of William Shakespeare and Francis Bacon had at the end of the sixteenth and into the seventeenth centuries. Although it is an account written by a foreigner, and not one in the cut and thrust of the Henrician court, perhaps it can be more relied on than might be thought. Those nobles and other courtiers within the court were trying to save themselves, whereas foreigners did not have to worry so much about their lives and so could report more accurately. It is interesting to consider.

* * *

So why is it important to consider Anne Boleyn through foreign eyes? Foreign ambassadors and their households were trusted to write honestly back to their masters and mistresses about what was going on in England. The events related in ambassadorial correspondence are probably truthful as the writers understood them. Opinions are often expressed, as in the letters of Eustace Chapuys, but the basic events themselves are likely to be true. When examining the opinions abroad about Anne and Henry VIII and their relationship, it can give an insight into what people really thought. In England, people were being constrained by the Acts of Supremacy and Succession of 1534 to accept Anne Boleyn, Princess Elizabeth, and Henry's position as Supreme Head of the Church in England. Abroad this was not the case, so opinions were more freely expressed.

Lancelot de Carles' poem relates many events in Anne Boleyn's life, though for some the veracity of his account is doubted because he writes in a poetic form rather than prose. That does not mean that the historical events he reported on are less than true. The French ambassadors of the period changed, whereas the Imperial ambassador was consistent across Anne's rise and fall. Eustace Chapuys is always an intriguing person to read the correspondence of, because he has such strong opinions about Anne Boleyn yet will never name her. Other ambassadors are more diplomatic, referring to Anne as the current queen and Katherine of Aragon as the former queen. For Chapuys, Katherine is always the queen and Mary the princess, Anne the lady or the concubine, and Elizabeth the bastard.

Chapter 6

Anne as Reformer

'During her life, the religion of Christ most happily flourished'[1]

Anne Boleyn is most often, and traditionally, seen as a Protestant, a catalyst for the Break with Rome and the English Reformation. Henry VIII's first wife, Katherine of Aragon, was seen as the epitome of Roman Catholicism. Her daughter, Mary I, followed in her footsteps in terms of religious belief, earning the epithet of 'Bloody Mary' for her persecution of Protestants, Anne Boleyn, 'the other woman', was seen as the complete opposite because Henry VIII broke with Rome in order to marry her when the Pope refused to grant an annulment of his first marriage. During Elizabeth I's reign, efforts were made to try and distance Anne Boleyn from the charges against her, portraying her instead as being dedicated to spreading the word of God.[2] But how Protestant, or otherwise, was Anne?

Looking at the evidence, it appears that Anne Boleyn was neither Catholic nor Protestant, or an evangelical as has also been suggested. She was a reformer of Catholicism with some Protestant leanings when it suited her. Because of these Protestant leanings, her public image has suffered. G.W. Bernard argues that Anne revealed in the Tower, and through her belief in good works, 'a deeply conventional Catholicism'.[3] It is not known how much of an influence Anne actively had on the Break with Rome, but Henry was not severing the connection with Rome for religious or theological reasons. He was in love with Anne and the Pope would not give him an annulment of his marriage to Katherine of Aragon to enable him to marry her instead.[4] When in the Tower of London after her arrest and condemnation, knowing that she would likely die but still hoping for forgiveness, Anne requested to have the sacrament placed in her room so that she could pray for mercy. After her trial she wanted to be shriven, again a very Catholic and conventional measure.[5] Anne's religion sometimes appeared to be a calculated affair which negatively affected her public image and which she could adapt to her own purpose. But she was pious, having been exposed in her early years to reform, which she remained passionate about.

Thomas Freeman argues that Anne Boleyn was not necessarily an evangelical or Protestant, though it is difficult to know for sure either way what her private beliefs were. He suggests that there were other reasons for her actions that some have attributed to her Protestant or evangelical beliefs; her charity and piety can be seen as 'good public relations' and her support of evangelicals and reformers can possibly be seen as her building a power base.[6] Anne's charity and piety could simply be seen as the actions of a queen, or of a woman with a true belief in God who wanted to help others. That did not necessarily cover up a nefarious purpose. Katherine of Aragon and Anne's other predecessors, as well as her Tudor successors, were all pious and doled out charity as expected of a queen, so that is not singular in any way.

However, Maria Dowling argues that Anne Boleyn was an evangelical and she claims that Thomas Cranmer, Archbishop of Canterbury, was careful during Anne's fall to distance their Protestant cause from her so that the 'radical ground' gained by her time in power would not be lost.[7] Bernard ascertains that John Foxe, author of the *Book of Martyrs*, believed that Anne's so-called practice of 'pious evangelical reform' automatically disproved the charges of adultery against her, because a queen and religious woman such as she could never have done such a thing.[8] Foxe's arguments about Anne's religious beliefs will be explored in more detail later in this chapter.

Eric Ives believed that Anne Boleyn was a Protestant because of her links with known reformers such as Edward Foxe, Bishop of Hereford, Hugh Latimer, Bishop of Worcester, and John Hilsey, Bishop of Rochester.[9] G.W. Bernard refutes Ives's arguments by saying that many writers of Anne as a reformer such as John Foxe and William Latymer were trying to influence the religious outcomes in the country so it was not in their benefit to portray Anne as a conventional Catholic.[10] There may be some credence in this argument. Nevertheless, it does not necessarily show Anne's Protestant fervour because she rewarded anyone who helped and supported her marriage to the king and her becoming queen of England, whether Catholic or Protestant.

Both Reginald Pole and Nicholas Sander were Catholic writers with Pole publishing in the 1550s and Sander in the 1580s. John Foxe and Gilbert Burnet were Protestant writers with Foxe publishing in the 1560s and Burnet in the 1670s. It is fascinating that one of the four writers discussed in this chapter was a century, give or take, after the others. That perspective can be interesting to see what sources have been drawn from to analyse and reach conclusions. Sander's work is the most enduring, written specifically to counteract Foxe's account of Protestant martyrs. Sander sees Anne as 'a harlot and seductress who led Henry into heresy, filled the court with fellow heretics, and gave birth, both literally and metaphorically, to the most monstrous heresy of all: Elizabeth'.[11] Sander's work intended to disparage Anne Boleyn in order to denigrate Elizabeth I, a Protestant queen. Many religious works in the period had an ulterior motive, either to support or denigrate a particular point of view or religious perspective.

Reginald Pole's *Defense of the Unity of the Church*

Reginald Pole was the son of Margaret Pole, and grandson of George, Duke of Clarence. Clarence was brother of Richard III and Edward IV, so Reginald himself had a claim to the English throne. The family was Catholic and against the annulment of Henry VIII's marriage to Katherine of Aragon, his remarriage to Anne Boleyn and the English Reformation. Pole was offered the archbishopric of York if he supported the king's annulment, but he refused and went into self-imposed exile on the continent around 1532. He would only return to England on the accession of Mary I in 1553 and would be created Archbishop of Canterbury, the last Catholic Archbishop of Canterbury in England. His work, the *Defense of the Unity of the Church* was intended to persuade Henry VIII to renege on his Break with Rome, banish Anne Boleyn from the court, and undo the annulment of his marriage to Katherine of Aragon, legitimising the Princess Mary and making her once again heir to the English throne.

Pole wrote to Henry VIII, sending him a copy of his treatise on 27 May 1536, just eight days after Anne Boleyn's execution. Henry VIII had earlier asked Reginald Pole to declare his position regarding the authority of the Pope. He sent the work to the king, along with a set of instructions for the person who delivered it to Henry. The instructions declared that, 'unless the truth was purely set forth, it might turn to the utter undoing of the king, and destruction of the quietness of the realm' as 'sore and grievous acts' had already been committed.[12] It was a little late to try and persuade the king to give up Anne Boleyn and restore Katherine of Aragon, as both ladies were dead by the time the work was sent to England. Pole goes on in his instructions, written in the days after Anne's execution, to ask the king to:

> ...take as favourable admonition of God the detection of the iniquity of her which hath been the original cause and occasion of all these errors and dangers, and to follow the advice of those whose conscience and fidelity to the king caused them, against their own private wealth and with great danger, to dissent from that matrimony.[13]

Pole asks the king to listen now to those who had spoken out against his marriage to Anne Boleyn, as they had been proven correct. The subtext is that these same people who spoke out against Anne were also against the Break with Rome, which was conducted in order to allow the marriage to come about. There is always a link between Henry VIII and Anne Boleyn's marriage and the advent of reformed or even Protestant religion in England. The Break with Rome later allowed Edward VI to take a harsher view on Catholics and push the Protestant Reformation further than his father.

Pole's work is primarily about maintaining the unity of the Church, and speaking out against the Break with Rome. There is a section entitled 'Henry VIII and Anne Boleyn' where Pole says directly to the king that, 'if you would cherish your own salvation' he needs to listen to what Pole says regarding Anne and the Break with Rome.[14] Pole raises a valid point about Henry VIII's scruples of conscience regarding his marriage to Katherine of Aragon, asking 'You had her as wife for all of 20 years without any fear of the law. If the law moved you, why did it move you so late? Had it never occurred to you at all?'[15] Probably around May or June 1531 Pole gave Henry an analysis of the difficulties surrounding the annulment, both political and international, even though he had, 'almost certainly at least tacitly', given his acquiescence to convocation's acceptance of the king's headship of the Church of England in February 1531.[16] Something was influencing Pole's change of mind, possibly a realisation of how far the king was willing to go to marry Anne Boleyn. It was not just a scruple of conscience over the validity of his first marriage. In *Defense of the Unity of the Church*, Pole goes on to explain that:

> You, a man of your age and with such experience, are miserably burning with passion for the love of a girl. She, indeed, has said that she will make herself available to you on one condition alone. You must reject your wife whose place she desires to hold. This modest woman does not want to be your concubine! She wants to be your wife. I believe that she learned from the example of her sister, if in no other way, how quickly you can have your fill of concubines. She, however, was anxious to surpass her sister by retaining you as a lover.[17]

The comparison between 'man' and 'girl' emphasises the age gap, with Henry VIII being aged 41 when he married Anne in January 1533, and she around aged 31 if we take 1501 as an approximate birthdate. It makes the relationship seem like it was not love at all, but lust of a man for a younger woman. And it was this which led to the king annulling his marriage to his first wife, not the law or his conscience at all. Pole specifies that Anne Boleyn would not be his 'concubine' but would only be his wife. There is also a sense of competition between Anne and her sister, whether real or imagined. Anne was determined to do better than her sister and not be pushed aside once she had been used.

The word 'concubine' is one that the Imperial ambassador, Eustace Chapuys, used consistently in reference to Anne Boleyn, never referring to her as queen.

Reginald Pole is not openly hostile to Anne Boleyn in his treatise, but he questions Henry VIII's motives in pursuing her, and the legitimacy of any marriage which may happen between them. If Henry's marriage to Katherine of Aragon was null and void, then so would any marriage with Anne Boleyn be. Pole questions:

> What kind of woman is this one with whom you are now associating in place of your repudiated wife? Is she not the sister of the girl whom you first violated and whom you kept with you for a long time afterward as a concubine? How, therefore, do you inform us you are seeking refuge from an illicit marriage? Are you here ignorant of the law that no less explicitly forbids you to marry the sister of her with whom you have been made one body, than it forbids you to marry her who has been made one body with your brother? If one is to be abominated, so is the other.[18]

Pole's focus appears to be on what is right and lawful. If Henry VIII believed his marriage to Katherine was null and void because they were in the forbidden degrees of affinity as brother and sister-in-law, then his marriage to Anne Boleyn would also be within the forbidden degrees of affinity as Henry previously had a relationship with Anne's sister, Mary Carey née Boleyn. If one is wrong, then so is the other. Pole is using logic to dismantle Henry's case. However, Pole does not appear to have been against the annulment right from the beginning. He was sent to Paris in October 1529 to help secure favoured opinions from the universities for the divorce. Pole would later 'make it appear' that he tried to avoid the assignment, but evidence suggests he succeeded in his mission and returned home triumphant.[19] Unlike other authors writing histories of the Reformation, either for or against, Pole does not seem in this work to be denigrating Anne herself. His focus is on Henry's actions and motivations.

Reginald Pole remained on the continent until Mary I came to the throne in the 1550s, so he himself would not face Henry VIII's wrath directly. Pole was made a cardinal by Pope Paul III in 1536 and was tasked with obtaining support for the Pilgrimage of Grace, a Catholic rebellion against the dissolution of the monasteries, in 1536–7. The rebellion petered out and the hoped-for international support never materialised. However, Reginald's family suffered for his opinions and their relationship to them. Reginald's brother, Henry Pole, 1st Baron Montagu, was executed by Henry VIII in 1539, and their mother, Margaret Pole, Countess of Salisbury, was executed in 1541, after two years' imprisonment in the Tower of London.

John Foxe's *Book of Martyrs*

Foxe's *Book of Martyrs* is an interesting text, the full title being *Actes and Monuments of these Latter and Perillous Days, Touching Matters of the Church*, published in 1563. It was foremost a polemical religious text, covering the lives of those who died or were killed and who promoted the Protestant religion, specifically in England and Scotland. Anne Boleyn is one such 'martyr' covered, though today historians cannot agree on exactly what Anne's religious stance was. Both Protestants and Catholics seemed to agree with regard to the significance of Anne's influence on the Reformation in England, but that is where agreement between them stops. Protestants see it as 'reforming' but Catholics as creating a 'schism'.[20] One word has a positive and one a negative connotation.

John Foxe himself is an interesting character. Ordained a deacon by Nicholas Ridley on 24 June 1550, in the reign of Edward VI, he attracted the support of William Cecil around this time.[21] The first edition of his *Book of Martyrs* was published by John Day on 20 March 1563. It was a large volume, about 1800 pages, and largely focuses on English history, but also recounts events on the Continent that affected English history; it contains a wide range of sources and reprintings, which account for the length of the work.[22] Foxe was determined to promote the Protestant religion, so his work is very biased in that direction throughout.

Foxe focuses on descriptions of Anne, enhancing her religious piety and promotion of what he sees as the true Protestant religion. The section is entitled 'The Death of the Lady Katharine, Princess Dowager and that of Queen Anne', making Anne's position as queen of England very clear and depicting Katherine of Aragon as the dowager princess, not a queen.[23] His point of view on their positions is made obvious right at the beginning. Foxe proceeds, after relating Anne Boleyn's final speech on the scaffold, to an overview of her:

> And this was the end of that godly lady and queen. Godly I call her, for sundry respects, whatsoever the cause was, or quarrel objected against her. First, her last words spoken at her death declared no less than her sincere faith and trust in Christ, than did her quiet modesty utter forth the goodness of the cause and matter, whatsoever it was. Besides that to such as wisely can judge upon cases occurrent, this also may seem to give a great clearing unto her, that the king, the third day after, was married in his whites unto another. Certain this was, that for the rare and singular gifts of her mind, so well instructed, and given toward God, with such a fervent desire unto the truth and setting forth of sincere religion, joined with like gentleness, modesty, and pity toward all men, there have not many such queens before

> her borne the crown of England. Principally this one commendation she left behind her, that during her life, the religion of Christ most happily flourished, and had a right prosperous course.[24]

This was obviously propaganda to promote the Protestant faith in England. The final line is what Foxe wants people to remember of her, though he goes on in the following paragraph to outline her 'manifold virtues' including distribution of alms and the appointment of reformist bishops, again with distinctly religious and specifically Protestant overtones.[25] Historian Thomas Freeman has written, however, that, 'to paraphrase a remark made to Anne's daughter, Foxe's book cannot be used as a window onto Anne's conscience'.[26] When writing about Anne Boleyn's religion in the aftermath of her execution, many writers had a distinct purpose to either promote or denigrate a person or belief system. G.W. Bernard suggests that Foxe had a twofold purpose in his writing: to influence the developing Elizabethan religious settlement, and by presenting Anne as 'a modest and virtuous patron of religious reform' he implied that 'so devout a lady could not possibly have been guilty' of adultery, incest, and treason.[27] Foxe's work was published in the reign of Anne's daughter, Elizabeth I, who was seen as a goodly Protestant monarch by Foxe, so Anne Boleyn was presented in perhaps a more Protestant light than her actual beliefs.

Regarding Anne Boleyn's execution in May 1536, Foxe espouses the idea that Henry VIII's affection for Jane Seymour and his desire to marry her was the sole reason for his execution of Anne. Foxe reports that Henry, 'the third day after, was married in his whites unto another'.[28] Henry VIII married Jane Seymour on 30 May 1536, eleven days after Anne's execution. It is the only real comment Foxe makes on the reasons for Anne's downfall and execution, choosing instead to focus on her religion and good works. But he gets the date wrong. If he gets something as fundamental as this incorrect, does it undermine other claims he makes? Anne's chaplain, William Latymer, wrote a work in praise of Anne which seemed to inform much of Foxe's information, and Foxe came to the conclusion that Anne's efforts were 'a heroic accomplishment for which she paid with her life'.[29] Anne did pay with her life, though some would perhaps disagree with the reason for it – was it her religious beliefs, her flirtatious nature, or her failure to deliver a king a son? It is probably more nuanced, and several things came together which meant the king wanted rid of her.

John Foxe writes of Anne's charitable work, based on testimony obtained indirectly from her silkwoman, Jane Wilkinson. Anne handed out clothing and alms to the poor, compiling lists of poor householders and allocating funds, and carrying a purse with her daily to distribute alms.[30] Foxe sees Anne as being charitable in introducing Henry VIII to the work of Simon Fish, called

A Supplication for the Beggars. He describes how she received the book from overseas when Fish was staying with William Tyndale, and Anne's brother, George, read it and advised her to show it to the king, which she did, in around 1528. Anne told the king that the man who wrote it had fled abroad out of fear of the cardinal, meaning Wolsey.[31] Fish returned to England in around 1530 when his wife interceded with the king for him, and after Anne Boleyn had introduced Fish's book to Henry. Foxe also recounts another version of the story, where the book was instead brought to the king's attention by one of his footmen, eliminating Anne from the story.[32] This version is recounted in just a couple of lines, rather than the space given to the version featuring Anne Boleyn which is put within the complete narrative of Fish's life. That suggests where Foxe believes the truth of the story is and is quite telling.

Writing in the reign of Elizabeth I, when *Actes and Monuments* was first published, Foxe very obviously sees Elizabeth as the rightful queen, and a godly Protestant daughter of her mother, describing how God was 'maintaining, preserving, and advancing the offspring of her body, the Lady Elizabeth, now queen, whom the Lord hath so marvellously conserved from so manifold dangers, so royally hath exalted, so happily hath blessed with such virtuous patience' that her reign cannot be compared to those who went before her – her brother Edward VI and sister Mary I.[33] Edward and Mary were incredibly militant in their beliefs – Edward towards Protestantism and Mary for Catholicism. Elizabeth did not seem to be so set, preferring to try and establish a middle ground and not to persecute either side, especially given the terror of Mary's reign. She wanted to keep the love of her subjects, which her mother, Anne, did not seem to ever have by all accounts, and her half-sister, Mary, had lost, to her detriment and sorrow.

Nicholas Sander's *Rise and Growth of the Anglican Schism*

Nicholas Sander's description of Anne Boleyn is probably one of the most enduring, including the idea that she had a sixth finger and several disfiguring marks. This has often been taken to mean that Sander was portraying Anne as a witch but is this true? His work was posthumously published in 1585 in Cologne by Edward Rishton, four years after Sander's death, entitled *De origine ac progresu schimsatis anglicani*.

It was finally translated into English from the original Latin for the first time in 1877 by David Lewis with the title *Rise and Growth of the Anglican Schism*.[34] It was published in Rome in 1586 and 1588, in France in 1587, and in Germany in 1594, with the Latin version reissued in 1610 and 1628.[35] It seems to have been an enduring work, with demand for copies in other languages, and reprints, largely in Catholic countries, though Germany had many Protestant areas. There was probably also interest still in Henry VIII as he was a larger-than-life figure who hugely influenced international politics in the first half of the sixteenth century. Sander portrays Anne as a 'sexually promiscuous schismatic'.[36] His work is responsible for modern views of Anne Boleyn as a witch. For example, she appears on the wall of the grand staircase in Hogwarts in *Harry Potter and the Philosopher's Stone* (2001).[37] It always seems that negative accounts have far more influence in the public mind than positive ones.

Sander points out that, 'it often happens that we are on the brink of ruin when we consider ourselves most secure'. Anne Boleyn was pregnant again by the end of 1535 but in January 1536, according to Sander, she, 'brought forth only a shapeless mass of flesh'.[38] This is an example of Sander's 'sardonic tone', almost mocking Anne that she had failed to give the king a son.[39] Sander was determined to make sure Anne was denigrated, which would also reflect negatively on her daughter, Elizabeth, who was on the English throne when Sander published his work. He reported that Anne blamed her miscarriage on 'the day I caught that abandoned woman Jane sitting on [Henry's] knees'.[40] Sander went on to say that Anne 'considered that her sin would be more secret if she sinned with her own brother, George Boleyn, rather than with any other' and that she was a woman 'excessively given to pride and self-love'.[41] His intention was to make Anne Boleyn out as guilty of what she was accused (adultery, incest, and treason), and of more besides. He exaggerates whatever evidence he could find to make Anne as black as coal. Sander's work was the first to compare Elizabeth I with Jezebel, like her mother, Anne Boleyn, was before her.[42] This connection clearly demonstrates Sander's purpose in using the mother to denigrate the daughter.

In *Rise and Growth of the Anglican Schism*, Nicholas Sander writes about his belief in God, that judgement will be given on everyone:

> The very next day after the execution of Anne Boleyn the king made Jane Seymour his wife. He had loved her and preferred her to Anne even while Anne was alive. The judgments of God are not less marvellous than they are just, rewarding everyone according to his works. As Anne supplanted Catherine, so Jane supplanted Anne.[43]

Sander believed that God was making a judgement on Anne's sin in supplanting a good Catholic queen and leading the king of England away from the true Catholic Church and allegiance to the Pope, into the sin of Protestantism. Sander has made an error here, however. He claims that Henry VIII married Jane Seymour the day after Anne Boleyn's execution, but it was actually eleven days later, on 30 May 1536. This is similar to the error John Foxe made, that

Henry married Jane three days later. It throws some of his assertions into jeopardy, getting something so fundamental incorrect. Henry and Jane were betrothed the day after Anne's execution. The assumption Sander appears to make is that Anne Boleyn supplanted Katherine of Aragon, then Jane Seymour supplanted Anne Boleyn, but it could be read as Protestantism had supplanted Catholicism, but that Catholicism will again supplant Protestantism. Sander makes another error saying that George Boleyn and the other men were executed on 22 May, when in reality it was on 17 May. His errors on simple things like dates undermine some of his other arguments.

Sander goes on to say that parliament met on 8 June 1536, with the king and council 'striving to save the schism they had begun', but many of the tenets were still Catholic, like a belief in transubstantiation (the belief that the bread and wine truly become the body and blood of Christ), the celebration of Mass, and clerical celibacy.[44] But the Break with Rome was maintained. Henry VIII would have no one set above him. Sander described the English people and old nobility as 'not only hating heresy but being almost universally catholic' and that they believed 'certain most detestable opinions should be condemned, if they could not have the Catholic religion preserved in its integrity'.[45] The implication is that, once Anne Boleyn was dead, the Reformation should have been undone, but Henry VIII was still determined not to have the Pope set above him. Anne was the catalyst for that happening in the first place, so Sander puts the blame on her shoulders, rather than those of the king himself, even though he maintained it.

Nicholas Sander's account is at least in part where suggestions of witchcraft have come from. But he does not actually link Anne Boleyn directly to witchcraft in his work. His focus is on Anne's involvement with heresy and denigrating her in those terms, linking to her daughter, Elizabeth I. There is a wider political agenda. We do not have the full indictment of the charges against Anne from May 1536, and it seems quite possible that parts are missing, so we cannot be entirely sure that there were not accusations of witchcraft in it. However, if witchcraft was mentioned, then it was not technically an offence in 1536. The Witchcraft Act was not introduced until 1542.[46] But accusations of witchcraft could result in the dissolution of a marriage, which is possibly where Henry VIII's mind was going in relation to Anne. He did not want another prolonged annulment case, as had happened with Katherine of Aragon, but wanted rid of Anne, to remarry and produce sons as soon as possible.[47] Henry had already had two wives, often seen as being of opposing religious views, who pulled him between them. He wanted to get away from that tension and that is what his third wife, Jane Seymour, could provide. Although she was a Catholic, after her attempt to intervene to get him to show mercy to the rebels of the Pilgrimage of Grace, she does not seem to have interfered in political or religious matters again, at least not in public. Having been through the religious controversies during his courtship of and marriage to Anne, Henry seemed to want to settle down. He needed rid of Anne and her passionate religious views in order to do that. Witchcraft was possibly something that was explored as a means to an end.

Anne's appearance is the thing that most comes from Sander's work and sits in the public consciousness. Eric Ives describes it as the 'monster legend'.[48] Portraying Anne as a monster was supposed to undermine her beliefs, including her promotion of reform, and encourage people to return to the Catholic church. Sander's description of Anne was damning:

> Anne Boleyn was rather tall of stature, with black hair, and an oval face of sallow complexion, as if troubled with jaundice. She had a projecting tooth under the upper lip, and on her right hand six fingers. There was a large wen under her chin, and therefore to hide its ugliness she wore a high dress covering her throat.[49]

Sander was not born until 1527, so would not have met Anne Boleyn in person. This was likely propaganda to portray Anne as a monster, witch and schismatic. Marks on the body were often used to identify a witch, who was said to have a pact with the devil. Eric Ives writes that a 'minor malformation' of one fingertip seems 'probable' and possibly a couple of moles, but not the 'disaster' Sander described.[50] No doubt Sander also believed, given his writing, that a pact with the devil explained her deviance from the Roman Catholic Church and embrace of what he believed to be heresy. It has been suggested that 'Sander was following the medieval and Neoplatonic convention of evil betraying itself through outward manifestations'.[51] The Neoplatonic tradition was that 'evil and wicked beings ought to be clothed in outward ugly features'.[52] This idea explains why it was so important to portray Anne as a monster physically, even if it was not true, to emphasise the supposed evil within her, as the woman who hoodwinked the king to abandon his wife and break with the English Church.

However, historian Sylvia Barbara Soberton explains that Sander may have just been elaborating on what he had already heard, because most of what he wrote already existed in contemporary sources, including by George Wyatt, son of Anne Boleyn's rumoured lover, Sir Thomas Wyatt.[53] Sander put his own twist on the stories he recounted to paint Anne as blackly as possible and besmirch her name and, by extension, that of her daughter, Elizabeth. Any sign of physical malformation was seen by Sander as symbols of 'religious deviancy'.[54] It was not Anne as a witch that Sander was promoting, but Anne as a heretic. These little details Sander added to his recounting were 'entirely fictitious' but also compelling, intriguing, and fascinating.[55] It helps to explains why these poor perceptions of Anne have survived down the years. As human beings, we always seem to remember the negative and the sensational, more than the truth. They were used to manipulate opinions and perceptions of Anne in the public eye. Sander's whole work was designed to damage Anne Boleyn and her Protestant views, and to reflect badly on Elizabeth I by extension.

Gilbert Burnet's *History of the Reformation of the Church of England*

Gilbert Burnet was Bishop of Salisbury, writing in the seventeenth century. He was a close confidant of William III, a committed Protestant, who was brought into England from the Dutch Republic, to replace his Catholic father-in-law, James II. He was part of both the Church of Scotland and the Church of England. Burnet wrote his work *History of the Reformation of the Church of England* in response to Nicholas Sander's *Rise and Growth of the Anglican Schism*. The first version of Burnet's work was published in 1679, a couple of years after Sander's work was first translated into French. This was the first of three volumes.

Early in his work, Burnet says that 'I know it is not the work of an historian to refute the lies of others', having just discussed some of the things that Sander raised in his work (as earlier in this chapter).[56] Sander was very dismissive of Anne, almost demonising her. But Burnet is sceptical of Sander's work, stating 'it leaves also a foul and lasting stain both on the memory of Anne Boleyn, and of her incomparable daughter queen Elizabeth'.[57] Like John Foxe before him, Burnet sees Anne as central to the beginning of the English Reformation because of her relationship with Henry VIII and her reformist views.

Anne Boleyn and Henry VIII co-authored a letter to Cardinal Thomas Wolsey which was badly burnt in a fire in 1731, with Henry signing it 'by your loving sovereign and friend, Henry R', and Anne adding her signature 'your humble servant, Anne Boleyn'.[58] The document was copied by Burnet in 1714 in preparation for inclusion in his work. It is because of this that we know what the letter said, and that it was co-authored and jointly signed. The fire destroyed all of Anne's signature apart from the first letter, and part of Henry's on the original document. It was demonstrative of Anne's growing influence that she could persuade Henry to write jointly with her to Wolsey, who was in charge of obtaining the annulment for Henry VIII from Katherine of Aragon in order for him to marry Anne. We cannot forget that it was because of the annulment that Henry VIII broke with Rome in the first place.

Burnet relates that 'Cranmer was looked on as the most learned' of the scholarly reformers, naming also Crome, Shaxton and Latimer, but that 'Anne

Boleyn had in the duchess of Alencon's court (who inclined to the Reformation) received such impressions as made them fear, that her greatness, and Cranmer's preferment, would encourage heresy'.[59] The duchess of Alencon was Marguerite of Navarre, who Anne would have met and been influenced by during her time in France as a teenager and young woman. The wind was blowing in a direction which pointed to divorce and a break with the Roman Catholic Church, and Anne was placed at the centre of that controversy. Burnet relates that it was down to Anne Boleyn that Henry VIII read Simon Fish's *A Supplication for the Beggars*, that she had 'put [it] in his hands' and he 'liked it well'.[60] The pamphlet condemned the Roman Catholic Church as corrupt and heretical, having too many of England's resources, making people pay for a place in heaven (known as indulgences), and speaks against the existence of purgatory because it does not appear anywhere in the scriptures. Anne Boleyn seems to have promoted a reading of the scriptures and spoke out against the corruption of the Church, so her beliefs can explain why she was eager for the king to read Fish's work.

To conclude this section, Burnet examines the papal bull of excommunication against the king, published after Anne's death, but which said, 'contrary to an inhibition made, put away his queen, and married one Anne Boleyn and had made impious and hurtful laws, denying the pope to be the supreme head of the church, but assuming that title to himself'.[61] The implication here is that Henry VIII's marriage to Anne and the Break with Rome were inextricably linked and that one would not have happened without the other. After quoting the bull in its entirety, Burnet writes that, if what was written in it was true, 'then the Pope is either clothed with the power of deposing princes; or, if otherwise, he lied to the world when he pretended to it thus, and taught false doctrine, which cannot stand with infallibility'.[62] There does not seem any doubt to me that Anne made this argument to the king in the fraught times of the Great Matter, to push the king to Break with Rome and take power to himself in order to marry her.

Modern Historical Viewpoints

Having examined a couple of accounts of Anne Boleyn's religion from the sixteenth and seventeenth centuries, it is also important to understand where the historiography stands today. Of course, there is still disagreement but the general consensus seems to be that Anne, like Henry VIII, was essentially a Catholic, but without the authority of the Pope, and wanting reform of the abuses of the Church from within, with more money going to charitable and educational causes rather than to Rome.

Elizabeth Norton writes that, to reformers, Anne was 'almost a saint' and that she had always been interested in religious reform, determined to promote it once she became queen, with her circle of both men and women around her who were interested in the new religious learnings.[63] Anne's interest in and passion for the new religious learning was probably developed during her time in France in the 1510s and early 1520s, through figures like Marguerite of Navarre. However, Retha Warnicke claims that there is 'no reason to believe Anne's support for schism predated that of Henry VIII'.[64] We do not know exactly what Anne learned in France, and perhaps anti-papal beliefs were not a part of the court there, or not something Anne necessarily believed in until she needed to make use of it to achieve her ends. Anne was not a fully-fledged Protestant and did not accept the key tenet of Protestant belief, that of justification by faith alone, though she was definitely anti-papal.[65] Justification by faith alone was the belief that God decides who is worthy of going to heaven, and that you cannot change his decision by good works. The Protestant belief is essentially that God decides himself, where the Catholic belief is that doing good works is the way to heaven, though forgiveness for sins can also be given through buying indulgences, a practice that the reformers believed was corrupt and should stop. Natalie Grueninger supports Norton's view that Anne was interested in religious reform but was not necessarily a Protestant. She did not believe in radical ideas like denying the Mass but did reject papal authority and took an interest in monastic reform and was deeply committed to the Bible.[66] She took the tenets she believed in and rejected others. In this, she very clearly had strong opinions and stuck to them.

Anne was a 'reformer by conviction' according to John Guy and Julia Fox, as she denied the tenet of justification by faith alone. She did not want to dismantle the Catholic faith, but to reform it from within.[67] Similarly, Amy Licence states that there was 'no doubting Anne's sympathies [were] with reformers' as, of books that can be attributed to Anne, seven were religious texts, of which six were reformist.[68] However, Guy and Fox also claim that Anne's apartments were 'hives of evangelical piety with her ladies studying the English Bible and sewing clothes for the poor', and that she 'retained an entire cohort of evangelical chaplains'.[69] Anne did put a lot of emphasis on her beliefs on the scriptures and some of her chaplains and bishops she appointed did go on to be burned at the stake for heresy, but that does not necessarily mean Anne was an evangelical. As we have seen she kept a lot of Catholic beliefs which reformers wanted rid of.

Lacey Baldwin Smith claims that Anne came from a 'Christian humanist-inclined family' as her father was in contact with Erasmus; there is 'little doubt' that Anne was influenced by Christian humanism and 'deeply wedded' to reading the Bible in both English and French.[70] She owned copies of both and, as queen, would encourage the ladies in her household to read the English Bible she kept on display in her rooms. Smith believes that Anne was an 'orthodox catholic' with 'Christian humanistic leanings'.[71] What we understand as humanism today is the belief that virtue and happiness should be the basis for life and that we can decide what gives our life meaning and makes us happy. Anne took the idea of virtue seriously, refusing to sleep with the king without marriage, exhorting her ladies as queen to be virtuous and keeping tight rein over her household, and she was passionate about charity and education. So, Anne was a pious and humanistic queen.

Eric Ives says that it was clear 'Anne was regarded as someone for reformers to turn to' and that her 'reformist stance was evident enough to be recognised in Europe'.[72] He says that it is important not to interpret material from Anne's life and reign according to 'religious alignments of later in the century' as doctrinal positions changed as the Reformation gathered pace.[73] That is important, because what was classed as Protestant or reformist belief in the 1530s was not the same as in the 1540s; it changed again in the 1550s, and again in the 1560s, in the period known as the mid-Tudor crisis, when each monarch had a different view on what the religion of England should be.

G.W. Bernard, in contrast to Ives, paints Anne's religion as political rather than personal, and not just for her, but for those around her, and those who promoted reform after her death, particularly in the reign of her daughter, Elizabeth:

> Dabbling with the new sects may for both Rochford and Anne have been more a matter of politics and radical chic than a matter of religious conviction. The Break with Rome, which had made Anne's marriage to Henry possible, had to be explained and defended ... Whether Anne Boleyn went much beyond the conventional and the political is much more doubtful than the thrust of recent writing allows. Anne was much more secular than the Elizabethan or modern portrait of her as a pious lady suggests ... what she revealed in the Tower through her belief in good works and her attachment to the sacraments was a deeply conventional Catholicism.[74]

It could be argued that Anne used religion to push Henry VIII to Break with Rome in order to marry her and have a son and heir. It could also be said that Anne's religious beliefs were manipulated after her death to paint her as either a Protestant martyr (in the case of John Foxe) or a heretical schismatic (in the case of Nicholas Sander), but she is generally seen in religious texts as more Protestant than she probably was. She believed in tenets of both Catholic and Protestant religion, which helped to give birth to the Church of England.

Thanks to Anne's position and growing influence through the 1520s and early 1530s, reformist ideas circulated more widely. Tracy Borman asserts that, by espousing religious reform, Anne helped the case for the annulment, but she also made dangerous enemies at court, as the religious conservatives put the blame for religious reform squarely at her door.[75] Anne did assist in the annulment case and the Break with Rome by introducing Henry VIII to works by William Tyndale and Simon Fish, but the blame cannot be laid just at her feet. For the Break with Rome to have happened, Henry must have strongly agreed with the ideas to put himself and the country through such turmoil. Anne may have planted the seed and acted as the catalyst, but it was a Henrician Reformation.

Chapter 7

Anne as Tragic Heroine

'The graves of the two unhappy Queens in the chancel remained unmarked by any memorial stone'[1]

Anne Boleyn's rehabilitation has been through a lot of stages, beginning in her daughter, Elizabeth I's, reign. Elizabeth did not have her mother and father's marriage declared valid, as Mary I had done with the marriage of Henry VIII and Katherine of Aragon, nor did she have her mother's remains reburied, as James I did with Mary Queen of Scots. But she made sure to honour Anne Boleyn in other ways, like taking Anne's falcon crest for her own, or keeping her mother's image in a ring she wore. The Victorians, in the nineteenth century, favoured presenting women as tragic heroines, for example, in Paul Delaroche's 'The Execution of Lady Jane Grey' painting. There are several romanticised images of Anne Boleyn, including a famous one of Anne in the Tower of London, painted by Edouard Cibot; one of Henry VIII and Anne shooting deer together, painted by William Powell Frith; Anne saying a final goodbye to Princess Elizabeth by Gustav Wappers; and Henry VIII's first interview with Anne by Daniel Maclise. There are also two historians from the period whose work will be examined in this chapter: Agnes Strickland and Paul Friedmann.

The Victorian period was also a time of exploration and innovation. There were restorations at the Tower of London in 1876 and 1877 and remains were exhumed in the Chapel of St Peter ad Vincula. These included the remains of Anne Boleyn, along with her brother George, Viscount Rochford, her sister-in-law, Jane Boleyn, Lady Rochford, and her cousin, Katherine Howard, along with several others. These exhumations were recorded in a book called *Notices of the Historic Persons Buried in the Chapel of St Peter ad Vincula in the Tower of London with an Account of the Discovery of the Supposed Remains of Queen Anne Boleyn* by Doyne C. Bell. There was a desperate need for repairs within the chapel as things were starting to fall apart and needed restoring, which would eventually make the chapel more in line with what we see today when we visit.

Queen Victoria herself also had a keen interest in Anne Boleyn, visiting her childhood home at Hever Castle in Kent when she was Princess Alexandrina

Victoria. This was three years before she became queen, on 13 September 1834, when she was aged 15. Victoria wrote about the visit in her journal that evening:

> At a quarter past 1 we drove with Lady Flora and dear Lehzen to Hever Castle. We arrived there at 3. This curious old place was the residence of Sir Thomas Boleyn, father of poor Queen Anne Boleyn. We saw the room where she used to live and a seat on which King Henry the 8th used to sit. We then mounted our horses.[2]

The fact that Queen Victoria showed such an early interest in Anne Boleyn and her story is probably at least part of the reason why the excavations were carried out during her reign. It is thanks to Victoria and Albert that there are now stones commemorating the executions of so many men and women under the Tudors, including Anne Boleyn. Anne was a tragic figure, wrongly accused and executed at the hand of her husband who had once passionately loved her and had torn England apart to marry her.

The noted novelist, Jane Austen, wrote *The History of England* in 1791, aged 15, and although not as serious a scholarly work as some others which will be discussed in this chapter, she wrote that 'this amiable Woman was entirely innocent of the Crimes with which she was accused, and of which her Beauty, her Elegance, and her Sprightliness were sufficient proofs, not to mention her solemn protestations of Innocence, the weakness of the Charges against her, and the King's Character'.[3] Just like it was posited in the work of Nicholas Sander that an ugly exterior appearance meant an evil spirit, hence he gave her a sixth finger, a swelling, and disfiguring moles, here we see Austen romanticising Anne Boleyn by suggesting that she was innocent of the charges of which she was accused because she was beautiful and elegant. These are the first arguments Austen puts across for innocence, followed by the weakness of the charges and the king's character.

In the nineteenth century 'Anne was considered morally dubious but probably innocent of the charges brought against her'.[4] There was evidence of her being flirtatious with a sharp tongue, which was not how women ought to be. Numerous Victorian writers in their histories emphasise Anne's 'feminine moral strength'.[5] What is sometimes difficult to reconcile is that the Victorians are often seen as being sticklers for morality and chastity. Anne Boleyn is often viewed as being morally questionable, because of what she was accused of, but things are not so black and white as they might appear, and people always have more to them. This is why the Victorian interest in Anne is so intriguing. There are always contradictions and evidence that may not match with the image a writer wants to present of their subject. Anne Boleyn was an ideal tragic figure because of the nature of her end, but it does not mean that she was perfect. Everyone has flaws.

Excavations at the Chapel of St Peter ad Vincula

After her execution, Anne Boleyn's remains were undisturbed until 1876 when exhumations at the Chapel of St Peter ad Vincula at the Tower of London took place at the request of Queen Victoria and Prince Albert. It was a part of the restoration work going on in the chapel which was looking a little run-down. It was ordered that the bodies be exhumed, identified, and reburied with name plaques to mark their final resting places.[6] The exhumations and identifications were recorded in a book called *Notices of the Historic Persons Buried in the Chapel of St Peter ad Vincula in the Tower of London* by Doyne C. Bell. Bell was present at the excavations, in his role as 'Secretary to Her Majesty's Privy Purse'.[7] In his preface, Bell remarks on the state of the chapel at the Tower of London:

> At Westminster Abbey and at Windsor due care and attention had been bestowed upon the Royal resting places, but when I came to the chapel of St. Peter in the Tower, I regretted to find that the graves of the two unhappy Queens in the chancel remained unmarked by any memorial stone, and the condition of the whole chapel was also such as could not fail to awaken feelings of a painful nature.[8]

Which two unhappy queens did Bell mean, as there are three queens buried under the altar in the chapel? Anne Boleyn, Katherine Howard and Jane Grey are all buried there. The fact that the graves remained unmarked for centuries suggests a lack of interest in the histories of the executed men and women buried there until the reign of Queen Victoria. That the royal resting places at Windsor and Westminster were taken care of implies it may have been the executed status of those buried in the chapel which meant that it did not receive as much care or attention. The Victorian period was a time of discovery, and Victoria's own interest in Anne Boleyn may have propelled more investigation into the graves and burial site more generally, as well as the lives of those who had been executed. It is under the reign of Queen Victoria that we see new regeneration of interest in the Tudors. For Victoria's interest, we have to be thankful, as who knows how much may have been lost had the chapel been allowed to fall into a state of disrepair.

Turning to the remains themselves, Victorian archaeologists described the neck bones as having been severed on a woman with a very delicate frame. The estimate was that the woman was aged between 25 and 30 at her death.[9] Given that the science of accurate dating was still in its infancy, these estimations may well have been incorrect. Or the skeleton they identified as Anne Boleyn's may not have been hers at all. There were several other women buried in the chapel, and a suggestion has been made that the bones had been disturbed so many times during works at the chapel over the centuries that they may have all gotten mixed up and Anne's skeleton may in fact be nowhere near where it is said to be.

Geoffrey Abbott, a former Yeoman Warder at the Tower of London, stated that the vault was opened and its contents viewed during the reign of Elizabeth I, though does not state his source. There was no vault, as the executed were buried beneath the chancel pavement, but given the fact that it was opened during the reign of Elizabeth I, still in living memory of the events, 'the information he recorded is likely to have been fairly accurate', though there is no way of verifying this.[10] The description Abbott gives from the 'anonymous visitor' is as follows:

> The coffin of the Duke of Northumberland rests besides that of the Duke of Somerset, between the coffins of the queens, Anne Boleyn and Katherine Howard, and next unto these last is the coffin of Lady Jane Grey. Then comes the coffins of Thomas Seymour, Lord of Sudeley and of the Lady Rochford; and lastly that of George Boleyn, that was brother to Queen Anne.[11]

This suggests that Anne and her brother, George, were buried at opposite ends of the chapel, and that Lady Rochford was buried beside her husband. However, Doyne C. Bell in his work on the excavations and restoration of the Chapel of St Peter ad Vincula in the 1870s, has Lord and Lady Rochford buried at opposite ends of the chapel, with Anne and George Boleyn buried beside each other.[12] Perhaps this suggests that at some point the remains of Anne Boleyn and Jane, Lady Rochford, have been mixed up, and it is unsure which lady is which. Bell does still have the two dukes buried between the two queens, though Jane Grey is not in the same line as the Boleyns, but in front of them, between her husband, Guildford Dudley, and her father, Henry Grey, 1st Duke of Suffolk. There is obviously a lack of agreement on the exact positions of the burials. This is because they were not marked at the time.

Queen Victoria ensured that Anne Boleyn's burial place was marked for the first time, even though today we are not entirely sure whether she is buried beneath it. Even Elizabeth I did not mark the resting place of her mother or have her remains moved somewhere else, perhaps unwilling to revisit the past and reopen old wounds. Elizabeth remained legally illegitimate, and her mother buried amongst traitors, but that did not mean she was forgotten. The alleged scaffold site was also marked at this time, 'making Anne more visible at sites where her history played out', including adding a 'faux Anne Boleyn bedchamber' at Hever Castle.[13] Of course today we know that where the current glass memorial on Tower Green is, was not in fact where Anne Boleyn, at least, was executed. Her scaffold was in the space between where the Waterloo Barracks now stand and the north wall of the White Tower.[14] But the memorial commemorates all of those executed on Tower Green under the Tudors.

Agnes Strickland's *Lives of the Queens of England*

Agnes Strickland is probably the writer we most commonly think of relating Anne Boleyn and the Victorians. She wrote her *Lives of the Queens of England* in 12 volumes which were published between 1840 and 1848 along with her sister, Elizabeth. The sisters adopted the motto 'facts not opinions', and the research was 'both pioneering and intensive' as they were initially denied access to the state paper office by the home secretary, Lord John Russell, but eventually gained permits through Lord Normanby and Henry Howard.[15] Agnes Strickland's name appears on the title page of all publications alone, despite being co-written with her sister, as she conducted all of the correspondence.[16] The work of the Strickland sisters is the first complete work of the queens of England and is invaluable as a resource, despite several things in the account now having been disproven, or at least questioned.

Susan Bordo relates that 'the Stricklands can make one squirm', but that their work is 'often plundered by male historians looking for colourful detail to enliven their own work'.[17] Histories written by women were not considered to be very good by the Victorians, and histories written by men were favoured. Strickland certainly had a way of creating an impression, and that a very poetic one. The chapter on Anne Boleyn in volume two begins:

> There is no name in the annals of female royalty over which the enchantments of poetry and romance have cast such bewildering spells as that of Anne Boleyn. Her wit, her beauty, and the striking vicissitudes of her fate, combined with the peculiar mobility of her character, have invested her with an interest not commonly excited by a woman, in whom vanity and ambition were the leading traits.[18]

The opening sentence on Anne uses the word 'romance', echoing the Victorian sentiment of Anne being a tragic figure, but then describes her as vain and ambitious, so perhaps not all her characteristics could be considered romantic. It comes from the tragedy of her demise, and her innocence in that. The sense you get from reading Strickland's description is that Anne Boleyn was a romantic and tragic figure because of her fate, that she was not likeable because of who she was. That is quite sad really, wondering what people would have thought of Anne had she not been executed, and how much she might still be talked about had she given the king a son.

Strickland covers a question which is still a focus of debate today; Anne Boleyn's year of birth and the order of birth of her and her siblings. She says that 'Lord Herbert … says expressly, that Anne Boleyn was twenty years old when she returned from France in 1521, so that she must have been born around 1501' and that she was the eldest daughter.[19] However, it is now generally accepted that Mary Boleyn was the eldest sibling, having been the first married in 1520, and her grandson, George Carey, believed Mary to be the eldest when seeking to claim the earldom of Ormond in the 1590s.[20] Given that the other claimant would have been Queen Elizabeth I herself, he must have been fairly sure of his rights. George Boleyn was likely the youngest of the three surviving siblings, given his later entry into court life than either of his sisters.[21] Continuing on the track of Anne's immediate family, Strickland goes on to say that Anne's mother, Elizabeth Boleyn, died in 1512 of puerperal fever and was buried at Lambeth, and that Thomas Boleyn remarried.[22] However, we know that this is not true, as Elizabeth Boleyn did not die until 1538, outliving both her son and younger daughter who had been executed two years earlier. There is no record of a second marriage for Thomas Boleyn either. He died just a year after his wife, in 1539. This is an example where some of Strickland's accounts have now been proven false.

Agnes Strickland has Anne Boleyn present at Greenwich Palace on 13 August 1514 when the marriage between Mary Tudor and Louis XII of France was celebrated, and in September of that year accompanying Mary to Dover en route to France.[23] However, Anne Boleyn was at the court of Margaret of Austria at Mechelen in the Low Countries prior to her arrival in France. She was not on the original list of attendants, where her sister, Mary Boleyn, appears, so it is likely that Anne was only in France in time for Mary Tudor's coronation in November 1514, having travelled direct from the Low Countries.[24] Once again, Strickland's research is now considered to be outdated. There is no evidence that Anne Boleyn returned to England in between leaving Margaret of Austria's court at Mechelen and joining Mary Tudor's court.

When Anne Boleyn returned to England and joined the court in 1522, she entered into some kind of relationship with Henry Percy, heir to the Earl of Northumberland, and Strickland claims that 'the pangs of jealousy occasioned by this intelligence, it is said, first awakened the monarch to the state of his own feelings' towards Anne.[25] We do not know exactly when Henry VIII first became interested in Anne, though it is generally thought to be sometime in 1525, or 1526, not as soon as she entered the English court and the service of Katherine of Aragon. Strickland possibly took her evidence from the writings of Cardinal Wolsey's gentleman usher, George Cavendish, who recorded in his biography of his master that the relationship between Anne and Percy 'came to the king's knowledge, who was then much offended. Wherefore he could hide no longer his secret affection'.[26] The dating of the love letters, as discussed in chapter two, puts the earliest around 1526 or 1527, so it does not seem logical that Henry VIII would have stopped Anne's relationship in 1522 or 1523 then waited for another three years or more before pursuing Anne. By 1527, Strickland states that 'Henry's new passion became obvious even to the queen, and occasioned her to upbraid him with his perfidy, but it does not appear that she condescended to discuss the matter with Anne'.[27] We do not really have any accounts of how Katherine of Aragon and Anne Boleyn lived together in the same household at the end of 1520s once knowledge of the king's Great Matter leaked out, though there is no evidence of any animosity between the two women prior to Henry's interest in Anne, so it was likely at least a cordial relationship initially.

Strickland goes on to discuss Anne Boleyn's involvement in the fall of Cardinal Wolsey, once again echoing the sentiments of George Cavendish. Strickland claims that 'Anne Boleyn had not forgiven, she never did forgive, the interference which had deprived her of her first love, Percy. The anger she had conceived against the cardinal on that occasion remained, after a lapse of six years, an unquenchable fire'.[28] George Cavendish related that 'Mistress Anne Boleyn was greatly offended, saying, that if it lay ever in her power, she would work the cardinal as much displeasure'.[29] It appears Strickland probably read Cavendish's account and mined it for her own work. There are several parallels in the incidents related.

There has been debate over the exact date of Anne Boleyn's wedding to Henry VIII. It has been suggested the pair were married at Dover on the day they returned from France, in November 1532, or in the chapel of Sopwell nunnery at St Albans, or even at Blickling Hall in Norfolk. But the common belief is that the couple were married on 25 January 1533 at Whitehall Palace by Rowland Lee.[30] It has been suggested that Lee was reluctant when he learned that he was being expected to conduct the marriage, but that the king assured him that the Pope had pronounced in favour of his divorce from Katherine of Aragon, and that he had the dispensation for his marriage to Anne in his possession. Strickland doubts the validity of this, saying in a footnote that Henry was 'weary of the delays attending the prosecution of the divorce' and its 'protracted tedium' so treated his marriage to Katherine 'as a nullity'.[31] In this case, Strickland agrees with modern historiographical thinking, though there are some historians who believe that Henry VIII and Anne Boleyn may have gone through some kind of preliminary commitment ceremony in November 1532, before the formal ceremony in January. This could help to explain why Anne was pregnant by the time of the January 1533 wedding. The two were already legally bound to each other so the January 1533 ceremony was a formality for them.

Agnes Strickland posits that Anne Boleyn's fall from power was essentially because she failed to make the transition from mistress to wife, and this is hugely important to understand as to the reasons why Henry could get rid of her, and why he appeared to find evidence of her guilt in her household:

> The levity of Anne Boleyn's manners was doubtless one great cause of her calamities. The lively coquettish maid of honour could not forget her old habits after her elevation to a throne, and the familiarity of her deportment to those with whom she had formerly been on terms of equality in the court of queen Katherine encouraged her officers of state to address her with undue freedom.[32]

Anne Boleyn, unlike her predecessor, Katherine of Aragon, already had court ties and friendships developed while serving in Katherine's household. But when she was made queen, there had to be more boundaries put in place between the divine consort and those who served her. From what we know of Anne's character, she could be haughty, but kept those who were her friends close to her. Anne struggled to put these boundaries in place when she became queen, just as she failed to adapt to Henry VIII's expectation of what a queen should be in his eyes. He wanted Anne to become submissive and compliant as Katherine of Aragon had been, but to outdo her predecessor by giving him a son. Anne's fiery temper and outspokenness, however, would not go away just because she was married.

In her description of Anne Boleyn's execution, Strickland writes that 'it was a case without precedent in the annals of England, for never before had female blood been shed on the scaffold; even in the Norman reigns of terror, woman's life had been held sacred, and the most merciless of the Plantagenet sovereigns had been too manly, under any provocations or pretence, to butcher ladies. But the age of chivalry was over'.[33] Anne Boleyn would be the first woman in England to be beheaded, but she would not be the last. Margaret Pole, Katherine Howard and Jane Boleyn would follow Anne to the scaffold within six years, also at the hands of Henry VIII. Strickland casts doubt on Henry VIII's masculinity, that he would send a woman to her death, calling him a 'sensual tyrant who gave the first example of sending queens and princesses to the block, like sheep to the shambles'.[34] Henry was always determined to be seen as masculine, which he believed enhanced his power. A son was the ultimate symbol of that masculinity, and Anne had failed, just as Katherine of Aragon had. Anne Boleyn's execution marked a turning point in the long Tudor century, where not even women were safe any longer because of the divisions in religion which had their roots in Anne Boleyn, and the problem of the succession, which Anne had failed to resolve in the king's eyes.

Stephanie Russo writes that 'Strickland's lack of belief in Anne's historical importance is stark' and that in the work, Anne Boleyn reverted 'to the role of (somewhat cynical) influencer'.[35] As much as Strickland writes about the queens of England, Anne comes across as someone with little agency of her own, subject to the whims of men and particularly that of the king. As an 'influencer' the suggestion is that Anne was unable to act on her own and could only attempt to influence the king in the direction she wanted him to go. Susan Bordo writes that female historians like the Stricklands were often derided as 'sentimental', 'gossipy', and 'trifling' as the history of women was seen as a 'specialised miniaturising focus'.[36] Women's history has taken centuries to become a respected specialism, and that is in part at least to Victorian historians who wrote about English queens like Anne Boleyn, led by the likes of Agnes and Elizabeth Strickland.

Paul Friedmann's *Anne Boleyn*

Paul Friedmann wrote a full biography of Anne Boleyn which was first published in 1884. His work is still popular among Tudor historians as one of the earliest full biographies of this executed English queen. Friedmann contrasts the characters of Katherine of Aragon and Anne Boleyn by describing Katherine as 'very simple and careless of show, praise, or glory … nor was she weak; she came quickly to a decision and was most firm in doing what she considered right' but, on the other hand she 'was narrow-minded, violent, and wanting in delicacy and tact'.[37] Friedmann goes on to describe Anne as 'acquiring all those arts and graces by which she was afterwards to shine' and that 'she was naturally quick and witty' but 'being extremely vain and fond of praise and admiration'.[38] Friedmann offers both positive and negative points about each woman, but the two are being juxtaposed against each other, which is not necessarily a helpful approach to take when the reason they were pitted against each other was Henry VIII. Both Katherine and Anne were women worthy of praise and discussion in their own rights, and not as comparative foils.

Anne is seen in Friedmann's work, not as 'the tragically wronged heroine of the Protestant Reformation' but a 'scheming adventuress'.[39] This is in contrast to many of the romanticised paintings and other images we see from the Victorian period. Bordo says that Friedmann, and the likes of James Anthony Froude and A.F. Pollard, whose work there is not the room to discuss here, give detailed histories of the king's Great Matter and the following events, but they do not achieve balance, perhaps frustrated with the 'idealised Anne of the Elizabethans and Romantics'.[40] Friedmann gives his opinion on Anne at the end of his work, admitting that:

> From Anne the English people received one of their greatest rulers, and for this gift they may well forgive such misdeeds as were not atoned for by long and cruel anxiety and a terrible death. Anne was not good; she was incredibly vain, ambitious, unscrupulous, coarse, fierce, and relentless. But much of this was due to the degrading influences by which she was surrounded in youth and after her return to England from France. Her virtues, such as they were, were her own.[41]

Friedmann, like so many modern writers, cites one of Anne's lasting influences and greatest legacies as her daughter, Elizabeth, but he does also say that 'Elizabeth never showed a spark of tenderness for the memory of her mother'.[42] We know that this is not true. Thanks to the work of Tracy Borman in particular, there are plenty of instances of Elizabeth respecting and remembering her mother. Friedmann goes on to say that 'we may pass no harsher judgement on her than was passed by Cromwell' who even when speaking of her destruction, extolled her courage and intelligence.[43] Even when speaking of the woman he had destroyed on the orders of the king, Cromwell could not help but to praise Anne.

The idea of Anne being surrounded by 'degrading influences' in her youth and on her return to England, it is not clear exactly to whom Friedmann is referring. His narrative picks up with the relationship between Anne Boleyn and Cardinal Thomas Wolsey, with little attention paid to the period before Henry VIII's interest in Anne. Friedmann does mention Queen Claude of France 'an excellent woman, who is said to have taken the greatest pleasure in the education of young girls'.[44] Anne certainly did have an excellent education abroad, in both the Low Countries and France, though Friedmann references little of it, recording that she had been intended to marry James Butler, but that the matter was given up in 1522 and that 'the events of Anne's life from 1523 to 1526 are not exactly known'.[45] This is true, Anne is much in the shade in this period, until we begin to see Henry VIII's intentions towards her become clear.

Henry VIII and Anne Boleyn's relationship was tied up with foreign affairs and diplomatic negotiations, as their relationship was central to the fate of

Katherine of Aragon, who was aunt to the Emperor Charles V. Friedmann argues that Henry 'fondly believed that the hatred of his subjects was mainly directed against' Anne and that he could triumph over his enemies 'if she were not in his way' and that he felt this way by the middle of 1535, not helped by the fact that Anne had lost her looks, probably worn out by stress and exertion.[46] Friedmann suggests that Henry had first spoken of getting rid of Anne in February 1535 but had been told that he must either keep Anne or take Katherine back and acknowledge Mary as his heir. But Friedmann's citation for this is a letter from Chapuys to Charles V dated 2 May 1536, not a source from the year earlier when this was said to have happened.[47] The letter from Chapuys said that the king 'had determined to abandon' Anne, even without the accusations of adultery as witnesses had testified that 'a marriage passed nine years before had been made and fully consummated between her and the earl of Northumberland' but that one of his council had told him that 'he could not separate from the Concubine without tacitly confirming … the first marriage'.[48] Here we see Henry VIII's determination that he could never be wrong. He waited until Katherine of Aragon was dead, and Anne had miscarried, before acting against her. Then he would not have to acknowledge that he had made a mistake in marrying Anne, or that his marriage to Katherine was valid.

Of the charges brought against Anne, Friedmann wrote that it was a 'pretended conspiracy' to murder the king, an 'amplification' of her conversation with Henry Norris over 'dead men's shoes'.[49] However, he also stated that:

> While I am strongly of the opinion that the indictments were drawn up at random, and that there was no trustworthy evidence to sustain the specific charges, I am by no means convinced that Anne did not commit offences quite as grave as most of those of which she was accused. She may have been guilty of crimes which it did not suit the convenience of the government to divulge.[50]

Friedmann is correct that there is no 'trustworthy' evidence which survives, although we have no record of exactly what evidence was presented at the trials of Anne and the men she was accused with. The dates in the indictments can largely be disproven, as discussed in chapter four, making them unreliable as evidence of her guilt. What Friedmann says about believing Anne guilty of 'offences quite as grave as most of those of which she was accused' is unclear. He does not reveal what these offences might be. Suggesting that they did not 'suit the convenience' of the government, perhaps implies some kind of slur against the king's power or masculinity, though Henry VIII had already been said to be a cuckold.

1. Late sixteenth-century panel portrait of Anne Boleyn, now kept at Anne's childhood home of Hever Castle, holding a red rose and wearing the famous 'B' pendant. The caption reads 'Anne Boleyn, Queen of England'.

2. Late sixteenth-century portrait of Anne Boleyn, now held at the National Portrait Gallery, depicts Anne wearing the famous 'B' pendant. The caption reads 'Anne Boleyn, wife to Henry VIII'.

3. Damaged 1534 portrait medal of Anne Boleyn, possibly created to celebrate the imminent birth of a son. Anne suffered a miscarriage or still birth in 1534, which could explain why this is the only one that survived.

4. A reconstruction of the 1534 portrait medal of Anne Boleyn by sculptor, Lucy Churchill, cast in bronze.

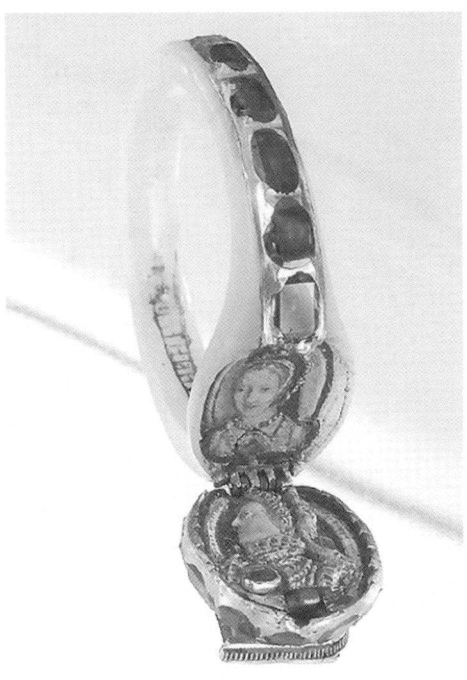

5. The Chequers ring, which belonged to Elizabeth I and opens to show two portraits, one of Elizabeth herself, and one which is probably her mother, Anne Boleyn.

6. A sketch by Hans Holbein thought to depict Anne Boleyn, labelled 'Anna Bollein Queen', of a woman in deshabille, possibly a preparatory sketch for a now-lost portrait or miniature.

7. A sketch by Holbein, possibly considered to be Anne Boleyn, shows a woman wearing a gable hood.

8. The Nidd Hall portrait, thought to be Anne Boleyn. The sitter wears an 'AB' jewel, though in later copies this is changed to a square jewel.

9. The Hoskins miniature of Anne Boleyn, which echoes both the Hever Rose and National Portrait Gallery images of Anne, again showing the 'B' pendant and wearing a French hood which Anne was said to favour.

10. A miniature from the Horenbout family workshop, said to possibly be of Anne Boleyn. It has, however, also been suggested to be Jane Seymour and Katherine of Aragon.

1. Hever Castle, the childhood home of Anne Boleyn and now the location of two of Anne's prayer books which have been recently discovered to hold erased inscriptions.

12. The Anne Boleyn Gateway at Hampton Court Palace. Henry VIII gained Hampton Court after Cardinal Wolsey's downfall and works were carried out throughout Anne's queenship.

13. The ceiling of the Anne Boleyn Gateway at Hampton Court. You can still see the entwined H and A initials and Anne's falcon emblem.

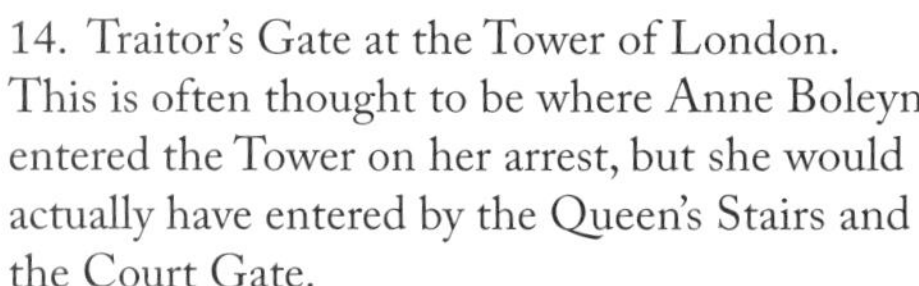

14. Traitor's Gate at the Tower of London. This is often thought to be where Anne Boleyn entered the Tower on her arrest, but she would actually have entered by the Queen's Stairs and the Court Gate.

15. The Bell Tower at the Tower of London. This is where Sir Thomas Wyatt was imprisoned and wrote his poem *Circa Regna Tonat*.

16. The Chapel of St Peter ad Vincula, where both Anne Boleyn and her brother, George, were buried. The other men were buried in the churchyard outside.

17. Anne Boleyn's memorial stone in the Chapel of St Peter ad Vincula. It was first laid in the reign of Queen Victoria, who wanted Anne's final resting place to be marked, though it's unlikely she's actually buried underneath it.

18. The glass memorial on Tower Green in the Tower of London. However, it does not mark the site c Anne Boleyn's death — the scaffold was between the White Tower and the Waterloo Barracks, abou where you queue for the crown jewels exhibit today.

19. A print of Anne Boleyn's execution showing Anne kneeling, blindfolded and praying, while the French swordsman takes his swing.

20. Anne Boleyn during her imprisonment in the Tower of London, as imagined and romanticised by Edouard Cibot. We see one of her ladies lamenting behind her, and a prayer book open on a table.

21. Anne Boleyn and Henry VIII shooting deer in Windsor Forest during their courtship, as imagined by William Powell Frith. It echoes Thomas Wyatt's poem *Whoso List to Hunt* with Henry as the hunter and Anne as the prey.

22. Anne Boleyn saying a final goodbye to Princess Elizabeth while in the Tower of London. We know Anne didn't see Elizabeth again after her arrest, so this is a very romanticised and tragic image, to tug on the heartstrings of anyone who saw it.

23. Henry VIII's first interview with Anne Boleyn. Henry VIII is as Holbein later painted him, though it would not have been how he looked when he first fell in love with Anne.

24. Anne Boleyn's printed Book of Hours *c*.1527 at Hever Castle. This is the book that Kate McCaffrey examined as part of her research which resulted in erased inscriptions being uncovered in the book. You can see Anne Boleyn's inscription at the bottom of the left-hand page.

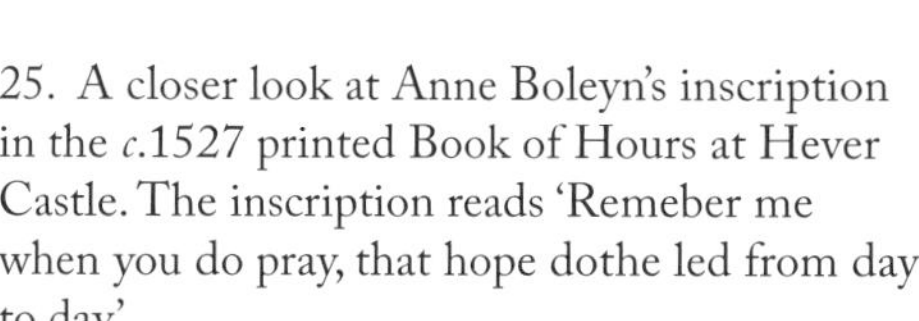

25. A closer look at Anne Boleyn's inscription in the *c*.1527 printed Book of Hours at Hever Castle. The inscription reads 'Remeber me when you do pray, that hope dothe led from day to day'.

Friedmann portrays Anne as 'a woman open to using sex to obtain what she wanted' and that she 'became a late Victorian femme fatale, in other words; a dangerous, glamorous woman who smarts and sexual appeal both raised her up and brought her down'.[51] Anne Boleyn is portrayed almost as a cautionary tale against being smart and educated, as well as possessing sex appeal, as the combination was dangerous both to the men around her, and to the woman herself who could be destroyed as a result.

Paintings of Anne Boleyn from the Victorian Period

The painting of Anne Boleyn in the Tower of London by Edouard Cibot and that of Anne saying a final farewell to Elizabeth in the Tower by Gustave Wappers are two of the most haunting, romanticised and tragic images of Anne's end. There is another painting of Anne hunting with Henry VIII in Windsor Forest by William Powell Frith which sees Henry and Anne's relationship as entirely romantic when looking at it on the surface, a happy couple hunting together. However, it is a visual representation of Henry as the hunter and Anne the prey. Daniel Maclise's painting of Henry VIII's first interview with Anne Boleyn is a huge contrast to Cibot and Wappers' paintings as they bookend the relationship. Cibot's and Wappers' paintings in particular sees Anne as a wailing woman in want of mercy but condemned on false charges. These images were 'more striking – and probably more influential – in creating a popular image of Anne as the romantic victim of Henry's tyranny' than any history book could be.[52] Anne is seen as a victim, again losing control of her own image, but we can see how perceptions are changing over time. These paintings can all be seen in the central plate section of this book.

Daniel Maclise's painting of Henry VIII's first interview with Anne Boleyn is the earliest chronological painting of the four as it depicts the first meeting. However, Henry VIII as seen in the painting is from the later Holbein mould, with the flat decorative bonnet, the wide silhouette, with the slashed doublet and short overcoat, with his legs on display which he seemed to be so proud of. The Holbein painting of Henry VIII in the 1540s has been imposed on an event from the mid-1520s and it feels a little incongruous. We see Anne Boleyn wearing a white gown, emphasising her chastity and virginity, and probably also a reference to her innocence of the charges of which she was accused, wearing an English gable hood, which we will see as a feature in the Victorian imagery of Anne, rather than the French hood we see in the most famous portraits of her. A servant is on his knees handing Henry a goblet and we see what appears to be Cardinal Wolsey in the background watching on. He almost looks like he is chewing on his fingers, an expression possibly of anxiety, almost as if he could see into the future, though of course we see this with hindsight, and it may have been a deliberate addition by the painter to allude to his fate and Anne's possible involvement in it. Anne Boleyn seems to be looking almost coyly to one side, not directly at the king as he stares unashamedly at her.

The Edouard Cibot painting, dated to 1835, is probably the most easily recognisable of the four. The figure on her knees with her head on the lap of a seated weeping woman seems to be Anne. She looks pensive and resigned, as Anne was said to be at the end. She is wearing a grey damask gown like the one Anne is reported to have worn at her execution, and an English gable hood. There has been a suggestion that it is in fact the seated woman dressed in black who is Anne Boleyn. Black was said to be a more expensive colour; hence some believe it is more likely that this is the queen. Personally, it seems that the figure kneeling is more likely to represent Anne. In the background is what looks like a Book of Hours or prayer book open on a table, perhaps alluding to Anne Boleyn's final confession, and her expression of her innocence when taking the Sacrament. The Imperial ambassador, Chapuys, reported that before and after receiving the Sacrament, Anne had affirmed 'on the damnation of her soul, that she had never been unfaithful to the King'.[53] She hoped when imprisoned in the Tower that the reformist bishops she had helped to promote would speak for her to the king and save her life. Anne looks upset but resigned in the painting, while the lady whose lap she is leaning on appears to be inconsolable.

Gustav Wappers' painting of Anne Boleyn saying a final goodbye to Princess Elizabeth is so haunting. There is no evidence that Anne saw Elizabeth again after her arrest, and it is difficult to believe that Henry VIII would have allowed the pair to meet again and say goodbye, just as he would not allow Princess Mary to say goodbye to Katherine of Aragon when she was dying. The painting has Anne sitting and holding the Princess Elizabeth in her arms, with the child's head against Anne's breast, possibly to enhance the idea of motherhood and an innocent child suckling from her mother. The young Elizabeth is wearing a white almost silken dress, perhaps to emphasise her innocence. Anne wears a dark gown with ermine sleeves, which enhances her royal status, along with an English gable hood, as she is recorded to have worn at her execution. Eric Ives wrote, based on a Spanish account, that Anne wore a grey damask gown lined with fur, an ermine mantle, and an English gable hood.[54] This is quite possibly what Anne is seen to be wearing in the painting, though the colour of her gown is perhaps a little dark. This suggests the painting may be intended to show a final goodbye on the very morning of Anne's execution.

The final of the four paintings discussed here is of Henry VIII and Anne Boleyn shooting deer by William Powell Frith from 1903. It shows Henry VIII in the guise of the Henry we see in the later Holbein portrait, with the feathered bonnet, and the slashed doublet with a loose coat over the top. In contrast, Anne Boleyn does not appear like any known portrait of her. She does not wear a hood but a hat with a feather, and a white gown, possibly symbolising innocence and chastity, as a representation of her innocence in the charges against her. She then has a dark long coat over the top. Henry stands behind Anne, looking at her as she looks ahead with her crossbow facing forward, as if she is looking at a deer. The fact that Henry is looking at Anne demonstrates that he sees her as the prey he is hunting. This echoes Thomas Wyatt's poem *Whoso List to Hunt* where it ends with the phrase '*noli me tangere*; for Caesar's I am'.[55] Anne is now out of touch for any other man, because the king is hunting her, and what he wants, he will have.

Susan Bordo has argued that 'if the Victorians "feminised" history, it had more to do with a gender ideology that men and women shared rather than which sex held the pen (or the brush)'.[56] The four paintings mentioned above were all painted by men, of a woman. It is an interesting juxtaposition to make. How might Anne have been perceived differently had it been a woman wielding the brush? Would she have been less romanticised as a victim and seen more as a woman with agency, brave and strong?

* * *

Lacey Baldwin Smith has said that the 'Victorians were both fascinated and repulsed by the pathos and brutality of the sixteenth century' but that many Victorian writers, despite believing Anne Boleyn not guilty of the charges against her, 'had difficulty imagining a government plot against her because it was presumed that proper British statesmen simply did not behave that way'.[57] Here, the Victorians have imposed their own beliefs and values onto events from over 300 years before.

The Victorians seemed to see Anne Boleyn as a tragic heroine, at least until the end of the period when opinions started to change. It is these changing views across the centuries which are often difficult to understand; what made these viewpoints change, and what were the influences which created the prevailing view? Anne 'neither controlled her own iconography nor enjoyed an undisputed reign as a Reformation heroine'.[58] Anne Boleyn had tried her best to take control of and mould her own image during her life. But none of us can control what people think of us after our deaths. All we can do is our best when we are alive. The manner of Anne's fall and death shaped the perception of her as tragic, while her involvement in the Reformation, helping the poor, and promoting those of learning formed the image of her as a heroine. Combined, these tragic and heroic elements are why the Victorians, and still people today, find her quite so fascinating.

Chapter 8

Anne on Stage

'From a blushing handmaid to his Highness'[1]

There have been some very interesting interpretations of Anne Boleyn, especially on stage, from William Shakespeare who began writing in the reign of Anne's daughter, Elizabeth I, through the works of Francis Bacon and John Banks, to the twenty-first century musical, *SIX*. People have probably read at least one of Shakespeare's plays, but *King Henry VIII* appears to be one of the lesser-known ones. With regard to the Bacon play, *The Tragedy of Anne Boleyn*, it is said that Elizabeth Wells Gallup did the deciphering of the play in the late nineteenth century. It is difficult to know whether or not she modified the play, although we have to assume that her own opinions coloured at least slightly the translation. John Banks's *Virtue Betray'd* is now out of print and seems to be largely unheard of. These three plays explore Anne Boleyn in very different ways as the writers had very different agendas and aims, though there is emphasis on Anne as the mother of Elizabeth. *SIX* is a very modern and musical retelling, contrasting completely with the earlier works, seeing Anne as a woman in her own right and pulling away from the idea that she would not be known without Henry VIII and Elizabeth I. To understand the plays themselves we need to understand the context of the times in which they were written.

There seems to have been a resurgence of literature on Anne Boleyn and the Tudors throughout the seventeenth and eighteenth centuries. Possibly this is because it was looking back to a Golden Age, during a time of civil war and strife. Plays in particular seem to have become more popular. It has been suggested that between 1576 and 1642 around 50 million people visited the theatre.[2] Since the first performance of Banks's work was not until 1682, it is fairly safe to assume that a lot of people would have seen the play if the theatre was so popular. The same could be said for the works of Francis Bacon and William Shakespeare. In the modern day, theatres are full and people will wait in an online queue to book tickets for shows as soon as they release. Enjoyment of theatre has not dimmed over the centuries.

Stephanie Russo, who wrote a book called *The Afterlife of Anne Boleyn*, has noted the 'interpretative potential of Anne' and her 'seemingly endless ability to reflect whatever the audience might want to see'.[3] These plays demonstrate several different interpretations of Anne Boleyn, focusing on her religion, motherhood, or sexuality, and reflecting opinions and the political context at the time of writing, as well as potential author bias. It is important to note not just the content of these stage adaptations of Anne's story, but the contextual influences on the writing.

William Shakespeare's *King Henry VIII*

William Shakespeare's play, *King Henry VIII*, was written jointly with John Fletcher, after a break from writing about English history. The play was known to contemporaries by the title *All is True* and testifies to a 'cultural nervousness' over competing politics and nostalgia for the optimism of the birth of Elizabeth I.[4] The alternate title suggests that Shakespeare was attempting to influence the historical record, though whether there was any truth in Anne Boleyn's purported reluctance in the play to become queen of England is unknown. Stephanie Russo says the play was set up as 'a reflection of historical truth'.[5] The play could easily be biased, if written in the reign of Elizabeth I, as Shakespeare did not want to upset the queen by portraying her mother as a temptress who seduced her father away from his first popular and pious wife, Katherine of Aragon, or as adulterous. The date of the writing of the play is contested, though it was certainly before 1613 which was when, during a performance of the play, a canon was fired as a special effect and set light to the roof of the Globe Theatre in London, which burnt down. The fire allegedly started during the scene where Henry VIII arrived at Wolsey's banquet and fell in love with Anne.[6] The play was first published in the First Folio in 1623.

By the mid-1600s Shakespeare's plays were not particularly popular. Sir William Davenant made *King Henry VIII* a success in 1663 with new scenery and costumes, and the actor Thomas Betterton portrayed a 'spectacular' Henry VIII, 'he being Instructed in it by Sir William [Davenant], who had it from Old Mr. Lowen, that had his Instructions from Mr. Shakespear himself'.[7] Shakespeare's plays seem to go through peaks and troughs, though there are some which appear to be perennially popular like *Macbeth* and *Romeo and Juliet*, which come back time and again. *King Henry VIII* does not seem to be one of these enduringly popular of Shakespeare's plays.

Shakespeare does not cover any events after the birth of Elizabeth I, seeing Elizabeth as the zenith of Tudor power and majesty. It makes sense that perhaps the play was written during Elizabeth I's reign, rather than under James I as it seems like Tudor propaganda, playing up to Elizabeth and in a way trying to rehabilitate Anne Boleyn's image, though she does not actually appear in the play all that often. Anne appears as a 'sexual motive for Henry and the incubator of Elizabeth'.[8] Shakespeare's main intention appears to have been to portray Elizabeth as England's saviour, and not to focus on the reputation of Anne Boleyn, who is sidelined a little, as Elizabeth's mother. Anne's queenship in the play is 'reduced solely to the mechanisms of the body' and the coronation scene was a celebration of the pregnant female body.[9] Anne is seen almost as a physical object to birth an heir, and not a woman in her own right. It has often been said that Elizabeth never spoke about her mother, and that Anne's execution in 1536 influenced Elizabeth's later decision never to marry.[10] But, as has been discussed in chapter 3, Elizabeth demonstrated her love and respect for her mother in other ways. There is plenty of evidence for Elizabeth's devotion to Anne Boleyn. Shakespeare may not have wanted to tackle some of the more controversial issues like Anne's fall and execution, and the fates of Henry VIII's subsequent wives.

Shakespeare's work would have been quite controversial, as this was Anne's first foray into drama and her reintroduction into the public sphere. She had appeared in a pageant in Elizabeth I's coronation procession alongside Henry VIII as parents of the queen, but it is the first fictional portrayal of Anne. The audience sees and hears very little about the Break with Rome and Anne's role in it, or any of the religious controversies which were flourishing at the time. Possibly that was seen as too controversial, alongside reintroducing a contentious queen to the public.

All of the characters in the play who are eliminated obstruct Henry's marriage to Anne and the birth of Elizabeth. The fall of these major characters in the play is important, not only to the play as a whole, but in foreshadowing Anne's own fall, though it is not shown.[11] None of those who were eliminated in the play seemed to be entirely guilty, or were not portrayed as such, possibly veiling Anne's own innocence in what she was later accused of. It appears more likely that those who died did so because they failed to do what the king wanted. In the end, this was Anne's own failing as well. It appears that the main reason for the fall of both Thomas Wolsey and Thomas Cromwell was their high level of influence. Although the play *King Henry VIII* does not get as far as 1540 and the downfall of Cromwell, Wolsey's fall is detailed. In the play, the Duke of Suffolk claims that Wolsey was using his influence with the Pope to halt the divorce, afraid of Anne's own influence.[12] David Starkey backs up this opinion, as Wolsey could easily manipulate the king's mind by giving him little gifts, and no doubt it worked the same way in international affairs.[13] Although Wolsey did not seem to see Anne's hand directly in his fall, he recognised that it was her upcoming marriage to the king that dislodged him, describing her as 'the weight that pulled me down'.[14] If Henry had not wanted a divorce then

Wolsey would not have failed, so probably would not have fallen, or at the very least he would have survived longer. In the same way, if Henry had not gone to so much trouble in order to marry Anne and then she failed, her ending, just three years after her wedding, probably would not have been quite so brutal.

What we do see of Anne Boleyn in Shakespeare's play seems to disagree with the historical record. The play often portrays her as timid, and not wanting the honours which were bestowed upon her, for example, the Marquessate of Pembroke, or not having any ambition. But it does seem to echo the relationship between them 'from a blushing handmaid to his Highness'.[15] This relationship is echoed in the love letters which Henry and Anne exchanged, in which Henry sees himself as Anne's servant.[16] What this suggests is that Henry is putting himself in the position of wooing Anne; a position unusual to him as most women fell at his feet. They both felt they were unworthy of each other, though more on Anne's side than Henry's. The public only saw Anne as being unworthy of Henry and this is possibly where her negative public image derives from – the public were disgusted when Henry VIII divorced his popular queen, Katherine of Aragon. Up until act two, scene three, Anne Boleyn has very few lines. This is possibly to demonstrate the difference in relationship between Henry and Anne, as Henry can say and do what he wants whereas Anne is subject to his whims. Even when she does speak in these early scenes it is short lines, though flirty. For example, 'you are a merry gamester' and 'you cannot show me'.[17] It is almost encouraging, but still holding back, a part of the game of courtly love in which Anne and Henry were so involved. In these instances, we see Anne Boleyn as a young woman, rather than the queen and mother of later years. She enjoyed her younger years at the centre of a vibrant court. This is all preliminary to the main point of the play: the birth of Elizabeth. The rest is largely unimportant to Shakespeare.

Kim H. Noling has conducted a detailed analysis of Shakespeare's *King Henry VIII*, and she notes that Anne's 58 spoken lines compared to Katherine of Aragon's 374 lines 'limits the audience's access to her character' as most of her speeches are restricted to a single scene.[18] Katherine of Aragon is certainly the central female character in the play. Anne appears in just three scenes and is entirely silent in one of them.

The major triumph of Anne Boleyn in the play is spoken about by two unnamed gentlemen in the coronation scene (act four, scene one). In this way, Shakespeare cleverly interposes what the people think of their new queen, although this does not seem to match the historical record either. Historians generally accept that Anne was an unpopular queen at the time. Joanna Denny, however, appears to think that Anne was popular among her new subjects, reporting that 'Anne's popularity [was because the people] were staunch believers in reform'.[19] Denny cites no evidence for this. Many of Henry VIII's closest friends were against the marriage, but they had to participate in the coronation or suffer the king's displeasure.[20] However, several prominent nobles did refuse to attend. These included Henry Stafford, 1st Baron Stafford (son of the executed Edward Stafford, 3rd Duke of Buckingham), Thomas Howard, 3rd Duke of Norfolk, who was Anne's uncle, and Henry Courtenay, 1st Marquess of Exeter.[21] In the play, however, the two gentlemen call Anne 'the goodliest woman', claiming that she had 'all the royal makings of a Queen' and that 'such joy [they] never saw before' in the people.[22] This seems contradictory to the historical record because the people did not seem to support the divorce or Anne as queen, and the coronation procession was allegedly almost silent and quite dull.[23] Shakespeare has seemingly used some artistic license in his portrayal of Anne Boleyn.

The Duke of Suffolk in the play seems to have supported Anne's marriage to the king but, in reality, Charles Brandon, 1st Duke of Suffolk, opposed it. Anne had alienated him by 1530 so Suffolk had gone to Henry VIII with tales of Anne's supposed involvement with the poet Thomas Wyatt before she came to court.[24] However, in the play Suffolk appears to support the marriage, calling Anne 'a gallant creature and complete in mind and feature' and he believed that her marriage to the king would lead to blessing on England.[25] The words 'gallant' and 'complete' suggest a wonderful young woman, perfect and accomplished, while the blessing Suffolk mentions is likely a veiled reference to Elizabeth I, her daughter and the future queen. In this way, Shakespeare portrays Anne Boleyn as the maker of the modern world, because Elizabeth's Golden Age opened up a new world. Her public image is slightly reclaimed because it was Anne Boleyn who gave England Elizabeth.

Francis Bacon's *The Tragedy of Anne Boleyn*

Francis Bacon in *The Tragedy of Anne Boleyn* appears to have been more assertive in his writing than either William Shakespeare or John Banks. He places the entirety of Anne's life on the page, rather than just bits and pieces. It is possible that Bacon was protected by his position within the court, or even that he had been commissioned to write the piece, although there is no evidence either way.

There are some conspiracy theories about Bacon's play from Elizabeth Wells Gallup who deciphered the play in the nineteenth century. She suggested that Elizabeth I was in fact Bacon's mother, hence Anne Boleyn was his grandmother. Alongside this, she claims that Bacon was in fact responsible for writing plays attributed to Shakespeare.[26] There is no evidence of either of these charges. Shakespeare's work has never been proven to be written by anyone else, except those he is known to have co-authored, like John Fletcher in *King Henry VIII.* Elizabeth's image as the Virgin Queen would definitely go against her having an illegitimate child, though there were rumours even when she was still alive that she had an illegitimate child by her favourite, Robert Dudley, 1st Earl of Leicester. The role of gossip and rumour in the sixteenth century Tudor court would have born witness if anything untoward or scandalous had happened and there has never been any evidence from the queen's ladies of a pregnancy, illegitimate child, or sexual relationship. The importance of these accusations in Bacon's work is that the woman who believed these things to be true had deciphered it, and she might have found evidence for her claims in the play itself.

Bacon's description of his work as a 'tragedy' immediately sets it apart from that of Shakespeare. Audiences are made aware that the play will cover Anne Boleyn's dramatic fall as well as her meteoric rise. Bacon's is the only play to be examined here that examines both aspects because, as will be seen, Banks only covers the period after Anne becomes queen and Shakespeare's work finished with Elizabeth's christening. For Bacon, the tragedy becomes a reality in the final speech of the play. It is not by Anne, or even by Henry, but the Earl of Arundel quoting Anne. The last line sums up Anne's image and even current perceptions beautifully: 'but Fame, truth's vindicator, shall to posterity transmit the message'.[27] What this implies is that Anne's fame after her execution and into the twenty-first century derives from her innocence. It also echoes the line in Anne's 1536 execution speech asking people to 'judge the best'.[28] Katherine Howard, the fifth wife of Henry VIII, was also executed for adultery. However, historians seem to always have believed her guilty, and she does not receive the same amount of attention as her cousin, Anne. Bacon seemed to have the right idea in that it is the most controversial cases that get the most attention, and it is the public that truly decide whether a person is innocent or guilty. Anne's innocence appears to have almost become fact across the centuries, despite her having been found guilty in 1536.

The end of the play appears to have been taken from several different sources. However, it also appears that later historians used the same sources. Agnes Strickland, for example, quotes 'from a private gentlewoman he made me a marchioness, from a marchioness a queen, and now he hath left no higher degree of honour, he gives my innocency the crown of martyrdom'.[29] This is quoted almost word for word in Bacon's play.[30] It is not a popular speech for historians to grapple with. Neither Eric Ives nor G.W. Bernard mention it, though in Bernard's case this may be because he is trying to prove her guilt. For Ives, the reason is harder to discern, though it is possible that he does not give the story much credence, as there is not really any evidence for it. Anne was unlikely to be so reckless, knowing that she would die, and her faults or mistakes would likely be taken out on her family in her absence. It has the feel of using dramatic license.

The first time that Henry sets eyes on Anne in the play is one of the most descriptive scenes, rather than the words actually heading anywhere. It focuses primarily on Anne's looks and personality. Henry picks up on Anne's 'wondrous virtue', 'chaste desires' and 'heavenly beauty bound'.[31] When Henry first started courting Anne it probably seemed to the court that playing on her virtue and chastity was hypocritical, but there is actually no real evidence that Anne had had any previous sexual relationships, or that she and Henry slept together before the end of 1532. Once they had agreed to wed, they wanted any child to be unquestionably legitimate. Henry goes further and describes her person; her being as 'full of spirit as the month of May', describing her lips 'ruby red grac'd with delight', eyes like 'twinkling stars in winter nights', and the general uniqueness of her appearance.[32] G.W. Bernard claims that Anne must have been quite beautiful for Thomas Wyatt, Henry Percy and Henry VIII to all fall in love with her.[33] Alison Weir says little about Anne's physical appearance but says that her charm and magnetism came from her personality, enhanced by her dark eyes which were very expressive.[34] This is in line with Henry's speech in Bacon's play describing Anne as being 'as full of spirit as the month of May'. Traditionally, it was to celebrate the arrival of spring, and a big celebration was called for. It seems like Anne was a breath of fresh air for the English court.

In one scene between Anne Boleyn and a nameless messenger from the king, Anne plays on her modesty, chastity and virginity in order to avoid a summons to his bed. She is then shocked when the messenger implies that Henry was thinking about marrying her.[35] In reality, their courtship was conducted in secret whereas in Bacon's work, it is conducted largely through messengers. There may have been messengers delivering letters between the pair in reality, but not privy to the private messages about marriage and the like. Until they are married there seems to be relatively few scenes in the play in which Henry and Anne feature together. In reality, even before the marriage, Anne was the primary woman at court over Katherine of Aragon, and Katherine was sent away from court in 1531. Anne was constantly wherever the court was residing.[36] In *The Tragedy of Anne Boleyn*, Anne claims that she is 'too mean to be [Henry's] queen, and yet too good to be [his] concubine'.[37] It appears that she is pulling away, not wanting to offend him by refusing to be his mistress, but knowing that Henry cannot get a divorce without a very good reason. However, the king's friend, Charles Brandon, had technically committed bigamy when he married Henry's sister, Mary Tudor, but it was seemingly sorted after the wedding by appealing to the Pope for a dispensation. It has been suggested that potentially Henry's divorce case would have been easier had he simply married Anne without waiting for papal approval and applied for a dispensation afterwards.[38] There was plenty of gossip about Brandon's marriage, so if Henry had done the same thing, no doubt it still would not have been considered binding, as any children would be of doubtful legitimacy. It was absolutely paramount for the children of a king to be of sound and legal parentage.

What is unique to Bacon's retelling of Anne Boleyn's story is the accusation of witchcraft, which is not implicitly made, but it is there, nonetheless. Shakespeare and Banks do not acknowledge this. The Duke of Norfolk, Anne's uncle, is seen telling Henry VIII that Anne planned to poison his eldest daughter, Mary, and that she had caused Henry's ulcerated leg in order that he might die so that she could marry one of her lovers.[39] Witchcraft itself is not mentioned but the insinuation is clear. The historical record tells us that, allegedly, on the night of Anne's arrest on 2 May 1536, Henry told his illegitimate son, Henry Fitzroy, that he was 'greatly bound to God for having escaped the hands of that accursed whore' as Anne had planned to poison him and Mary.[40] There is no real evidence for this except for the word of Eustace Chapuys, the Imperial ambassador to England, who was biased towards Katherine of Aragon and her daughter, Mary, against Anne Boleyn and her daughter, Elizabeth. His reports cannot be wholly trusted, though it would have been in his best interests to report the truth to his master, Charles V. Even if Henry had said this to Fitzroy, he may not have truly believed it. It is quite possible the comment came from anger. The idea of a witchcraft charge is often used to highlight the breadth of the charges against Anne, although witchcraft is not mentioned in the surviving part of the indictment.[41] In the play, Henry is devastated and angry at Anne's betrayal calling her a 'lewd minx' and declaring that he will withdraw to 'furnish me with some swift means of death for the fair devil'.[42] The terminology is very reminiscent of witchcraft as witches were said to make pacts with the devil, and make sexual bargains with him.

Bacon's play is interesting because there is a definite sense that he tapped into public feeling and reaction at the time about Anne. He quite probably talked to people who had known Anne or had family who knew Anne, and had recollections of what was believed, more so than Shakespeare. Bacon himself was born in 1561 and his father, Sir Nicholas Bacon, was Lord Keeper of the Great Seal under Elizabeth I. His family had a history of court service, so in all likelihood would have known someone who knew Anne Boleyn.

John Banks's *Virtue Betray'd*

John Banks's play *Virtue Betray'd* is now virtually unknown it seems. At the time it was written, the English Civil War had just finished, Oliver Cromwell was dead, and Charles II restored to the throne. It is possible that Banks was reasserting the right of Charles II to the throne and the importance of monarchy. The divine right of kings was still a controversial issue after the Civil War and demonstrating the legitimacy of Elizabeth I through the legal marriage of her parents, Henry VIII and Anne Boleyn, showed that the divine right of kings was still a valid concept which underpinned the monarchy. This is one possible aim of Banks's work, although it could merely have been a scholarly interest in one of the most tumultuous periods in English history. With Elizabeth I's reign almost out of living memory, it probably felt safe enough to write about Anne Boleyn.

The distinct position of Anne in history according to Banks is as a 'hapless victim' of royal tyranny and Catholic conspiracy.[43] She is also a 'tragic, entirely virtuous woman callously divided from the love of her life', meaning Henry Percy, by a 'tyrannical and lascivious' Henry VIII.[44] Anne is portrayed as an entirely innocent victim who died at the hands of others, her reputation destroyed. But she is also depicted, especially at the beginning of the play, as lacking in ambition, and Henry VIII is portrayed as a 'violent rapist'.[45] This places Anne and Henry at opposite poles, painting Anne as entirely good and Henry as entirely bad. It is black and white rather than shades of grey.

Virtue Betray'd was staged at the Dorset Garden in London for the first time in March 1682. It has been suggested that with *Virtue Betray'd* and *The Albion Queens* (a play examining the relationship between Elizabeth I and Mary Queen of Scots), Banks pioneered the 'she-tragedy' which seemed to come into being in the late Restoration period. It rejected the poetic justice of previous plays in favour of a 'persistent emphasis upon the suffering of an innocent heroine'.[46] In contrast to how Anne Boleyn is usually portrayed as a seductress and marriage destroyer, Banks depicts her as an innocent victim. The difference between Banks's work and that of Bacon and Shakespeare is that it begins with Anne's wedding to Henry VIII. It ignores the controversial sections of Anne's involvement in the divorce and the Break with Rome. It focuses on Anne as queen, and the power she wielded.

The title alone, *Virtue Betray'd*, is intriguing as it does not even make it immediately clear who the play is about. Banks saw Anne as a virtuous and chaste woman who was betrayed. Right at the beginning of the play in the first scene, it becomes obvious that Anne feels betrayed by Henry Percy, the future Earl of Northumberland. Their engagement was broken off, but Percy was to marry another as if he and Anne had never been together. Anne ignores the fact that she has married later to become queen of England, as likely she did not have much of a choice. It implies that Anne was still in love with Percy, even after her marriage to Henry VIII; '[Percy] hangs heavy on her heart and in her Eyes'.[47] In reality, Percy always insisted that he and Anne had no romantic relationship.[48] In real life, if Anne was still in love with Percy surely someone at the court would have commented on it; particularly the ambassadors, who had nothing to fear from Henry's wrath. Their masters would have expected to know anything going on, especially in relation to the royal family. There are no surviving comments from ambassadors about any kind of relationship between Anne and Percy, aside from the letter from Percy in May 1536 that he and Anne were never betrothed.[49] Whether Anne felt betrayed by Percy in reality is unclear, but he did not seem to put up much of a fight when their relationship was ended.

Henry VIII also eventually betrayed Anne. He had loved her but when she failed to deliver a living son, he turned on her. In the play, Henry has been betrayed by Anne, but if she was innocent, then it is the other way around. Henry claims he has 'more horns than any Forest yields'.[50] What he means is cuckold's horns. Adultery on the part of a woman was more severe than on the part of a man. A woman's adultery could affect the division of titles and wealth, or the succession to the throne, if it was not known who had fathered a child.[51] For queens this was even more important, because it could be of detrimental effect to the country. Betrayal is a key theme in Banks's work as the title suggests.

Because Banks examines Anne's role as queen, there is a definite focus on monarchy and corruption within it. People who exposed the evils of the sixteenth-century court were punished because they showed the weakness of the monarchy at the time.[52] This applies not only to Anne Boleyn, but also to the men who were accused alongside her: her brother George, Francis Weston, Henry Norris, William Brereton, and Mark Smeaton. The degree of their so-called crimes meant that the succession had been put into jeopardy and the king had been disgraced. The story of Anne Boleyn was no doubt relatively familiar to audiences at the time, but Banks reshaped it to focus less on Anne's story and more on the monarchy as a whole.[53] The corruption of the monarchy in this play stems less from Anne than from Wolsey. Anne seems to make the monarchy corrupt through her relationship with Henry Percy, but Wolsey makes it corrupt through his manipulation of Henry VIII. This same manipulation can be seen in the Exclusion Crisis of the 1670s and 1680s where several men were attempting to manipulate Charles II into declaring them his heir. For example, the Duke of Monmouth and the Duke of York, who were both claimants to the throne. This can be compared to Henry VIII and Anne Boleyn, where both Anne and Katherine of Aragon were trying to influence Henry over the succession, along with his ministers like Wolsey and Cromwell. Childlessness was also key to both periods, as both Katherine of Aragon and Anne Boleyn failed to have a son, and Catherine of Braganza, wife to Charles II, did not have a single surviving child, male or female. This could explain why Banks was using the story of Henry VIII and Anne Boleyn in order to highlight an important issue in the time in which he was writing.

The play is primarily a political one, with a religious angle. It centres on a Catholic plot to depose the Protestant Anne Boleyn and take England back into the Roman Catholic fold. A literary critic, Tracey Miller-Tomlinson, has suggested that the political angle would have resonated powerfully in the time in which Banks was writing.[54] Henry VIII's bastardisation of his and Anne's daughter, Elizabeth, echoed the confusing issues of succession in the 1680s after the tumultuous period of the Civil War, execution of Charles I, and the Interregnum. There were several claimants to the throne, and rumours flying around of a possible coup: the Popish Plot (1678–1681). The Popish Plot was a fabricated conspiracy to kill Charles II, like the charges against Anne that she plotted with her lovers to kill Henry VIII. The claimants to the throne were seen as being very similar to those in the time of Henry VIII. The future Mary I was seen as being the legitimate claimant to the throne in many people's eyes. Similarly with the Exclusion Crisis, there was both a legitimate claimant (the Catholic future James II) and an illegitimate claimant (the Protestant Duke of Monmouth). This was the greatest fear of Henry VIII – that he would not have a legitimate son to succeed him on the throne – and it is echoed in the decisions of Charles II. The succession issue is partly the reason why Anne Boleyn was ultimately executed, and Katherine of Aragon was put aside before her.

The future Elizabeth I does appear in Banks's play, although she does not feature in any scenes with her mother. A key scene is when Elizabeth confronts her father with his intentions to put Anne to death. This could never have happened in reality as Elizabeth was only 2 years old when her mother died. This is another example of historical license in Banks's work, in order to put across a political point: that there will always be those who question decisions, and you can never satisfy everyone, someone will always be hurt. Elizabeth was aged up to make a political point. A lot of the words and phrases used to describe Elizabeth echo earlier phrases used to describe Anne; for example, 'woman's rage', 'sparkling reason', and 'prettiest innocence'.[55] There are plenty of accounts of Anne's rage, particularly when Henry VIII took a mistress. Alison Weir described Anne as having become 'haughty, overbearing, shrewish and volatile' and constantly arguing with her husband.[56] Anne found it difficult to move from the position of mistress to that of wife. Qualities acceptable in a mistress were not considered suitable in a wife. It was these qualities which turned some members of her extended family against her, notably her uncle, the Duke of Norfolk. In the early part of the play, Anne is described as having 'Innocent Charms'.[57] This echoes descriptions later in the play of her daughter.

Innocence appears to be an attraction of the Howard woman, as Henry would later find with Katherine Howard who was not as innocent as she looked.

There are several allusions, even within the first scene of the play, which suggest Anne's eventual end. In Rochford's first speech he says:

> And may my Sister's crown sit lighter on
> Her Brow, than does the Honour upon mine;
> Something of boding whispers to my Soul,
> And tells me, Oh! This marriage will be fatal –
> Methinks I see a sword ty'd to a Thread,
> Small as a Hair, hang o'er Our Pageant Greatness:
> Believe me, Friend; Thrones are severest Touch-stones;
> And, like the Emblem of their Guard, the Lyon,
> All but of Royal-Blood they will destroy.[58]

What is particularly interesting about this is that it is using historical hindsight to add another dimension to the play and being obvious about it. Many works fail to acknowledge the benefits of hindsight on stage shows. There is no way Anne could have known her fate, or people around her could have guessed it either, no matter what people whispered in the streets during her life. Rochford even appears to know the method of death. The executioner of Calais was brought over from France to behead Anne with a sword instead of the traditional English axe.

Banks obviously did conduct plenty of research in the writing of this play, but he neglected to use some of the best known parts of Anne Boleyn's story. The most obvious issue with historical license in Banks's play is that Cardinal Wolsey died in 1530, three years before Anne Boleyn became queen, yet in Banks's work he is still alive at Anne's execution in 1536. This is in addition to Princess Elizabeth having been aged up in order to confront her father. Banks appears to have changed the historical record in order to suit his own purposes in detailing the plight of Charles II and Catherine of Braganza by using events from a century and a half earlier.

Historical accuracy aside, however, the foretelling of Anne's death is a running theme throughout the play. Anne can foresee her fate, but she cannot run from it. Her family uses her as a means of 'social promotion' while they also have other demands of her, as does the king and court.[59] Her family wanted more titles, wealth, and influence. The king wanted a queen and a son and heir to his throne. The court wanted a queen they could be proud of, as Katherine of Aragon was, but also a queen who could produce an heir. Anne failed both the king and court, even though Elizabeth I would turn out to be a very successful ruler, but she did not fail her family. Anne's father, Thomas Boleyn, was made

Earl of Wiltshire and Ormond and Lord Privy Seal in 1529, the third highest office in England.[60] This patronage is not really discussed in Banks's work, as it focuses more on the wider political situation. Banks is trying to influence the politics of the time in which he was writing, using Henry VIII and Anne Boleyn as an example of the power of monarchy.

The play demonstrates the danger of a disputed succession. Civil war could break out if there were too many claimants to the throne, as seen in the fifteenth century with the Wars of the Roses. This use of overlapping time streams is not unusual in literary works, as it is inevitable that works will be influenced by the times in which they were written. Banks's work is just more obvious about it.

Toby Marlow and Lucy Moss's *SIX The Musical*

SIX The Musical was first staged at the Edinburgh Fringe Festival in 2017, written by Toby Marlow and Lucy Moss. It seems strange now that this musical is such a recent invention as it is playing in London's West End, Broadway, and is touring both the UK and the US. It is a celebration of girl power and resilience:

> From Tudor Queens to Pop Princesses, the six wives of Henry VIII take to the mic to tell their tales, remixing five hundred years of historical heartbreak into an 80-minute celebration of 21st century girl power. These Queens may have green sleeves, but their lipstick is rebellious red.[61]

In the end, the queens decide to write an alternative version of history with different endings for each of the wives to what actually happened. It is certainly a new retelling of an old story and one of female power and rebellion; the most modern version of the six wives yet seen. 'Greensleeves' is a riff on the song that Henry VIII is alleged to have written for Anne Boleyn, though it is questionable whether it was indeed written for her. The character of Anne in the show wears a short green dress with puffed sleeves, fishnet tights, and diamante boots. Her hair forms doughnuts on top of her head with spiked ornaments and the rest is left loose. It is quite a rebellious look, echoing Anne's rebellious and free spirit.

Each queen takes turns singing a song about their experiences with Henry VIII in the order they were married to him, but before Anne Boleyn's song there is an introduction where the other queens sing about her, introducing her as the most famous and controversial queen, who changed history, and making the wry point that she is usually the one people actually care about. But that she paid the ultimate price in the end.[62] Anne Boleyn does seem to be, out of all of the six wives, the one who gets the most attention, has the most books written about her, and causes the most arguments and controversy. She certainly changed history: mother of Elizabeth I, catalyst for the Break with Rome and the dissolution of the monasteries, and the first crowned English queen to be judicially executed. Her portrayal in *SIX The Musical* is that of a temptress, a woman with a plan. But did she have a plan? That is up for debate. She did not plan to become queen from the moment Henry VIII began pursuing her. It may not have crossed her mind until Henry asked her to marry him, whenever that happened in their courtship. We know that Henry VIII did not initially intend to marry Anne, as he asked her to be his mistress.

It is also up for debate whether Anne chased the king, or if he pursued her. It is possible that Anne tried to pull away from the king because she did not want to be his mistress and it seemed impossible at the time for her to be his wife. Marlow and Moss in *SIX* challenge the idea that Anne was a 'self-aware schemer', and that she in fact did not intend to cause the chaos she did, but could not do anything different when presented with those circumstances.[63] It makes good theatre and entertainment and puts Anne Boleyn and the other wives under the spotlight for new audiences to discover, and hopefully to go away and find out the real history.

Anne Boleyn's spotlight song in *SIX* is entitled 'Don't Lose Ur Head', a play on the fact that she did, in fact, lose her head. With a refrain throughout where she defiantly tells those around her not to worry, not to 'lose their head' (a play on do not be angry), the Anne Boleyn we meet in *SIX* is clear that despite her actions, she had never meant to cause any harm.[64] This is suggestive of the idea that Anne got caught up in the affair with Henry VIII almost against her will until she was too far in that she could not get out and just had to stick with it. She was a victim of the king in the end, but she also played the game of courtly love very well and made huge gains for herself and her family. It cannot be said that she entirely failed, even if she did ultimately lose her head. The musical influences for Anne Boleyn were Lily Allen and Avril Lavigne.[65] If you've listened to either of these then you can see the musical similarities.

Anne's song runs through her life from the French court, through her marriage, to her demise.[66] There are several lines where Marlow and Moss are obviously aware of the mythology and research surrounding Anne Boleyn but have consciously gone against it, particularly in relation to the part she played in the politics of the day.[67] Most historians believe that Anne was in fact very much into politics, and had almost a natural affinity for persuasion and, some people believe, manipulation. She was involved with the divorce case and the beginnings of the English Reformation, introducing Henry VIII to works by Simon Fish and William Tyndale. Further on in the song, there is another suggestion that Anne was pushed into the situation she found herself in by her father, who advocated for her to capture the king's attention.[68] There have been suggestions that Anne Boleyn was pushed into a relationship with the king by her father, uncle, or brother, whether because Henry had grown tired of her sister, Mary Boleyn, who had been his mistress, or because her family had noticed the king's interest and wanted to use that to their own ends. Marlow and Moss jump on this claim to explain why and how Anne and Henry came to be together. In a musical, it is difficult to go into the ins and outs of a relationship which is never as simple as having a single explanation, and it does work within the context of the song.

When the song moves into the relationship itself, Anne jokes about moving in with the king's wife and then goes on to say to Henry that he needs to make up his mind about which of the two women he wants to be with.[69] This points to the fact that there was an uncomfortable ménage à trois where Katherine of Aragon, Anne Boleyn, and Henry VIII all lived together at court for a while, until Henry told Katherine to leave court in 1531. She would not see Henry again. Anne was known to have spoken bluntly to the king, worried that he would cast her off, so she was pressuring him to deal with the situation. The Imperial ambassador, Eustace Chapuys, reported that Anne said to Henry VIII, 'Did I not tell you that whenever you disputed with the Queen, she was sure to have the upper hand? I see that some fine morning you will succumb to her reasoning, and that you will cast me off'.[70] There are also some instances where Anne's fiery temper comes through in the song as she slights her rival, Katherine of Aragon, that she is past it, and then crudely touches on Henry's alleged impotence.[71] The latter probably comes from George Boleyn at his trial where he was asked whether his wife, Jane, Lady Rochford, had ever told him that Anne confided to her that Henry 'was no good at sex with women, and that he had neither prowess nor force'.[72] It is very obvious that Marlow and Moss have consulted the original sources in order to build the song.

At the end of the show, the wives agree that it is fruitless to compete; in actual fact, it is they that make Henry interesting. In a demonstration of girl power they agree to take back the narratives of their own lives. Anne's version of her own life is to write songs for Shakespeare, borrowing some of Henry's lyrics from Greensleeves.[73] She steps out of Henry's shadow and makes a life for herself. The suggestion is that all of these women are incredibly capable on their own and that a man does not define them and is not the reason why they have become famous. They might have been known today even without being defined as a wife of Henry VIII and that Henry himself is better known, precisely because he was married to each of these women.

* * *

The major change between the writing of William Shakespeare, Francis Bacon and John Banks is the political situation. Anne Boleyn's daughter, Elizabeth I, was still alive when Shakespeare was writing, and Bacon appeared to want to pay homage to her. However, when Banks was writing, it was to influence the wider political context, rather than present a personal perception. As Anne Boleyn and Elizabeth I came out of living memory, it became easier to write about them without fear of repercussions. *SIX The Musical* is entirely different. It is a musical and very much a 'show' in a way that earlier stage perceptions of Anne are not. In *SIX*, Anne Boleyn is the sexy one, determined to win the competition of the most hard done by wife because she was beheaded. She is sassy in a way that is very modern, and we do not see in earlier productions. The focus is also on the women, rather than how they relate to Henry VIII.

The main thing about Anne Boleyn is her notoriety. The stage shows discussed here pull together all kinds of aspects of Anne Boleyn's life and character, but individually they focus on very different parts, rather than the whole. Stephanie Russo claims that part of Anne's fascination lies in 'tracing the way she disrupted ideas of medieval queenship'.[74] Perhaps that explains why Anne is so fascinating – she was a new kind of queen, and her steps to the throne were so very different to her predecessors. Anne Boleyn's journey demonstrated that crowned monarchs were not necessarily safe, something which would be borne out in the cases of Mary Queen of Scots and Charles I. It seems, in adapting Anne's life for the stage, many of the factual elements have been dismissed or manipulated. Playwrights attempt to influence politics in the time they are writing rather than presenting a real depiction of times past.

Chapter 9

Anne on Film

'My Elizabeth shall be queen, and my blood will have been well spent'[1]

Anne Boleyn and the Tudors more generally have been an in-demand topic in media in the twentieth and twenty-first centuries and are only growing in popularity. Partly this appears to be due to the controversy, sex, and murder that are an acknowledged part of the sixteenth century in England. Glenn Richardson has suggested that the story of Anne Boleyn has 'all the right ingredients' for a good film, including power, lust, and tragedy.[2] Filmmakers are not just intrigued by the historical record, but by the scandal that rocked the court and how that translates into a good television series, film, or novel. Hence, history takes a back seat. History is fictionalised because it offers a rich source of material, and gaps in the historical record can be filled with the writer's and actor's imagination.

Thomas Freeman suggests that 'films have a remarkable ability to illuminate and animate past events, but they also distort our perception of them'.[3] Films can bring the past to life for many, but they cannot portray every single possible interpretation of the surviving evidence, and much evidence is not clear-cut. A filmmaker will generally choose from among the available interpretations which one best suits the film's purpose and dramatic arc, limiting the knowledge distilled to the audience to what the film wants to achieve. Ian Kershaw has claimed that a film or television show is at its weakest 'where an issue is highly contentious and subject to widely differing interpretations' as interpretation and debate are the lifeblood of history, but film and television are more 'directive' and debate muddies the waters.[4] This idea of film being weak when there is a contentious issue is important to consider in the case of Anne Boleyn. She can be incredibly divisive and contentious among historians and on social media, and most people will have a favourite screen portrayal, whether it's Genevieve Bujold in *Anne of the Thousand Days*, Claire Foy in *Wolf Hall*, Natalie Dormer in *The Tudors*, or one of many others. But when a new portrayal comes out, there are always questions over how Anne will be portrayed: seductress and homewrecker, religious reformer, traitor, or a woman pushed by the men around her. It is often difficult to convey all of the complexities of Anne Boleyn in a single film or television series.

An increase in historical interest has brought up the idea of identity in fictionalised portrayals, particularly in film. Although focused on Anne Boleyn, examining these portrayals also reveal very differing and changing perceptions of Henry VIII. Today, 'impressions of Anne and Henry are coloured by fictional representations'.[5] It is impossible for them not to be, because there are so many fictional portrayals in films, television shows, and in novels, and they are widely disseminated. It is not just the identity of figures that has changed, but also national identity more widely. James Chapman has suggested that eras which are most fictionalised are those whose image of national identity add to British 'greatness'.[6] The Tudor century is incredibly popular to fictionalise, along with the two world wars. England's national identity was forged in the Reformation, and Anne Boleyn was a key part of that. England's power was then cemented with the defeat of the Spanish Armada by Anne's daughter, Elizabeth.

There are really three era of screen adaptations about Anne's life with the early ones culminating in the release of *The Private Life of Henry VIII* in 1933, the revival after the release of *Anne of the Thousand Days* in 1969, and the twenty-first century wave including shows like Showtime's *The Tudors* (2007–2011) and *The Other Boleyn Girl* (2008). Stephanie Russo describes cinematic Anne Boleyns as being 'far more uniform than those found in novels' and 'usually agentic, ambitious and intelligent women, even when plot elements of her story are treated very differently'.[7] As will be seen in chapter eleven, Anne Boleyn on the page is portrayed in a wide variety of ways, with the emphasis on different parts of her life. In a way, the film is almost more restrictive because you have a very limited window of time to put across her story and to keep the audience engaged, and thus some aspects of her character are pulled out more than others.

We often view the past with rose-tinted glasses, as a time of great discovery and development that led to what we know today and in a way shaped our national identity. Film theorist, Linda Hutcheon, has suggested that while films were not made to be 'historically accurate' it makes little sense to speak of them as 'historically inaccurate' either.[8] Historical events are generally not adapted for the screen to be historically accurate but for dramatic and entertainment purposes. They are adapted to bring in the audience, entertain them and make money. Hence why films and television have so much sex and violence and less politics. Another theorist has said that a historian is first and foremost concerned with accuracy as far as possible, whereas the producer of a film is interested instead in the visual impact and entertainment.[9] This implies that accounts perceived as being historically accurate and fictionalised films are not really compatible.

There will always be historical inaccuracies. Thomas Freeman illustrates a very important point which is that:

> The content of historical films is actually a matter of considerable importance since they reinforce and perpetuate, if not actually create, myths about the past that are very difficult to shift or dislodge.[10]

For example, one of the myths that seems to be very persistent is that Anne Boleyn slept with her brother, George, in her desperation to conceive a son. On social media, people have been seen to cite the film of *The Other Boleyn Girl* as evidence for this. They appear to struggle to grasp that this is a fictional portrayal, dramatised for effect, and that the film is not evidence that this event happened. It is a worrying development in the 500 years of cultural history surrounding Anne Boleyn that some people assume that what these portrayals show is absolute fact. This chapter will discuss some of these assumptions and what the surviving historical evidence can tell us about the reality of what actually happened.

The Private Life of Henry VIII (1933)

The Private Life of Henry VIII is a film from 1933 starring Charles Laughton as Henry VIII and Merle Oberon as Anne Boleyn. Looking at some of the posters which were produced to promote the film, the slogans focus on some of the more gory or controversial aspects of Henry's reign, with one poster declaring 'Every woman got it in the neck – eventually' and another saying 'What a King! What a Man! What a Lover!', capitalising on the idea Henry himself no doubt would have approved of: his sexual prowess and masculinity. Only two of Henry's six wives 'got it in the neck' so the first tagline is untrue, but it is dramatic. But it can be said that, in this film, Henry is 'more of a victim than a victimiser' particularly in the portrayal of his final three wives.[11] Anne Boleyn's appearances are confined to the first twenty minutes and we as the viewer are encouraged to believe in her innocence.

The only part of Anne Boleyn's life we see in the film is her end. The portrayal of Anne's execution in *The Private Life of Henry VIII* is interesting. It is almost glamorised rather than made to be devastating. Oberon's looks may have appealed to the director, Alexander Korda, for 'invoking a sense of Anne's glamorous French appeal'.[12] Anne did have a sense of exoticism on her return to the English court from France in 1522. Lancelot de Carles, who was in London at the time of Anne's execution in 1536, reported that you would never have thought her English, but a Frenchwoman born.[13] So perhaps Merle

Oberon's casting as Anne was to bring out the exoticism in her, though Anne is not the focus of the film, and she is dead within the first twenty minutes. The interest is not in Henry and Anne's relationship. The film opens on the day of Anne Boleyn's execution, also said to be the day that Henry VIII married Jane Seymour, though the latter event actually happened eleven days after Anne's death. The two events are juxtaposed in order to portray Henry as callous and uncaring about Anne, looking to the future and hopes of a male heir, rather than the past. Katherine of Aragon is effectively ignored, with the title card reading that 'her story is of no particular interest – she was a respectable woman. So, Henry divorced her'.[14] The immediate implication, therefore, is that the film will focus on the more controversial and gory aspects of Henry VIII's life and reign, beginning with the execution of his second wife.

A group of ladies in the first scene are told that the 'A' initial in Henry VIII's bedding needs to come out and be replaced with a 'J'. As they work, they talk about Anne Boleyn's fate and her replacement, asking whether she was really guilty because 'all her lovers confessed' but under torture, and that 'she was as innocent as you or I'.[15] The women believe that the king is executing Anne so that he can marry Jane Seymour, and joke that 'yes, that's what they mean when they say, "chop and change"'.[16] The viewer is supposed to believe Anne Boleyn innocent of the charges against her, although the suggestion is that she was only accused of adultery; not even the incest charge with her brother is mentioned, let alone the treason charge. Adultery alone at this time was not punishable by death. Only one of Anne's supposed lovers, Mark Smeaton, actually confessed to adultery, but denied treason. The other men all maintained their innocence to the end. There has been an idea that Mark Smeaton was tortured in order to confess; whether that was physical or emotional is unclear. Smeaton was a commoner so his fate would have been hanging, drawing, and quartering without the king's mercy, so it is possible he was offered the quicker death of beheading in exchange for his confession, or even to be let off if he confessed. But the conversation ends on an almost comic note with the 'chop and change' remark, downplaying the tragedy of Anne Boleyn's end.

There is one other particular thing of note about *The Private Life of Henry VIII* and the scenes of Anne Boleyn's preparations for death and Henry VIII's preparations for his new marriage. That is that one of the women removing Anne's initials from the king's bedding is her cousin, Katherine Howard, who would go on to marry Henry as his fifth wife. It is thought that Katherine was only born around 1524 or 1525 so she would only have been maybe 11 or 12 years old at this point, not the grown woman we see Henry flirt with. It is disturbing to see, knowing the history with hindsight, and seeing Henry's callousness as he awaits the execution of one wife, is about to marry another, and flirts with a later one. Katherine Howard is the wife who is at the centre of *The Private Life of Henry VIII*, rather than her cousin, Anne.

When William Kingston wrote to Thomas Cromwell that Anne had said, 'I heard say the executioner was very good, and I have a little neck', she was reported to have laughed as she said it and put her hands around her neck.[17] Anne is said to have veered during her imprisonment from hope, to tears, to hysterical laughter, and back again. Merle Oberon does not laugh as she delivers the line, 'and I have such a little neck, haven't I?'.[18] She instead says it 'wistfully, as if in resigned acceptance and ... with a touch of narcissism'.[19] It is interesting to consider how Anne might have said it, as we only have the report that she did say she had a little neck and laughed, but was the laugh hysterical, sarcastic, accepting, sad? We will never know the answer. Anne must have been in such a whirl of emotion and despair that trying to put ourselves in her shoes at this point is incredibly difficult. No one today can really understand her position.

Thomas Freeman writes that director, Alexander Korda, 'emphasises glamour and stylishness rather than terror or tragedy, in his depiction' of Anne's death.[20] Before her execution, while in the Tower of London, the viewer sees Anne asking for a different mirror to be brought to her to examine her hair, and asks, 'will the net hold my hair together when, when my head falls?' and then, 'isn't it a pity to lose a head like this? Still, they will easily find a nickname for me. Among the queens of England, I shall be "Anne sans tete"'.[21] This idea of Anne declaring her own nickname comes from a letter written by the Imperial ambassador, Chapuys, on 6 June 1536, a couple of weeks after Anne's execution, where he says that the night before her death Anne 'talked and jested' that the people would not find it hard to invent a nickname for her as they would call her 'la Royne Anne sans tete', and then she laughed.[22] Though given that this was not written in Chapuys' original account of the execution to Charles V, or recorded in any other source, we cannot be certain whether this actually happened. The almost glamourisation of Anne's execution in *The Private Life of Henry VIII* continues once it is over as a man who witnesses it says to his wife, 'Well, one must admit, she died like a queen', to which his wife replies 'yes, and that frock, wasn't it too divine?'.[23] The focus is taken away from the terror and fear Anne must have felt, and the tragedy of an innocent woman having been executed, to focus on something more mundane.

Anne of the Thousand Days (1969)

Anne of the Thousand Days is a film based on a Broadway play and starred Richard Burton as Henry VIII and Genevieve Bujold as Anne Boleyn. This portrayal of Henry and Anne's relationship is a favourite and suggests that Anne did not really want Henry and tried to push him away continually. The Internet Movie Database (IMDb) has reviews from ordinary people, rather than critics, of films and television shows and one review describes *Anne of the Thousand Days* as the product of a cinema in transition, a classic from the sixties, and a 'rare achievement'.[24] A review from 1970 in *The New York Times*, just a year after the film's release, does not seem very fond of it, describing it as 'a sort of epic battle of the sexes', but it is also a product of its time as the review also claims that the success of the film came from the 'real intelligence' of the actors in it.[25] Burton and Bujold do a fantastic job as Henry VIII and Anne Boleyn, portraying their fiery relationship.

The film was adapted from a play of the same name which premiered in 1948, written by Maxwell Anderson. Anne Boleyn's 'celebrity as a perceived witch in the 1960s' was acknowledged by scriptwriters in the film, in lines missing from the original play.[26] This includes Henry proclaiming 'I am accursed!' after Anne's final miscarriage.[27] In a previous scene where Thomas Cromwell speaks to Anne about her unpopularity with the people, he tells her that, 'the people say that you are a witch-queen'.[28] It is a clever cultural reference playing into what ideas were at the time of the film rather than in Anne's lifetime. But witchcraft is a popular notion in many of these screen adaptations. Bujold's performance as Anne Boleyn in the film gained an 'enthusiastic critical reception' which was an exception to the 'lukewarm – and frequently hostile – reviews that the movie received when it opened'.[29] Bujold's performance as Anne is 'an Anne for the 1960s women's liberation movement: she has self-determination, intelligence, agency, and ambition'.[30] We can never forget to consider the times in which a drama was created and released, and an 'Anne who could challenge and laugh at Henry, even as she faced death, was an Anne that was suited to the sensibilities of the 1960s, and one that has arguably become even more desirable today'.[31] Bujold's performance is certainly the standout of the film and remains this author's favourite, though Richard Burton also has a commanding presence on screen. The pairing holds the film together as they negotiate the sunshine and storms of Henry VIII and Anne Boleyn's relationship.

One of the most interesting aspects of *Anne of the Thousand Days* is that Anne is very open about her relationship with Henry Percy, telling her parents that she loves him and will marry him. She is also very open about her previous physical relationships, telling Percy that she is not a virgin, that she had sex in France and even before that.[32] We do not see her being so open with Henry VIII, probably knowing that it would ruin her chances with him and her future prospects as well. Though there is also a distinct sense that Anne did not intend to marry the king, or even to sleep with him, so it was not important to disclose. By the time she agreed to marry him, it was too late to reveal the truth. A sexual relationship before marriage would reflect negatively on Anne's character and morals and have an influence on whether she was perceived as being guilty of adultery. We do not have the kind of concrete evidence that either proves or disproves the nature of Anne's relationship with Percy, though Percy himself wrote to Thomas Cromwell in May 1536 when Anne was imprisoned in the Tower, to deny any kind of betrothal between them.[33] There is no evidence of Anne having had a sexual relationship prior to Henry VIII, but that is not conclusive, as it would not necessarily have been recorded.

In the film, Cardinal Thomas Wolsey breaks up the relationship between Anne and Percy and tells Anne that 'when Henry of England turns his eyes on a girl, she can hardly look away', to which Anne responded that 'I shall not go the way of my sister. You would be wise to anticipate my answer and spare His Majesty any annoyance'.[34] When Wolsey tells Anne of the king's interest in her, her sister, Mary, is heavily pregnant with the king's child. It demonstrates Henry's callousness towards women, that he believes he can have whoever he wants and then just discard them. Anne will not be one of many. At the ensuing meeting between Henry and Anne, Anne is dismissive of him when he says that 'you see before you not the king, but a poor fellow, as uncertain, as eager, as hopeful, as afraid, as any man that ever fell in love' and he tells her that 'what you want, you shall have' to which Anne responds 'if I have you first'.[35] No Anne Boleyn on screen before 'had ever been so proudly defiant, so insistent on her own autonomy'.[36] She seems to understand the way that Henry thinks; that everyone wants him and that he will give them money and titles to pay them off. At this point in the film, Anne is broken hearted and what she wants she cannot have as Henry has married Percy off to another woman. Henry VIII remains at Hever for a few weeks after this conversation, trying to persuade Anne to give in to him. They ride out of Hever and stop by a lake. Anne is determined to tell Henry exactly what she thinks of him, and it is cutting, that she has seen what he is, 'spoiled and vengeful and bloody', mocking his poetry and music. The final nail in the coffin was her comment that 'you make love as you eat, with a good deal of noise and no subtlety'.[37] Henry struggles to hear from someone who is not admiring and appreciative of him. Henry has been loved and pandered to his whole life, and it seems that Anne was the first person to really disagree with him and tell him what she actually thought about him. Henry VIII certainly became bloody and vengeful. It is debatable just how much Henry was a tyrant before the late 1520s and the annulment case, but there were certainly early indications in his arrests of Empson and Dudley in 1509 and their executions the following year, and then the execution of the Duke of Buckingham in 1521. Henry already had form for being bloody and vengeful prior to the introduction of Anne Boleyn into his life.

When Henry VIII begins to fall for Jane Seymour, Anne Boleyn immediately acts, sending her to Northumberland, 'as far away as I could send her since we don't own Scotland' as 'she has the face of a simpering sheep, and the manners. But not the morals'.[38] There is no record in the contemporary sources that Anne succeeded in sending Jane away from the court, though she had attempted it with another woman that the king had shown interest in. The Imperial ambassador, Eustace Chapuys, reported that 'in order to conceal from the public his love for Jane Seymour, the King has made her reside seven miles from this city'.[39] This was reported at the time of Anne Boleyn's execution, so it does not seem that Jane was sent away when Henry was courting her, only at the point when he knew there would be rumours and he wanted to make sure that he was seen to be just in his proceedings against Anne and not acting out of lust. In *Anne of the Thousand Days*, there is also an element of blackmail in this conversation, with Henry and Cromwell manipulating Anne into bringing Jane back to court, with Anne concluding 'if I bring Jane Seymour back, you will have parliament pass the Act of Succession'.[40] The implication is that, unless Anne brought Jane back to court, Henry VIII would not pass the Act of Succession which made Anne Boleyn's children heir to the English throne.

One of the most memorable scenes and quotes in the entire film is from Anne Boleyn's confrontation in the Tower of London with Henry VIII, although there is no historical evidence that Henry ever visited Anne in the Tower during her imprisonment. In fact, Henry seems to have immediately tried to forget anyone who he decided to get rid of. He refused to see Anne Boleyn, Katherine Howard, Thomas Wolsey or Thomas Cromwell after their arrests, so this scene seems to be an addition for dramatic flair. In the film, Anne sarcastically informed Henry that she was guilty of the crimes of which she was accused, and in the face of his anger cried out 'but Elizabeth was yours … she's a Tudor'. Even facing her own death, Anne is determined to protect her daughter, fiercely. She declares that 'Elizabeth – child of Anne the Whore and Henry the Blood-Stained Lecher – shall be Queen! … Elizabeth shall be a greater queen than any king of yours!' and that 'my blood will have been well spent!'.[41] This does tally with Anne's devotion to her daughter, the future Elizabeth I. However, Anne could not have known of Elizabeth's future, and this is what we see with films – the benefit of hindsight allows us to make much of linking Anne's execution and Elizabeth's Golden Age. Susan Bordo writes that 'Bujold's fire, issuing from her petite frame and elfin face, her hair dishevelled, her dark eyes glittering with pride, desperation, hurt, and vengeance, transformed the potentially hokey into an indelible, iconic moment'.[42] It is one of the most memorable moments in any Tudor film or television show. Bujold puts everything she has into the performance, and she unravels in front of you, knowing that she will die at the hand of her husband, but determined that her daughter will triumph. Henry becomes violent and slaps Anne in the face of her pride, but she remains defiant.

Just moments before Henry visits Anne in the Tower for the final time, she laments over the state of her relationship with, and marriage to, Henry which lasted 'one thousand days. Just a thousand. Strange. And of those thousand, one when we were both in love, only one when our loves met and overlapped and were both mine and his. And when I no longer hated him, he began to hate me'.[43] Susan Bordo says she always loved that speech for its 'psychological acuity about the kind of love that is fuelled by challenge and pursuit'.[44] It echoes Thomas Wyatt's poem *Whoso List to Hunt* with Henry as the hunter and Anne as the prey, ending with the line about how she was, 'wild for to hold though I seem tame'.[45] Anne has tried her best to give Henry VIII a son, but failed, and she has lost her agency in the quest for a male heir. The focus is on Anne's role as a wife, and it seems like 'the quest for historical agency appears a waste of time at best, a deadly undertaking at worst'.[46] Anne tried to forge a place in the world but ended up at the sharp end of an executioner's blade. She did not manage to forge historical agency for herself but, in a sense, she did manage it for her daughter, though Elizabeth I was also constrained at times by her sex.

There has also been a suggestion from Thomas Freeman that a filmgoer likes to see a satisfactory ending otherwise they feel a little cheated.[47] There is no satisfaction in Anne Boleyn being executed for crimes she did not commit, but there is a kind of joy in knowing that Anne will be vindicated through the reign of her daughter. Both *Anne of the Thousand Days* and the next film under discussion in this chapter, *The Other Boleyn Girl* from 2008, finish with a shot of the young Elizabeth after her mother's death. The end focus is not on Anne's death, but on Elizabeth's future. Sadly, there is no final speech from Genevieve Bujold as Anne Boleyn on the scaffold. We see her kneel and then the canon fires. This allows the audience to imagine the feelings and emotions, not just of Anne, but of the watching crowd and even of the king himself.[48] Though the historical record has Anne recorded as making a short speech, this is omitted for dramatic effect in this case. It's a scene fraught with emotion: sadness, despair, and betrayal.

Susan Bordo interviewed Genevieve Bujold for her book *The Creation of Anne Boleyn* and asked her who she would choose to play Anne Boleyn today. Her response was that 'maybe it's selfish, but … the way I feel … No one. Anne is mine'.[49] Even nearly fifty years later, Bujold still feels protective over Anne. People do seem to feel some kind of possessiveness and protection of Anne, but Genevieve Bujold's portrayal of Anne, for me at least, is the definitive one.

The Other Boleyn Girl (2008)

There have been two films made of *The Other Boleyn Girl*, originally a novel by Philippa Gregory published in 2001. The earlier 2003 film is the less well known of the two and stars Jared Harris as Henry VIII and Jodhi May as Anne Boleyn. The 2008 film features Eric Bana as Henry VIII with Natalie Portman as Anne Boleyn. It is the 2008 film which will be the focus here. Historian David Starkey describes Gregory's work as 'good Mills and Boon'.[50] This may be a little over the top for Gregory's work, which is enjoyed the world over, but there is no question that her work is not as historically accurate as the likes of Hilary Mantel, though it has been said that Mantel's is harder to read and far denser with more characters and political manoeuvrings to keep on top of. *The Other Boleyn Girl* in many ways has 'catered to an audience familiar with the more negative sides of Anne's personality'.[51] Gregory's is not a perception which is sympathetic towards Anne Boleyn, though given it is told from the perspective of Mary Boleyn rather than Anne herself, perhaps we are seeing the sibling rivalry and jealousy come across. Anne appears selfish, rude and manipulative through most of the film, and the original novel, until it all comes crashing down around her and she struggles to come to terms with it. It is often difficult to stomach and makes you root more for Mary, the often-overlooked sister.

When Henry VIII first falls for Mary Boleyn, Anne is angry as it had been intended that she be the one to catch the king's attention, but a riding accident meant that Mary was caring for the king when he awoke. He says to Mary that, 'you've been here all the time, how could I have overlooked you?' and she responds that 'next to Anne it's easy to do'.[52] Mary seems to be used to being overlooked, as she comes across as the more docile and caring sister, where Anne is more upfront and forthright. Susan Bordo astutely recognises that Henry turned to Mary because Anne had humiliated him by being the more expert rider.[53] Elizabeth Boleyn then tells Mary that she has been summoned to court, and Anne, frustrated, lashes out at Mary that 'all I know is that the man didn't know who you were. He was with you in that room for half an hour and came out besotted'.[54] In the historical record, much of Henry VIII's relationship with Mary Boleyn is shrouded in secrecy, and we do not even know the duration of the relationship. The only reason we probably know about the relationship at all is because Henry VIII later had to apply for a dispensation to marry Anne. G.W. Bernard argues that the dispensation was required because of a prior relationship within the forbidden degrees of affinity.[55] A letter from George Throckmorton backs up Henry VIII's relationship with Anne's sister, Mary, as he recorded a conversation with the king where he thought his conscience might be troubled if he married Anne 'for it is thought ye have meddled both with the mother and the sister', but Henry replied, 'never with the mother'.[56] The letter does come from after Anne's death, but it does not seem like the kind of conversation one would forget, especially when writing about it to the king.

Anne Boleyn is sent away to France after her relationship with Henry Percy is broken up, despite a marriage and consummation. Norfolk states that she will stay there 'until you have learnt your lesson' and 'until your father has forgiven you'.[57] We do not know exactly what happened between Anne Boleyn and Henry Percy, although Cardinal Wolsey's gentleman usher, George Cavendish, certainly believed the pair were promised to each other.[58] It is on Anne's return from France in *The Other Boleyn Girl* that Henry VIII comments 'I find you much changed, Mistress Anne' when she is not afraid to enunciate her views on a woman's position and how she can be a match for a man, – 'it's a question women have asked themselves for some time. But we can see that men do have some value, so we accept them as equals'.[59] She claims that great men rise above petty squabbles and are able to forgive and forget, to have generosity and humility, recognise his match in others and not be threatened by it, in women as well as in men. But we also find Anne to be ambitious and ruthless; it seems her enforced exile has made her re-evaluate her priorities, to close off her heart almost. When her sister, Mary, is pregnant with the king's child, Anne has been flirting with the king, and while Mary is in labour in the next room, Henry asks Anne if he can have hope of her, claiming that he 'will never lie with my wife nor speak to your sister again'.[60] When Mary gives birth to a son within minutes of this declaration, Anne chooses that moment to say that he may hope, and he walks away from his mistress and his son. Anne's ambition, and even spite against her sister, overcomes everything else. Perhaps Anne still rues the fact that Mary managed to win Henry over when she failed at the beginning of the film and takes her revenge. Anne then visits Mary as she recovers from the birth, and Mary tells her to 'take care because he'll only do to you what he's done to me'. Anne's response is that 'you shouldn't have given yourself so lightly' and that 'love is of no value without power and position'.[61] Anne proudly claims that when she gives the king a son it will not be a bastard to which Mary replies 'you reach too high, as always'.[62] Perhaps Anne had thought she had power and position with Henry Percy, who would one day be the earl of Northumberland, but she found the ultimate power with the king of England. No one could unseat her if she gave the king an heir.

One of the most disturbing and controversial scenes in the film is where Anne Boleyn, having given birth to Elizabeth and miscarried a child that she has not told the king about, is speaking with her siblings. She states that 'soon the truth will be out. That I cannot bear children. He will have me burned, as a witch'. When Mary realises that Anne is intending to lie with another man to conceive a child to replace the one that she lost, and that the man she intends is their own brother, Mary cries out 'I can't listen anymore, it's monstrous!'[63] In the film, the incest charge against them derives from the fact that George's wife, Jane Boleyn, has overheard the conversation. Jane is a popular figure to be accused of giving evidence against her husband and sister-in-law but there is no real contemporary evidence to suggest that she did. Julia Fox argues that 'a myth evolved, seeing her execution as a much deserved, if belated, retribution for giving false testimony' against Anne and George.[64] This in fact began with the work of the martyrologist John Foxe, and was not posited, as far as we know, at the time. In *The Other Boleyn Girl*, Anne claims that her life depends on George sleeping with her and them conceiving a child. Mary refuses to have any part in it and so, in the end, does George. The pair undress and sit on the bed, but in the end, George says, 'I can't. I'm so sorry, Anne. I can't', to which Anne replies, 'I'll tell the king in the morning. Let's pray he takes pity on me'.[65] The popular idea of incest seems to derive from *The Other Boleyn Girl*, but with no actual evidence in the primary sources, and being able to disprove many of the dates and places listed in the indictment for the adultery and incest charges, it seems absurd to think that it could be true. Anne and George would not have been left alone long enough by Anne's ladies for anything to happen between them, no matter what screen adaptations might show.

The viewer witnesses Anne Boleyn's trial in *The Other Boleyn Girl*, and she demonstrates her boldness, keeping hold of the mantle of queenship when she declares as she enters the courtroom that 'it is a sad day for England when nobles do not rise for their queen', to which her uncle, Norfolk, replied 'and even sadder when that same queen is charged with adultery and incest'.[66] Anne is almost using her position as armour in this scene; she does not necessarily believe her queenship will save her, but it comes across almost as if she knows that having continuing to act as queen will help her to get through it. Norfolk asks Anne how she pleads, and she pleads not guilty, then addresses directly the charge of incest against her, that 'the love I have for my brother is the natural love any sister would have for someone with whom she's grown up, nursed when sick, played with as a child'.[67] She concludes by telling her judges that their verdict will be judged by God. Although Anne and George did consider incest in this film, they did not actually commit it. Her innocence comes across in her certainty of her plea. The final sentence is suggestive of Anne's final recorded words: 'if any person will meddle of my cause, I require them to judge the best'.[68] But she is also declaring her innocence in her certainty that she will be judged favourably on the day of judgement, where her accusers will not, for declaring an innocent woman guilty, despite what the king may desire. Her exchange of glances with her one-time love Henry Percy is devastating as he declares her guilty; Anne's shock in this moment suggests that she had still expected him to stand by her after more than a decade. She is shaking and in shock at her condemnation.

We do not get a final scaffold speech from Anne – she mounts the scaffold and then sees her sister receive a letter from a royal guard, and the hope infuses her face, as it does that of Mary when they lock eyes, but when Mary opens the letter, we hear Henry's voice reading it, telling her that 'you risked your life coming to court and were only spared because of my respect and affection for you ... you will not be shown the same clemency a second time'.[69] Henry closes the letter by saying that he hopes God will have mercy on Anne's soul. Despite what Henry had told Mary in an earlier scene, that he 'would do nothing to hurt any part of you', in response to Mary's plea for Anne's life that 'she's my sister, and therefore one half of me', Henry does not keep that promise.[70] We have no evidence that Mary Boleyn returned to court after her secret marriage in 1534 to William Stafford, or that she saw her brother or sister again. It is incredibly unlikely that she was at the executions of either of her siblings and probably hid herself away in the country to mourn. But in *The Other Boleyn Girl* Mary receives the letter from Henry and within a couple of minutes, Anne is dead in front of her. The viewer then sees Mary march into the palace and take Princess Elizabeth, the only part left to her of her sister.

In an interview, Philippa Gregory, author of the book *The Other Boleyn Girl*, claimed that 'Mary's story is one of absolute independence and victory, triumph of common sense over the ambition of her sister Anne'.[71] Bordo questions this, thinking that somehow sex is allowed, but ambition is not and that it seems to be 'an opportunistic, infinitely malleable' kind of feminism.[72] It is interesting to consider these different opinions. Ambition, of course, is a natural part of life for many, no matter whether you lived in the sixteenth century or the twenty-first, and we do not need to deride it or make it seem that it is not sensible. What *The Other Boleyn Girl* does well, is to juxtapose two sisters with very different values, and demonstrate the perils of the Tudor court.

* * *

What you get with a film is a big screen, and often big budget, rendition of historical events. It is not intended to be historically accurate, but dramatic and entertaining. Opulent costumes and beautiful locations come together to create a visual feast. The audience gets the full power of aesthetics which allows them to see the scaffold, facial expressions and emotions which are never quite reached in the novel versions discussed in a later chapter. They rely on words where films rely on pictures. Picture is a faster way of conveying an emotion or a look between two characters. Things can be conveyed in a single second rather than a sentence or two. Thomas Freeman says that:

> Film is just too powerful a medium for its messages to be ignored and our understanding of the past too crucial for us to be indifferent to the errors, untruths and distortions conveyed in historical films.[73]

For historians, it is a balancing act to discuss the historical inaccuracies and dramatic changes made to recorded history for the benefit of entertainment and, often, money. Awareness of the errors and changes in historical film does not necessarily have to diminish our enjoyment of these films, but a care is needed to ensure that changes made for dramatic benefit do not become historical fact in the eyes of the audience. We cannot ignore cultural history and how it impacts our view of the past. Essentially, Tudor history is still being made today, not only by new discoveries, but new points of view and perceptions of key figures like Anne Boleyn.

Chapter 10

Anne on the Small Screen

'Those eyes of yours are like dark hooks for the soul'[1]

Anne Boleyn on the small screen, in contrast to the big screen, is given more chance to tell her story. Serialised television shows provide ample opportunity to go into more detail and tackle some of the smaller details and side stories. Thomas Freeman discusses historical films, but this can just as easily be applied to historical television dramas, saying that filmmakers attach a lot of importance to the aesthetics like sets and costumes, and less to the historical accuracy, whereas a historian would reverse these priorities.[2] But a serialised television series is not going to draw in audiences if it was entirely historically accurate because that probably would not make for great viewing. And a serial means that you want people to tune in to multiple episodes, week after week, so you need the drama to keep people coming back for more. The drama and entertainment value weighs more with producers and directors than accuracy because their intention is not to be accurate, but to manipulate the facts for dramatic purpose.

One of the most popular television adaptations of the Tudor dynasty is Showtime's *The Tudors*, broadcast between 2007 and 2010, starring Jonathan Rhys Meyers as Henry VIII and Natalie Dormer as Anne Boleyn. Natalie Dormer seems to be a favourite as Anne Boleyn, and *The Tudors* is probably the most quoted Tudor drama on television. Anne Boleyn only features in seasons one and two, aside from a ghostly appearance in the very last episode of the show, appearing to her dying husband and declaring her innocence, along with her pride in her daughter. It has been argued that *The Tudors* 'is Tudorist because it deals directly with the ways in which historical cliché – particularly surrounding Henry VIII – works in the popular imagination'.[3] *The Tudors* as a television drama is very cliched and on social media people say things like 'well it was on *The Tudors* so it must be true'. The truth is actually more complicated than a television drama could ever depict, because not everything, including all the nuances, can be portrayed on screen, so things are often simplified or left out.

Claire Foy played Anne Boleyn in a small screen adaptation of Hilary Mantel's *Wolf Hall* in 2015. She was nominated for a television BAFTA for her performance. Foy would go on to play another queen, a young Queen Elizabeth II, in *The Crown.* Her portrayal shows a more ambitious and less sympathetic Anne than Dormer's. We also do not see the beginning of Henry VIII and Anne Boleyn's relationship, as the story begins in 1529 with Wolsey's fall and Cromwell stepping up. We get a condensed period compared to *The Tudors*, though *Wolf Hall* is only six episodes of an hour each, compared to the two series of *The Tudors*, which total twenty episodes of an hour each.

This chapter will also discuss the performance of Jodie Turner-Smith in *Anne Boleyn* from 2021, the first black actress cast as Anne Boleyn. New perceptions cannot be overlooked and are a sign of the society that we live in today. This will be discussed alongside other dramas including *The Six Wives of Henry VIII* from 1970, with Dorothy Tutin as Anne Boleyn, and *Henry VIII* from 2003 with Helena Bonham Carter as Anne.

What is interesting is how much some of these film and small screen adaptations have in common. They all have access to the same historical sources, but there is no doubt that new adaptations of the Tudors on screen are acquainted with existing versions, so may take elements from older adaptations and combine them. This can precipitate and encourage older myths and inconsistences. Some newer versions of Tudor stories, particularly when it comes to Anne Boleyn, are mixes of what has gone before and some new perceptions. Sometimes it works better than other times, as with anything.

The Tudors (2007-2010)

Showtime's *The Tudors* first aired in 2007, beginning the story of Henry VIII in 1518, nine years into his reign, as his marriage to Katherine of Aragon was beginning to fall apart and he was desperate for a male heir that he did not believe she would provide. This is where Anne Boleyn enters the story in the show. The Internet Movie Database (IMDb) has reviews from ordinary people and one review describes the show as being historically inaccurate and indulging in twenty-first century culture which is 'tabloid-obsessed'.[4] It does come across almost as a tabloid-style show, and you can certainly tell it is modern, with none of the sensibilities of the sixteenth century. It is 'a flashy, soapy, sexually charged romp which is more about watching beautiful people in a ridiculous narrative than understand a set of historical events or concepts'.[5] All television dramas are made with an eye to audience viewing figures and keeping them coming back for more, which is often more important to the production companies than historical accuracy. *The Tudors* is obviously based on research as it uses some quotations from letters and other evidence, but that is manipulated to suit the dramatic purpose.

What has become popular in modern television series and films is a quote or tagline that sums up the series, sometimes quoted on a promotional poster or over the credits at the beginning. For *The Tudors* this is 'you think you know a story, but you only know how it ends; to get to the heart of the story, you have to go back to the beginning'.[6] This only appears over the season one credits. It is dropped for seasons two to four. It encourages us to think about Anne Boleyn, not as the executed adulteress, but as an ambitious woman who fell in love and tried to get the best for herself. It also urges us to be open-minded about Henry VIII, thinking not of him as the overweight tyrant we see in the iconic portrait by Hans Holbein, but as the young, athletic, and handsome man he was for the first two decades and more of his reign. The idea is not to assume that you know everything and to rethink stereotypes. It is very good advice and one that should not just be applied to television drama or film, but to historical evidence and arguments as well – never take things at face value.

There is often a lot made of the fact that Henry and Anne's relationship was quite tumultuous with peaks and troughs throughout their courtship and marriage, characterised by fervent arguments and passionate reunions. Their turbulent relationship is often portrayed in *The Tudors* and one such argument focuses on the fact that Henry was not yet free to marry Anne, yet they had been committed for two or three years. Anne was angry that she had been waiting for so long to marry the king and that, 'in the meantime I could have contracted some advantageous marriage and borne sons, which is a woman's greatest consolation in this life. But instead, I've been wasting my time and my youth for no purpose at all!'. She goes on to say that 'it's too late. Your wife won't let you go, I should have realised', to which Henry replies, 'Stay here, I beg you, Anne. I'm the King of England!'.[7] If the rumours about Anne Boleyn and Henry Percy were true, perhaps this was Anne's frustration about the end of that relationship coming out. Had that marriage gone ahead, Anne could have been married for six or more years by 1530 and borne several children. The length of time it took for the king to obtain his annulment meant that Anne had lost most of her youth to waiting, and she probably feared that her childbearing years were slipping away and she would not be able to give the king children by the time they were able to marry. If this was the case, she would be cast off as Katherine of Aragon was. Henry VIII had never had to beg for a woman before Anne, and it was new for him. He thought his position as king would win Anne over, and the insinuation is that Anne should yield to her king if he requested it. It seems to have been a recurring theme with Anne getting frustrated at the amount of time it was taking for Henry VIII to get an annulment of his marriage to Katherine of Aragon so that they could marry. Anne was not getting any younger, and her chances of having a child were slipping away. If Anne was born in 1501, then she was 31 or 32 by the time of her marriage and that was considered old to be birthing a child, particularly a first child, at the time.

Historical evidence also points to this instability and the uncertainty of the relationship being a theme of their arguments. In one particular letter, Anne claimed that she had been wasting her time and threatened to leave the king, suggesting Henry VIII was forced to appease her in bringing down Thomas Wolsey.[8] Anne is portrayed in *The Tudors* as being at the centre of Wolsey's fall, and pushing for more measures to enable her marriage to go ahead. In a scene where Anne Boleyn reveals to Henry VIII that she has a new motto, she teases him by asking him to find the motto somewhere on her body, and while he teases her, Anne tells him that someone is stalling on the divorce. When Henry names Cardinal Lorenzo Campeggio, who was the Pope's representative in England, Anne responds, 'no, someone else. Someone much closer to you'.[9] She uses the king's desire to get what she wants. *The Tudors* puts Anne Boleyn at the centre of a circle which includes Thomas Howard, 3rd Duke of Norfolk, and Charles Brandon, 1st Duke of Suffolk, to bring down Wolsey. This idea that Anne Boleyn was at the centre of Wolsey's fall comes from the account of George Cavendish who had Anne saying that 'if it lay ever in her power, she would work the Cardinal as much displeasure' as he had done to her.[10] As Wolsey is trying to claw his way back into royal favour, Anne makes sure that he is unable to, introducing Henry to the work of William Tyndale, to which Henry VIII responded, 'this book is a book for me, and for all kings'. Anne responded, 'and there are other books like it ... books which Wolsey deliberately kept hidden from you'.[11] The insinuation is that Wolsey was stopping Henry seizing the power, which was rightfully his, and thus Wolsey had subverted the king. The suggestion that Henry was anything less than all-powerful would have been anathema to him, and he would have done whatever was necessary to prove himself powerful, masculine, and in charge.

Anne Boleyn's coronation is a pivotal moment in *The Tudors*. But the most important part of the series of scenes which form the coronation is just after the coronation itself when Anne meets Henry prior to the coronation feast. We see the shift in the way Henry VIII sees the relationship with Anne in this scene. Anne emerges from Westminster Abbey as Henry is speaking to Cromwell, and Henry asks Anne how she liked the city and that everything was well done. Anne responds that 'it was more like a funeral than a parade' as no one shouted, and people kept their hats on their heads. Henry VIII responded that he wanted her to be happy and smile, 'remember, you are my queen now', and when Anne tried to talk further about the response of the people to her coronation, he emphasised 'I said, you are my queen'.[12] There is a distinct sense that Henry expects Anne now to obey him in everything, and to be the queen he expects her to be. This is where Anne's mistake is, that she failed to adjust to the move from a mistress with all of the power in the relationship, to a wife and queen who Henry expected to be submissive and obey him. In this scene we see Henry assert his power in this moment of triumph for Anne. We see his deep sorrow just months later when Anne gives birth to Elizabeth, and a distinct sense that Henry feels Anne has betrayed him and not lived up to her promise to deliver him a son when he says 'you and I are both young. And with God's grace, boys will follow'.[13] It comes across as a threat, and a promise to act against her if she fails again. But maybe that is seen with hindsight. Tracy Borman wrote that Henry must have been humiliated and disappointed, given everything he had gone through to marry Anne.[14] But it did not mean that the marriage was over at this moment, as some have supposed. There was no reason to suggest that Anne would not go on to have more children. The first one was healthy. She would, however, certainly have felt the pressure to conceive again quickly after Elizabeth's birth and hope it would be a son.

During season two, Anne's marriage to Henry VIII is seen to unravel fairly quickly. The birth of Elizabeth followed by a miscarriage made it clear to Anne that Henry was looking at other women, and that her position was dependent on the king's love and affection, as well as her producing a male heir to inherit the English throne. After her first miscarriage in *The Tudors*, Anne is visited by her father, Thomas Boleyn, 1st Earl of Wiltshire and he asks what she did to lose the baby. When Anne says nothing, Thomas sums up her position as follows: 'from now on we must all be careful, you especially, not to lose the king's love. Or everything is lost. Everything. For all of us'.[15] Thomas recognised that Anne's position, and that of the whole Boleyn family, rested on her retaining the king's love and producing a son. She did not have the international backing that Katherine of Aragon had, and she could be in more danger than the former queen if she failed. However, in *The Tudors*, Thomas Boleyn is portrayed as self-scheming, determined to get the best for himself. We see him distancing himself from Anne after her arrest and when told that he would lose his offices and position at court, he responds with 'so I am to keep my earldom?'. The Duke of Suffolk is outraged that this is all he can think about, shouting, 'Did you watch your son die? What about your daughter, will you watch her suffer? Will you watch her die? Tell me, Boleyn, was it all worth it?'.[16] Thomas Boleyn's ambition and need for position and wealth is central to his character in the television show. But he did die in March 1539, just three years after the executions of his son and daughter, and his wife had died the year before him. The fates of their children had to have shaken their parents, and may have contributed to their early deaths, though Anne was already concerned about her mother's health when she was in the Tower.

The execution scene of Anne Boleyn at the end of season two is masterful. Natalie Dormer in that last scene was beautiful; the balance of emotion in her face, movements and speech was perfect. She showed fear, acceptance tinged with hope, and determination to die a 'good death'. The writers did their research, using extant records of Anne's final speech to make it realistic and capture the reality as far as possible. Dormer's Anne Boleyn not only yields herself to justice and praises the king, but also claims that with her death she atones for any crimes she has committed. However, Anne was not blindfolded in the scene, as she likely was in reality. In an earlier scene with Archbishop Thomas Cranmer, Anne outlined some of her other faults, that she had not always shown the king the respect he deserved given what he had done for her, for example. But she continues to declare her innocence in charges of adultery and treason.[17] Her real recorded execution speech demonstrates the same, her refusal to speak of the charges, 'I come hither to accuse no man, not to speak anything of that whereof I am accused and condemned to die'.[18] Her refusal to speak of the crimes for which she was about to die is unusual as those about to be executed usually acknowledged their guilt, or at least that they were sinful. Anne does none of this. Had she been guilty of these crimes and failed to declare them she would have been condemning her soul, which in such a religious age was unthinkable.

In the scene where Anne makes her final confession to Archbishop Thomas Cranmer, she is cleansing her soul before her death. A final confession could be very influential. If you went to your death without having confessed your sins, then it was believed that you would fare poorly on the day of judgement. Anne's final confession could be compelling evidence of her innocence of the charges of which she was accused. In *The Tudors*, she says that 'I solemnly swear on the damnation of my soul that I have never been unfaithful to my lord and husband, nor ever offended with my body against him'.[19] She admitted she had not always shown the king the humility he deserved considering his kindness to her but that she had done nothing else against him. Anne closes her confession by saying that 'God has taught me how to die and he will strengthen my faith'.[20] Anne had the courage and faith in her own strength and her innocence. Of course, we do not know what Anne actually said in her confession, though we do know that she made one. The details do not seem to have been recorded or, if they were, they have since been lost or destroyed. Declaring on the 'damnation of my soul' is a strong conviction and would have carried weight in such a religious society, whether Catholic or Protestant. In *The Tudors*, Anne makes the distinction between being 'unfaithful' and offending 'with [her] body against him', meaning she did not commit sexual acts, and did not love others either. She admits that she had not always 'borne towards him the humility' she owed him given what he did for her, quite possibly referring to their tumultuous arguments and her sharp temper at times.[21] Anne in this moment knows that she will die because the king wants it, and that his love for her had changed to hate. Anne died what would be thought of as a 'good death' as she alludes to in this speech, with acceptance and praise of the king, without declaring the miscarriage of justice which led to innocent people being executed. The fact that Anne's execution scene is portrayed simultaneously with Henry VIII's consumption of a swan, said to represent eternal love because they mate for life, is disturbing, and shows his complete callousness towards his once great love.[22] Henry is portrayed as being indifferent to Anne's death and, in fact, welcoming it, as a means for him to marry Jane Seymour.

The Tudors is a very popular drama, with Natalie Dormer's portrayal of Anne Boleyn seeming to be many people's favourite representation of the doomed queen. Despite some complaints about the inaccuracy of casting in terms of appearance of the actors, like Jonathan Rhys Meyers as Henry VIII, Dormer captures Anne's tempestuous personality, wit, intelligence, and her fear as things begin to unravel in a brilliant way. Stephanie Russo says that 'it is undeniable that Natalie Dormer's performance as Anne Boleyn has been extremely influential, even formative of our contemporary understanding of Anne Boleyn'.[23] Even if things are not entirely historically accurate, Anne's essence is there on screen.

Wolf Hall (2015)

Hilary Mantel's novels have received critical acclaim for their portrayal of Thomas Cromwell, who was wound up in the fate of Anne Boleyn. The trilogy consists of *Wolf Hall* (2009), *Bring Up the Bodies* (2012) and *The Mirror and the Light* (2020). The first two feature Anne Boleyn heavily as a character and have been adapted for the small screen. The third book has now also been adapted for the screen, though does not feature Anne as a key character, as she was executed at the end of *Bring Up the Bodies*, and at the end of the television series *Wolf Hall*. We see flashbacks of Anne in the televised version of the third book, as her fate haunts Thomas Cromwell. Alongside Mark Rylance as Thomas Cromwell, Damian Lewis stars as Henry VIII and Claire Foy as Anne Boleyn. Foy would go on to give an award-winning performance as a young Elizabeth II in *The Crown*.

Foy's performance as Anne Boleyn is beautiful and nuanced. In *Wolf Hall* Anne speaks with a noticeable French accent, which is not seen in other portrayals. It is quite possible Anne had a French lilt to her voice as she left England in 1512 for the Low Countries, then France in 1514, and did not return to England until around 1521 or early 1522. This section of Anne's life is often either overlooked or underplayed on screen in favour of the more controversial aspects of her relationship with Henry VIII and her tragic fall and execution, so it was fantastic to see this slightly different take on Anne. The accent does not happen in all of Anne's speech, we see it particularly in her pronunciation of Cromwell's name, which she says more like 'Cremuel'.[24] The first time we actually meet Anne and hear her speak, this is almost her first word. Other characters have spoken about Anne and her role in the fall of Cardinal Wolsey in various scenes, before the viewer actually gets to meet her, so we are being set up to think of Anne as ambitious, and ruthless, determined to be queen at any cost. The idea is put in our heads before we see the character and, of course, everything is seen through Cromwell's eyes, so it is his opinions of her in these moments that are portrayed, which is very clever. The viewer does not see or know anything that Cromwell does not.

Stephanie Russo writes about how 'Foy's performance emphasises Anne's haughtiness and lust for power, which alienates all around her; Mary and her other ladies-in-waiting seem to take delight in denigrating her, either to her face or behind her back'.[25] The role of Mary Boleyn in telling her sister, Anne's, story in *Wolf Hall* is fascinating. Played by Charity Wakefield, Mary seems to be fed up with her sister and her constant teasing and plotting. As Anne and Cromwell discuss Wolsey's fate and how it would be impossible to get an annulment from the Pope without him, Mary interjects about Anne that 'she's not getting any younger'.[26] Anne refuses to rise to it. After Cromwell's initial conversation with Anne, Mary waylays him as he is about to leave, and says, 'God, I thought she would slap you. My sister likes a good fight' and that she still had not slept with Henry but allowed him to 'pull down her shift and kiss her breasts', to which Cromwell responded, 'Good man if he can find them'.[27] Mary teases Anne to her face but is also willing to tell Cromwell what she knows and denigrate her sister for her ambition and lesser looks. Anne was certainly said to not be as attractive as her sister, though her charms were said to be in her wit and intelligence.

In the next episode, we again see Mary Boleyn and Thomas Cromwell talking together, as Mary confides that Anne refused to become the king's mistress, saying that 'this isn't France and I am not a fool like you, Mary' as she knew her sister was once the king's mistress and 'she sees how I am left, and she takes a lesson from it'.[28] Thinking about how Mary was left, it seems that Anne and their father cut her off after her secret second marriage in 1534, and Mary had to write to Cromwell to ask him to intercede with her family, saying that 'they are so cruel against us'.[29] Mary was probably pushed down the family pecking order once she lost the king's favour and Anne replaced her, not wanting to be reminded that the king had slept with one sister and intended to marry the other. In *Wolf Hall*, Mary goes on to declare that 'my father says I'm a mouth to feed and my uncle often says I'm a whore'.[30] The two sisters are being juxtaposed against each other, with Anne as the favoured one because she brings the position and favour to the Boleyn and Howard families where Mary is seen as a disgrace, unable to hold a king. Cromwell and Mary are again talking together in episode three, when Mary says that Anne is 'selling herself by the inch. She wants a cash present for every advance above her knee'. Cromwell then asks for an official position, knowing that Anne would be able to get it for him. Mary says that 'she made Tom Wyatt a poet and Harry Percy mad. I'm sure she has some idea of what to make you'.[31] Although they both acknowledge Anne's power, they also recognise the damage that has been done in order to make it happen and know that more will need to be done before Anne can sit on the throne of England. Mary Boleyn does not feature in *Wolf Hall* after the coronation scene, though we do not actually see or hear about her secret second marriage, she just vanishes. The relationship we see between Mary Boleyn and Thomas Cromwell in *Wolf Hall* gives an insight into a very different Anne/Cromwell relationship to that which we see in Showtime's *The Tudors*, with a crueller and more manipulative Anne.

In one conversation between Anne and Cromwell, Anne demonstrates her developing religious beliefs, admitting to Cromwell that she has read the works of William Tyndale and that 'The subject must obey his king, as he would God. Do I have the sense of it? The Pope will learn his place'.[32] But this is the only direct reference to Anne's religious beliefs in *Wolf Hall*. She then goes on to relate that a piece of paper was found in her bed with Henry VIII, Katherine of Aragon and herself drawn on it, but herself without a head – 'Anne sans tete'– and tasks Cromwell to find out who put it there.[33] We see a similar scene in *The Tudors* with playing cards left on a table in Anne's apartments. In *Anne of the Thousand Days*, Anne makes a joke about the same nickname. We know that this comes from a letter written by the Imperial ambassador, Chapuys, a couple of weeks after Anne's execution, when he claimed that the night before her death Anne joked that the people would call her 'la Royne Anne sans tete'.[34] There are plenty of instances in both television and film portrayals of Anne that can be linked back to contemporary sources or other accounts written later on, which suggests that filmmakers are doing some research into the original sources, though manipulating them for dramatic effect.

The third episode marks the big change in Henry VIII and Anne Boleyn's relationship when the pair sleep together for the first time. Mary Boleyn tells Thomas Cromwell, on the visit to Calais in 1532 to meet Francis I of France, that 'she's in his arms. Naked as she was born. She can't change her mind now'.[35] Mary goes on to say that Henry 'made her a binding promise. They're married in God's sight, and he swears he'll marry her again in England and crown her queen'. Mary then alludes to her past relationship with Henry, telling Cromwell that 'if he's shy, Anne will know how to help. I've coached her'.[36] This comes from the idea that Henry VIII may have been temporarily impotent at various points. It was said that Jane Boleyn, Anne's sister-in-law, had been told by Anne that the king was impotent.[37] However, Henry did not seem to struggle to get either Katherine of Aragon or Anne Boleyn pregnant, though it did take longer to get Jane Seymour pregnant, and none of his last three wives ever conceived with the king. So, if this suggestion is true, it seemed to come on in later life.

Thomas Cromwell and Anne Boleyn have a definitive break, but it is often said or shown to be over religion, but in *Wolf Hall* it happens when Anne tells Cromwell to take one of his 'young men' to see Lady Mary, daughter of Katherine of Aragon, and to compromise her. As Anne explains it, 'all that's needed is for her to make a fool of herself in public, so she loses her reputation', but Cromwell refuses to be a party to it, saying 'that's not my aim. Those are not my methods'.[38] Cromwell is often seen as being ruthless, but *Wolf Hall* shows him to have lines he will not cross. He is a more sympathetic character, against Anne's more ruthless and ambitious character. Anne ends the discussion by stating that 'since my coronation there is a new England. And it can't subsist without me. I'm warning you, make terms with me, Cromwell. Before my child is born'.[39] This is the moment it seems where Cromwell realises that it is either him or Anne, but Anne is safe as long as she is pregnant and there is a chance that she could give Henry VIII a son.

There is another confrontation between Anne Boleyn and Thomas Cromwell in the final episode, after Anne's final miscarriage in January 1536. Anne is angry that, when Henry fell from his horse and was thought dead, Cromwell sent for Lady Mary and did not appear to think of Anne or her daughter. Anne says that 'at the first opportunity, you've betrayed me', but Cromwell did not see it as betrayal but pragmatism.[40] He could not hold the throne for an infant or an unborn child, when there was a popular grown woman who the people would fight for. Anne angrily argues that Cromwell thinks he is a great man and that 'you think you no longer need me' but that he has forgotten 'those who've been made can be unmade'. This is a fact to which Cromwell responds, 'I entirely agree'.[41] It is something Anne should also have remembered. This sets up Anne Boleyn's end, and the fact that Cromwell was the one who orchestrated the events which led to her execution.

We see Henry VIII telling Cromwell that he wants Anne gone, possibly into exile, but Cromwell understands that only either he or Anne can survive, not both, and so he acts first to bring charges against her, afraid that otherwise she still has the power to bring him down. The execution scene itself is interesting because we see Anne Boleyn give the full execution speech, which is well known and was discussed in chapter four. But the scenes of the execution are interspersed with a discussion Cromwell had before the execution with the French swordsman, examining the sword which would kill her. As Anne walks to the scaffold, Thomas Cromwell's son, Gregory, asks why she keeps looking up at the Tower, to which Cromwell replies 'because she thinks there's still hope'.[42] If Anne still thought there was hope at that time, it must have been crushing to be kneeling on the scaffold waiting for the sword swipe. However, once her brother, George, had been executed two days earlier, Anne probably lost all hope, and realised she would die, that there would be no reprieve.

Other Television Dramas

There are three other dramas which will be focused on in this section, though there are a huge variety that have been made and televised over the years. The twenty-first century has really seen them take off. The oldest of those discussed here is *The Six Wives of Henry VIII* from 1970 starring Keith Michell as Henry VIII and Dorothy Tutin as Anne Boleyn. Also discussed will be *Henry VIII* starring Ray Winstone as Henry, and Helena Bonham Carter as Anne from 2003. A more recent adaptation from 2021 is *Anne Boleyn* with Jodie Turner-Smith in the titular role and Mark Stanley as Henry VIII. These are all very different adaptations of the Anne Boleyn story, so it is worth examining them in more detail.

Dorothy Tutin's performance as Anne Boleyn in *The Six Wives of Henry VIII* in 1970 is told across two episodes as she is introduced in the episode about Katherine of Aragon, and then gets her own episode afterwards. In the first episode Anne is seen to be rather calculating and disdainful, whereas in the second episode based on Anne's story she comes across as more nuanced and rounded. The characterisation in the first episode is 'hardly surprising' as it is intended to elicit sympathy for Katherine.[43] Retha Warnicke argues that Tutin's Anne is 'a more calculating character that is obviously based on the Sander/Chapuys model'.[44] These earlier portrayals of Anne see her as very calculating and ambitious, whereas in some of the twenty-first century versions we see more reluctance on Anne's part to be with Henry, at least at first. The series as a whole can be described as a 'subdued, very proper British series'.[45] There is none of the overt sex that we see in the likes of *The Tudors*, and a distinct sense of a woman's proper place being played out.

One of the very first scenes in Anne's episode – episode two – is fascinating as we really see the sunshine and showers, passionate arguments and making up, that characterised their relationship and led to the breakdown during their marriage. The scene is after the birth of Princess Elizabeth and begins with

Anne examining a window, 'they have now worked our arms, the royal and those of Anne Boleyn' and you can hear the pride in her voice, that she has made a royal match.[46] She goes on to remind Henry of their early months and years, that 'we had no fears then. No evil tongues to come between us', but it escalates into an argument when she declares 'you do not bed with me'. Henry declares that a woman is no heir, to which Anne retorts 'fit only for your bed, it seems!', and Henry responds, 'you call me liar, you call me a whoremaster. I'll leave you 'til your temper's cooled'.[47] It escalates fairly quickly from remembering the happy times when they were first in love, to an argument about heirs and possible affairs. But the argument is forgotten as soon as Anne declares that she is pregnant, carrying the heir. When things get out-of-hand, she seems to know how to manage Henry and calm things down, and sets her mind to manipulating the situation, that 'I would have those who say that I'm not the rightful queen gutted on Tower Hill. I would have them scattered like offal when my son is born'. Henry responds that 'so they shall be, should you bear me a son' and ends the conversation with the words 'pray for a son'.[48] This final line comes across as threatening in the tone, that he will only act against those who demean Anne once she gives him a son, and if she does not, then the threat is left implicit.

The second of the three dramas is *Henry VIII* from 2003. Helena Bonham Carter's Anne Boleyn 'is ambitious because she understands the limited power that women have within the Tudor world' and she knows and understands that her safety with Henry is dependent on her having a son, and that safety and security can only come from a good marriage.[49] Susan Bordo describes Bonham Carter's performance as 'fine but indistinguishable from Helena Bonham Carter in any other role' and describes the whole production as 'a pretty decent TV movie that no one remembers anymore'.[50] Bonham Carter has had such a variety of roles, including the late Queen Mother in *The King's Speech*, and Bellatrix Lestrange in the Harry Potter films, that she cannot be pigeonholed.

What was enjoyable about Bonham Carter's portrayal of Anne Boleyn was that she seemed to instinctively understand Henry VIII. In her first audience with him, requesting permission to marry Henry Percy, she flatters the king but not the simpering flattery of others, but a more nuanced style appealing directly to what is most important to him – conquest of France. Anne comments that 'comparisons are meaningless, Your Grace. Since France belongs to England, whatever attributes its court might have are yours anyway'. And goes on to imply that the King of France was disappointing, that 'talk among the ladies in France was not so favourable'.[51] She then wiggles her little finger to illustrate her point, and Henry bursts out laughing. Anne has made an impression and when she and Percy leave, Henry whispers to Wolsey. We do not hear what is said but a following scene shows Cardinal Wolsey breaking up Anne and Percy's relationship, that the gap in their stations is too great being an earl's son and a knight's daughter.[52] Before the relationship was broken up, however, Percy and Anne have a moment to talk, and Percy is very obviously proud of Anne's performance, commenting that the king hung on her every word, to which Anne responds that 'Henry Tudor is a vain man and vain men are easy to flatter into submission. Quite the opposite to my husband'.[53] Anne has immediately read Henry's personality, and he does not come across favourably. Referring to Percy as her husband, the couple clearly believe that they have gained permission for their marriage, but it is the following scene where they are torn apart. Anne has made too much of a favourable impression on the king.

The final drama to be examined here is *Anne Boleyn*, which was a three-part mini-series broadcast in the UK on Channel 5 in June 2021. It starred Mark Stanley as Henry VIII and Jodie Turner-Smith as Anne Boleyn. The drama received mixed reviews generally, although Turner-Smith's performance received largely positive assessments. However, she did not capture the essence of Anne's character that we see in the contemporary sources. The series focused on only the last five months or so of Anne's life rather than the courtship, which has been told so many times, so Anne's changeable nature, fears and despair turning to hope and laughter, as well as her runaway tongue, should have been evident. The performance, however, was lacklustre.

In one scene where Anne is pregnant for the final time, just after Henry VIII's jousting accident in January 1536, Anne comments that 'it is good to see you up again, and with an appetite'.[54] It almost seems like a sly dig at Henry, commenting on his appetite, but it is also as if the fight has gone out of her, where the contemporary sources have Anne fighting to the end. She was pregnant, hopefully with a son, so as much as she would have been scared, this was also a moment of hope, that she might be able to save herself. Anne goes on to ask Henry 'did you order your horse to be killed?' to which he replied, 'I've no use for an animal that won't obey me'.[55] The implication being that Anne needed to obey Henry and fulfil her purpose to produce an heir. The threat is implied that if she does not, he will get rid of her and replace her with someone more conformable.

The controversial casting of black actress, Jodie Turner-Smith in the title role was covered in pretty much every review, with many remarking that Anne Boleyn was white, so why is she played by a black actress? Comments were made that a white actress would never be cast to play a prominent black woman, so why is the other way around acceptable?[56] They may have a point over the casting of black versus white actresses, in that if a white woman was cast to play a prominent black woman, there would be an outcry, but it is a sign of the times in which we live that a black woman can be cast to play a prominent white woman. Mark Stanley who played Henry VIII said in an interview, about the casting of Jodie Turner-Smith, that:

> It was all about this being the right person for the job, rather than what we as a society might perceive as the 'right look' for the job. Anne Boleyn was beautiful, witty, vibrant, intelligent and Jodie is all of those things. She brought our Anne to life in a way another actress couldn't.[57]

This can be a controversial subject to talk about, but casting the first black woman to play Anne Boleyn cannot be ignored. It reflects on today's culture that we are a more multi-cultural society with people from all kinds of nationalities, races, and backgrounds. This is why it is important to examine cultural history and examine fictional portrayals in context, not just in terms of the historical facts presented, and dramatic changes, but the aims of the filmmaker, and the time in which they were produced, as well as the reception of them upon release.

* * *

What these small screen adaptations and portrayals of Anne Boleyn give us, that the big screen film versions discussed in the previous chapter do not, is more space and time to tell these stories and to examine a few more of the nuances and supporting characters. For example, Thomas Cromwell is often seen as the instrument for Anne's fall from power, as in *The Tudors*, whereas we see a more sympathetic portrayal in *Wolf Hall*. The docu-dramas have different focuses when it comes to Anne, with *Anne Boleyn* only really exploring her downfall. The older docu-dramas discussed here, *The Six Wives of Henry VIII* and *Henry VIII* go through all six wives, how they overlapped and what made each one singular. Some focus on her fall, or religion, or her relationship with Henry VIII, though it has not been possible to discuss them all here.

What we do learn from examining these small screen adaptations of Anne Boleyn's life and reign is that there is so much within her life and her character that makes for exciting and dramatic viewing. But it is difficult to include everything; so many portrayals focus on a couple of aspects, rather than the entirety. It does mean that, if the viewer is not aware of the real history, then they are missing crucial aspects which may colour their views of Anne Boleyn and Henrician England. As much as we all enjoy historical dramas, it is important to acknowledge that they are not intended to be accurate and cannot be used as historical sources.

Chapter 11

Anne on the Page

'When you spend your life in the shadow of the throne, you're always afraid of blades'[1]

Novels about Anne Boleyn are plentiful. From works by Jean Plaidy and Philippa Gregory to Hilary Mantel and Suzannah Dunn, there are a wealth of choices. There are also less obvious options like Jennifer C. Wilson and Laura Andersen. All of these works offer different perspectives of Anne. Philippa Gregory's novels seem to be favourites for film and television adaptations while Hilary Mantel's novels have twice won the Man Booker Prize for fiction. Their works are discussed in chapters nine and ten 'Anne in Film' and 'Anne on the Small Screen' rather than as novels here. Although fictionalised, these novels do have their roots in history. Historical novels, particularly on the Tudors, have had renewed attention with the likes of Gregory and Mantel. There are lots of issues discussed around the growing field of historical fiction including historical representation in the popular realm, bringing sidelined women to the fore, and engaging with postmodern history through fiction.[2] These all come out in the more modern novels of the twenty-first century in particular.

David Starkey has claimed that historians need to stop taking historical fiction writers so seriously as 'the idea that they have authority is ludicrous'.[3] He goes on to say that historical events and people, such as the wives of Henry VIII, are too important to be fictionalised. However, historians are never going to be able to stop history being fictionalised, and it does introduce people to periods of history who might not otherwise be interested, and perhaps even encourages them to look further into the facts. Fiction is now encouraging the historians of the future. It has been suggested that authors 'romanticise the past despite, or perhaps because of, its brutality'.[4] It is the drama, romance, and violent ends which people seem to find so gripping to read. G.W. Bernard acknowledges that fiction writers and filmmakers use history to good effect in creating drama, but he also recognises that because the representations are so popular and powerful, they risk people believing the falsehoods that are portrayed.[5] Executions are often described in novels in detail which 'belongs to a fetishised and imagined world rather than the lived past'.[6] If people choose to believe fiction rather than look into the fact then that is their choice. We can only hope that people are interested enough to investigate further.

Historical novels of the twentieth and twenty-first centuries occasionally give a list of sources against which readers can check historical accuracy and read more about the subject. These include Philippa Gregory's *The Other Boleyn Girl* (2001) and Jean Plaidy's *Murder Most Royal* (1949). What is intriguing about this practice is that writers do not seem to necessarily pay full attention to the sources they quote and often deviate from them, whether consciously or unconsciously for dramatic purposes. These sources are intended to give the novel a sense of accuracy, and often you can easily tell whether the writer has done their research or not. Historical novels are becoming more popular as history becomes more accessible.

Modern novelists are free to address the more contentious issues contemporaries would not have dared to touch. Hilary Mantel has said that an author has to consider what they owe to a novel and to the readers as they do not want a two-dimensional story, barely dramatised.[7] Licence is taken with historical fiction to encompass the social issues of the day, like the increased interest in sex. Perhaps, however, it is not merely an increased interest in sex, but a sense of increased freedom and lack of inhibition to discuss sexual matters. Novels about Anne Boleyn often include sex scenes, as she is seen as the woman who destroyed Henry VIII's first marriage, so naturally she is often portrayed as a sexual or sensual figure. Anne in a way manipulates Henry using her sexuality, taking advantage of the fact that he was desperate to have her. But in the end, she 'became the victim of her own methods'.[8] It was Anne Boleyn's perceived flirtatious and sexual behaviour which brought her down, and it was Jane Seymour rejecting Henry VIII's advances, just like Anne had done a decade before, that may have given Henry the push to get rid of Anne permanently. Disapproval of Anne Boleyn in the sixteenth century was about her supposed sexual immorality. In the 1930s, fiction writers began to build an image of Anne as the 'evil sorceress she ought to have been' in their eyes.[9] Anne as a sorceress is a 'relatively recent concept'.[10] It is largely the modern media which has created the witch image. It certainly adds drama to the many fictional portrayals created in the twentieth and twenty-first centuries. Examining the contemporary sources, the focus is on Anne's sexual behaviour and her religious beliefs, and it is important to remember that Anne Boleyn was never accused of witchcraft. It was not even a crime in England until the introduction of the Witchcraft Act in 1542. It is, however, very prevalent in historical novels.

As already mentioned, execution and Anne Boleyn's violent end often features heavily in fictional portrayals of her. Philippa Gregory has George Boleyn saying to his sister, Mary, that, 'we're Boleyns. When you spend your life in the shadow of the throne, you're always afraid of blades'.[11] It sums up what is often so fascinating about Anne Boleyn. Henry VIII changed the face of England in order to marry her, but just three years later it was Anne's own husband who signed the warrant for her execution. Portraying Anne Boleyn's execution in novels plays a role in creating perceptions of Henry VIII as a tyrant and impacts on Anne's own characterisation. Anne 'is not only witness to Henry's violence but fuels it. Where Henry is represented as tyrant, she is often the Lady Macbeth who encourages him'.[12] Anne Boleyn is seen to have created the tyrant that Henry VIII became.

Jean Plaidy's *Murder Most Royal* (1949)

Jean Plaidy's work is the oldest fictional work discussed here. It appears to be a more traditional recounting with Henry pursuing Anne rather than her seeming to go after him. One sentiment expressed by Anne Boleyn in *Murder Most Royal* is that she cannot be a queen, as Henry already has a wife, and she claims, 'your mistress I will not be!'.[13] Anne Boleyn was the first person to refuse Henry anything directly, as far as we know. His former mistresses, Bessie Blount and Mary Boleyn, had given in when he asked them to. It is perhaps this change which meant that Anne had such an influence on history. It was her refusal to sleep with the king without being married that led to the Break with Rome and the dissolution of the monasteries. It also helps to explain why she still fascinates historians, film makers, and fiction writers today.

First meeting the king in the gardens at her home at Hever Castle, Plaidy's Anne Boleyn feigns ignorance of who he is, not impressed with court gallantry, saying that the English are 'somewhat clumsy when compared with those of the French court'.[14] Anne knows that the king is sleeping with her sister, Mary, and is angry, so she teases him, claiming that 'they say I am as French as I am English' when Henry calls the French 'a perfidious set of rascals'.[15] This is the beginning of their story in the novel. After a year of being loved by the king, Anne reflects on how she has changed:

> She had grown hard, calculating; she was not the same girl who had loved Percy so deeply and defiantly; she was less ready with sympathy, finding hatred springing up in her, and with them a new, surprising quality which had not been there before – vindictiveness.[16]

Being loved by a king, and knowing that your relationship with him is unpopular, would make a woman harder, more protective, and likely to strike out. What we know of Anne's character suggests she was proud, and ambitious, and became haughty as her position as the king's future wife became popular knowledge. In the novel Anne revels in being 'the shining light, the star, the most beautiful, the most accomplished of women, greatly loved by the King'.[17] As the novel progresses Anne has to suffer as she loses this position at the centre of the king's universe and sees herself replaced by others, pushed aside.

Plaidy seems to make more of Henry VIII's relationship with Jane Seymour and its impact on Anne's position than the likes of Philippa Gregory or Hilary Mantel. She suggests that Jane was angling from the beginning for Anne's position, and both she and Henry were playing a waiting game to see if Anne produced a son. Perhaps Anne saw the similarities between her and Jane as between her and her predecessor, Katherine of Aragon. It has certainly been suggested that Jane had been groomed to take Anne's place, although whether this actually happened is debateable.[18] The relationships between the women in Anne Boleyn's story are so important to her rise and fall. When awaiting the birth of her child, Anne laments, 'what if history were to repeat itself! What if that which had happened to Queen Katherine was about to happen to Queen Anne! Would she be asked to admit that her marriage was illegal?'.[19] It would come to pass, so we see Plaidy using hindsight to create tension in the story, and a sense of building to something inevitable. It was not inevitable at the time, but the knowledge of how Anne's story would conclude gives authors a way to build tension and drama.

Anne Boleyn confronts Henry when she is pregnant and awaiting the birth of her child, as she believes that he has had an affair, 'if you must amuse yourself, I would prefer you did not do it under my eyes and with one of my own women!' to which Henry says to himself, 'Am I to be defied by one wife, dictated to by another?'.[20] Anne was not like Katherine of Aragon, who came to understand that confronting Henry over his extra-marital liaisons only resulted in an argument, it did not stop the king. But Katherine defied Henry in refusing to accept the annulment of her marriage. Anne was so used to having Henry all to herself, over the seven years of their courtship, that she could not seem to stomach him having relations with other women. Anne's character meant that she would not accept being second best. Henry responds directly to Anne, 'you close your eyes, as your betters did before you! ... you ought to know that it is in my power in a single instant to lower you further than I raised you up'.[21] This scene is evidenced in a letter from the Imperial ambassador, Eustace Chapuys, to his master, Charles V, the Holy Roman Emperor. In a letter dated 3 September 1533, Chapuys related that Henry VIII 'told [Anne] that she must shut her eyes, and endure as well as more worthy persons, and that she ought to know that it was in his power to humble her again in a moment more than he had exalted her'.[22] This must have frightened Anne, as she knew that her position depended on maintaining the love of the king, and in producing a son.

Anne Boleyn's final scenes in *Murder Most Royal* involve Plaidy quoting her execution speech almost word for word as Eric Ives quoted it, using phrases like 'I am come hither to accuse no man' and 'if any person will meddle with my cause I require them to judge the best'.[23] The last is perhaps the most memorable line from the records of Anne's execution speech. It echoes the belief that Anne was innocent of what she was accused and how she asked others to look kindly on the records of her life and reign. Plaidy also outlines in the novel a fear that Henry VIII and Thomas Cromwell felt in allowing Anne to speak on the scaffold, but she claimed that 'all the bitterness had gone out of her'.[24] She probably feared for the fate of her daughter and the rest of her family including her parents and sister. According to Plaidy's retelling, Anne also was unaware that her brother had perished before her. Anne did not dare to declare her innocence more openly, as if she said something against the king or his justice then the repercussions could land on their families. That would be enough to make anyone behave.

Suzannah Dunn's *The Queen of Subtleties* (2004)

Suzannah Dunn's novel *The Queen of Subtleties* is told from a dual perspective – one from Anne Boleyn herself, and the other from Lucy Cornwallis, a woman described in the novel as the king's confectioner. The author's notes at the end describe how a 'Mrs Cornwallis' is recorded as having been the king's confectioner, but that not much is known about her, except that she was given a house in Aldgate for her services.[25] It is an interesting approach, to combine telling the story from the subject's point of view, and then basically from a fictional character's point of view alongside. Perhaps this approach was chosen because it gives more of an outsider's perspective on Anne's story, and there is a bit more licence for fiction and drama outside of Anne's own perspective.

The novel begins with Anne Boleyn talking to her daughter, Elizabeth, reflecting on her life before her execution, believing that her daughter will 'be told lies about me, or perhaps even nothing at all … portraits of me will be burned. You'll probably never even come across my handwriting because my letters and diaries will go the same way'.[26] With hindsight, we know that many of Anne's possessions were destroyed. We do have some of her handwriting, because she wrote in her Books of Hours which survive in the collection of Hever Castle, but a lot of letters and the like were lost, along with probably several portraits. We have later copies, but only a damaged medal as a contemporary image. Anne writes about her history, that she 'grew up to be a Frenchwoman.

I came back to England as a Frenchwoman. There are women in France who are strong, Elizabeth, because they're educated'.[27] Anne attributes her success to her education and her time spent in France and how it taught her what it means to be strong. Anne writes that 'England was changed forever. It had to be done. I got old England by the throat and shook it until it died'.[28] Anne does not come across in Dunn's novel as at all apologetic for the chaos she had brought to England; conversely, she is proud of the change she has wrought in the country. Elizabeth Norton writes that Anne 'had the personality and drive to change history'.[29] She certainly did change history and left a legacy in her daughter, who would continue to shape England.

As the novel progresses, the reader hears of Anne's frustrations at how long the annulment case is taking, 'It's all I ever hear! Poor you and your difficult situation! What about me? … I could have married someone else … I could have had children … I could be having a proper life'.[30] Anne then discovered that Katherine of Aragon was still mending the king's shirts, and Henry could not understand why this was a problem for Anne, claiming that 'she likes mending my shirts, it gives her something to do', to which Anne responded, frustrated, 'mending your shirts is a wifely duty. Do you understand? What other wifely duties does she still perform for you?'.[31] This incident comes from a letter sent by the Imperial ambassador, Eustace Chapuys, to Charles V. Chapuys wrote that Anne was furious at the gentleman who had delivered the cloth to Katherine, and 'abused the bearer in the King's very presence'.[32] Henry is trapped between two strong women, both of whom are stubborn and want to be his wife, but neither are willing to give in and let the other triumph.

Anne Boleyn's trial on charges of adultery, incest and treason plays out in the novel. How, when the jury found her guilty and her uncle, the Duke of Norfolk, had to read out the sentence, 'can you believe it – he was snivelling. Leaking. Red-eyed, red-nosed' as he pronounced the sentence of burning or beheading according to the goodwill of the king.[33] Norfolk and Anne had allegedly fallen out well before her arrest and trial, and Norfolk probably sat as the judge based on his prominence as one of two dukes in England at the time (the other being the king's friend and former brother-in-law, Charles Brandon, 1st Duke of Suffolk) and wanting to distance himself from his disgraced niece and nephew. Norfolk seemed to have the luck to be able to save himself. He would perform the feat again when another niece, Katherine Howard, married the king and was executed, also for adultery. In the novel, Anne spoke to the men who condemned her, saying that she 'realised that I hadn't been the ideal wife – and a king does need an ideal wife – but it seemed, after all, regrettably, that I wasn't wife-material. I'd done him no greater wrong than that, though'.[34] That was Anne Boleyn's greatest flaw – she failed to make the expected transition from mistress to wife. As a mistress, Henry was at her mercy and she could technically still walk away, though the king probably would not have allowed her to. As his wife and queen, there was an expectation from the king that Anne would be a devoted and loving wife, not get involved in politics, and produce plenty of children. Anne's natural character meant that she would not hold her tongue or fade into the background like Katherine of Aragon had. She would continue to speak out on politics and religion, and push for the rights of her daughter, although failing to produce the expected and promised son.

Like the beginning, the novel also ends with Anne Boleyn speaking about, and indirectly to, her daughter, Elizabeth. She knows she will not be there to see her daughter grow up, and that she will suffer as a result of her mother's fate. Hindsight means that authors of historical novels can allude to the future of a character, as Dunn does here:

> I should take this opportunity to pass down some motherly wisdom, shouldn't I? I know what I should say: if you want to keep your head, keep it down. But my guess is that you – Tudor, Boleyn – will run the risk of losing it anyway, one day, so I say this: be your mother's daughter and hold it high.[35]

Unlike other fictional retellings of Anne Boleyn's story, the reader does not see the actual execution take place. The novel ends in Anne's lodgings in the Tower of London the night before the execution as she tries to figure out why this is happening to her and what has led her to this point. Dunn's viewpoint is that it is the world that surrounds Anne that prompts her behaviour: the Tudor world not the woman herself.[36] But the final sense we have of her in the story is of her bravery, courage, and spirit. She recognises herself in her daughter and knows that daughter is part Tudor and part Boleyn, a powerful combination.

Laura Andersen's *The Boleyn King* (2013)

Laura Andersen has not written a traditional narrative of Anne Boleyn, but rather an alternative history, a what could have been had Anne Boleyn not miscarried for the final time in January 1536. What if that pregnancy had resulted in a birth, and that of a son? Then if that son became king of England after Henry VIII's death? Henry IX, known as William in this story, is king of England, with his uncle, George Boleyn, as his regent and his mother, Anne, as a key advisory figure. His sister, Elizabeth, is at court, part of an inner circle with Elizabeth's friend, Minuette Wyatt, and William's friend, Dominic Courtenay. It is a fascinating what if – one which many people will have considered, if Anne had given Henry a son – and it is the first novel in a trilogy.

The prelude to *The Boleyn King* is dated 28 June 1536 when, in reality, Anne Boleyn was already dead, but in this version, it is when Anne gave birth to a son. This was the result of the pregnancy which actually ended in miscarriage in January 1536. Historian J.E. Neale describes how 'never was fortune more cruel', as Anne 'had miscarried of her saviour'.[37] This novel explores what might have happened had Anne not miscarried and in fact birthed a son which saved her from the fate of May 1536. The prelude describes how Anne had birthed a healthy daughter, Elizabeth, just three years earlier, 'but she had not been afraid that time' as she was newly crowned and accepted as queen 'and she had been absolutely certain that the child she carried then was a boy'.[38] The prelude concludes with a suggestion of Anne's actual fate in May 1536, but in the novel it is relief, 'Anne shut her eyes again, so as not to weep openly. Henry will be pleased, she thought, and I ... I will remain queen'.[39] In *The Boleyn King*, Anne is terrified that she would be overthrown and replaced if she failed to produce a son, and there is a mention that Henry VIII had taken Jane Seymour as his mistress during Anne's pregnancy. Of course, in reality Jane Seymour would replace Anne as queen. This final line in the prelude, we see Anne's relief in the realisation that the production of a son saved her. The question of what could have happened to Anne had she not given birth to a son is raised later by George Boleyn to his royal nephew and niece:

> I do not think you appreciate how deeply resentment of your mother still runs. Make no mistake – religion may be the driving force, but Anne has always been the flash point. If William had not been born a boy ... if Henry had not been so taken with his healthy son ... Anne came perilously close to losing more than just her crown in the year before William's birth. Henry was always unpredictable and easily persuaded in his tempers.[40]

With hindsight today, readers know what actually happened to both Anne and George, and the suggestion here is that it happened because Anne failed to provide Henry with a son. That was certainly a part of it, but there were other political and religious considerations which came into play to bring her down.

The reader first meets the dowager queen Anne Boleyn when her daughter, Elizabeth, visits her in her chambers. Elizabeth says that she had 'heard her mother cut a lady to shreds with her tongue for an uneven hem or a slight stain'.[41] There are reports of Anne's sharp tongue, for example before her marriage to the king when Henry VIII quarrelled with Katherine of Aragon and Anne is said to have retorted that one day Henry would cast her off, 'farewell to my time and youth spent to no purpose at all'.[42] Anne was said to hold her household to very high standards. She must have known that she would always be compared to her predecessor, Katherine of Aragon, and did not want to be found lacking. In the novel, when Elizabeth enters her mother's room in the story, she sees Anne with 'a Tyndale Bible open on her lap'.[43] This description echoes contemporary sources of Anne Boleyn's religious beliefs, and her introducing Henry VIII to the works of William Tyndale through his *The Obedience of a Christian Man*. This is a very interesting and insightful scene into Anne Boleyn, and what her potential relationship with Elizabeth could have been like had the two had the chance to develop that. Elizabeth is reunited with Minuette in this scene, and she describes how Anne would have 'frozen any other woman with a stare of ice for such behaviour' when the two hugged delightedly, but that Elizabeth 'would have been hard-pressed to name a single woman whom her mother considered a friend. She had always preferred men'.[44] This is another allusion to Anne's actual fate, accused of adultery with five different men of the court. She seemed to fall out with her sister, Mary, after Mary's secret second marriage, and there have been suggestions that she also fell out with her sister-in-law, Jane Boleyn, Viscountess Rochford, who joined a gathering in support of Princess Mary, reported by Jean de Dinteville, the French ambassador.[45] This must have been a huge blow to Anne and her family.

The novel says that Henry VIII gave Anne Boleyn the right of 'femme sole' against the objections of his council before he died.[46] This was a legal position which allowed Anne to act with her own wealth and property without the consideration of her husband. Margaret Beaufort, Henry VIII's grandmother, had been granted the same status once her son, Henry VII, became king. Anne tells Elizabeth to see to it that 'your brother never has cause to regret your independence' to which Elizabeth responds, 'I will act in all ways as you would'. Anne Boleyn answers, 'That is what worries me'.[47] Again we see that flash of Anne Boleyn's spirit, and that of Elizabeth. It is easy to say like mother, like daughter in this scene. There is contemporary evidence of the fiery temper of both women, and one can imagine Anne giving Elizabeth advice as she grew up, had Anne not been executed before Elizabeth was 3 years old.

In the novel, Anne Boleyn dies in summer 1554 at her childhood home of Hever Castle, having retired from the court due to illness. The progress of Anne's final days is charted in the novel through letters written by Minuette who was with her. In one letter, Minuette writes that, 'Her Majesty does not mince words, either in praise or in condemnation. Her marriage could never have been serene, but hearing her talk, I wager she found more pleasure in arguments with Henry than she ever would have found in a placid existence with a less dominant husband'.[48] From what we know of Anne's character, she enjoyed debate and would never have settled for hiding her opinions or her natural character. This is why she appears to have struggled, or even failed, to make the anticipated change from dominant mistress to subservient wife. She could play the game to get what she wanted. At the end of her life in the novel, Anne Boleyn goes back in her delirium to January 1536, 'the blood ... I've been bleeding since yesterday. Since the moment of Catherine's internment ... If I lose this child – the very month of her death – the people will say it is God's will. That it is God himself denying me. Denying my marriage'.[49] This is a prime example of a fiction writer using hindsight to make a point. This moment in January 1536, when in reality Anne Boleyn miscarried for the final time, is said to have been the beginning of the end for her, though there is some debate on exactly when it was that Anne was doomed, and it may not have been as early as January 1536.

What alternative history novels like this give readers is a chance to imagine what might have happened had just one thing changed. *The Boleyn King* is the first of a trilogy, and there is a second connected trilogy where Elizabeth I still becomes queen, and what could have happened if a big what-if of her reign was changed. It is fascinating to imagine how things might have been different, and to see the historical figures we know in situations we are aware they were not in.

Jennifer C. Wilson's *Kindred Spirits* (2016)

This book, or book series, is probably the most obscure of the ones discussed here. It does not take place in the Tudor period, but in the modern day and features Tudor figures as ghosts at the Tower of London, Westminster Palace, and other places. Each book focuses on different ghostly figures. The first book, *Kindred Spirits: Tower of London*, features Anne and George Boleyn, Richard III and his brother, George, Duke of Clarence, Katherine Howard, and Lady Jane Grey, among others. The group of ghosts are living in Tower as it is open to twenty-first century tourists, and they prank the guests and re-enactors while dealing with their own ghostly squabbles and histories.

The story opens with a conversation between Anne Boleyn and Richard III, but in a relaxed way, with Richard asking, 'Where's George?' and Anne responding, 'Yours or mine?'.[50] A joke between the two of them, as both had brothers called George executed within the Tower, and whose ghosts were still around. The opening scene also plays on a key part of Anne Boleyn's imagery, describing 'the pearls of her favourite necklace winking in the sunlight, and the famous "B" glistening. She still never took it off, pinning it to her dress with a brooch during her headless periods'.[51] The tone varies throughout the book between fun and serious, and this opening chapter is a good example of that. A tour guide at the Tower describes how Anne entered the Tower through Traitor's Gate and Anne whispers into the ear of a young student 'and I never left' with a 'mischievous grin'.[52] Nowadays, we know that Anne did not in fact enter the Tower through Traitor's Gate, but at the court gate, one of three riverside entrances.[53] Richard III gets angry when he hears a guide referring to him as a child murderer of his nephews, the Princes in the Tower, but Anne tries to explain they all have labels: 'You aren't the only one. I mean, I'm supposed to be a witch, Katherine [Howard]'s a whore, my brother, well…'.[54] Anne Boleyn was never accused of witchcraft, but it is still a common misapprehension, and one which is widely used in historical fiction. Anne is usually considered to be innocent of the charges against her, whereas her cousin, Katherine Howard, seems to be generally considered to have been guilty. George Boleyn is thought to have committed incest with his sister, though this is thought to be completely unfounded and unproven. It still is a popular theory to appear in historical fiction, notably Philippa Gregory's *The Other Boleyn Girl.*

The incest accusations against Anne and George Boleyn are addressed more directly later in the story, when Anne relates to her brother a story that she heard two girls discussing in the Tower. The story goes that, 'apparently, George … we had several children, all boys, who all survived, and their descendants survive to this day!', with George responding, 'does it really not trouble you, that people still harp on at that vicious old rumour?'.[55] Rumours continue to spread, even though they are completely outlandish and would not have been possible. Anne was surrounded by her ladies all of the time, and one or more of her ladies would have needed to assist her to commit adultery or incest, but none of them were ever accused. This is in contrast to Katherine Howard where her lady, Jane Boleyn, Viscountess Rochford, the widow of George Boleyn, was arrested and executed alongside her mistress. Eric Ives writes that 'Lady Rochford connived with Katherine Howard but was charged and executed; nobody was charged with abetting Anne Boleyn' and that to ignore this 'is to miss the point'.[56] Anne's response to George's question echoes what we see in a lot of historical fiction novels, that emphasis on Anne's triumph through her daughter, Elizabeth:

> At the end of the day, I have won the battle. And the war, for that matter. My Elizabeth was such a great Queen for England, and for that I will be eternally proud. And also, in history, surely the real winners are those who are remembered? Would I have been such a tragic, romantic heroine today, if I had successfully produced heir after heir for Henry, and done nothing of note? I doubt it.[57]

Anne would have been proud of Elizabeth, no doubt. Henry VIII was so determined that he needed a son to succeed him, but that son died young, and Mary I died childless, allowing Elizabeth to accede to the throne. Probably the three most remembered figures of the Tudor period are Henry VIII, Elizabeth I and Anne Boleyn. Henry because of his six wives and the Break with Rome, Elizabeth for the defeat of the Spanish Armada and presiding over England's supposed 'Golden Age', and Anne largely for her eventual fate, but also her role in the Reformation. Had Anne produced sons for Henry she probably would not be remembered as much as she is in the public mind, because it is the controversy surrounding her execution that keeps her story alive.

There are lots of reflections from the ghostly Anne Boleyn, reminiscing to 500 years ago when she was alive and queen of England. She looks back to the day of the May Day jousts in 1536 and how Henry VIII behaved completely normally to Henry Norris just hours before the latter's arrest, and how Henry had received the news of Mark Smeaton's confession around the same time and decided to act.[58] Even at a distance of nearly 500 years Anne still seems to struggle to understand it, how 'a king who had torn up his marriage, the church, and his relationship with Rome, just so that he could marry her' could have done what he did, though her time on the throne 'hadn't been all bad'.[59] Anne Boleyn attributes her fall to her lack of a son, 'when no more living babies were forthcoming, male or otherwise, Anne could do nothing but watch as, month by month, her power diminished'.[60] Anne's lack of a son was certainly damaging to her. If she had a son, she probably would not have been unseated and executed. Henry VIII would not have wanted to question the legitimacy of a son, though if a son had been born to Henry and Anne, his legitimacy would not have been accepted by Catholic Europe, much as Elizabeth's was not.

Alison Weir's *Anne Boleyn: A King's Obsession* (2017)

Alison Weir is a prolific writer of both fiction and non-fiction on the Tudors, but her *Six Tudor Queens* fiction series is a triumph. Each of the six books in the series covers the life of one of Henry VIII's wives from the wife's perspective, and *Anne Boleyn: A King's Obsession* is the second book in the series. We see Anne Boleyn as a girl, through her time in the Low Countries and France, her courtships with Henry Percy, Thomas Wyatt, and then the king, her marriage, and her tragic end. Weir had to represent Anne as a feminist because 'to do otherwise would have been perceived as failing to respect Anne's modernity'.[61] Feminism is a complex concept when it comes to applying it to sixteenth century figures and applying the expectations of a twenty-first woman to a sixteenth century one is to misunderstand a woman's position at the time. Weir manages this sympathetically, by not placing Anne as a modern woman, but as one grappling with new ideas.

When Henry VIII begins paying court to Anne Boleyn in the novel, Anne confides in her sister, Mary, who had already had an affair with the king. Anne says that 'believe me, I understand now how it was for you, although he insists you consented' and Mary's response is 'that's not true! He made me!'.[62] The implication here is that Henry could have any woman he wanted, whether they consented to his affections or not. He expects Anne to just fall into his arms, but she declares to Mary that 'I am not willing, and mercifully he has not tried to force me' to which Mary responds 'you are lucky. He is the last man you should tangle with'.[63] When Anne Boleyn does give in to Henry, it is with a caveat – that she will not be his mistress, but only his wife. Weir has Anne resisting Henry for an extended period, aware of how her sister was treated and not wishing to submit herself to the same fate. She could not have known she would face a worse fate at the hands of her husband but we, the reader, are all too aware of how the story will end.

Henry continues his pursuit of Anne relentlessly, giving her gifts and begging her to be his. He does not attempt to force himself upon her, as he did with her sister in this story, though the reasons are not made entirely clear why he felt the need to force himself on one sister but not with the other. Henry asks Anne to become his mistress, that he would love and honour her, and give her whatever she wanted, but Anne's response is fired back: 'I would rather lose my life than my honesty, which will be the greatest and best part of the dowry I shall bring my husband'. When Henry responds that he will live in hope, Anne's answer is that 'I understand not, most mighty King, how you should retain such hope. Your wife I cannot be, both in respect of my unworthiness, and also because you have a queen already. Your mistress I will not be! And now, sir, I beg leave to return to my duties'.[64] George Wyatt reports a similar speech in his work, written in the reign of Elizabeth I, that Anne knew the king was married so rejected his speech of love, and that 'in such sort as what so ever tended to regard of her honour she should not to scorn'.[65] Anne was determined not to become another of Henry's cast-offs and it is notable that Weir has obviously used the original sources to form some of the speech of the characters.

Weir's novel relates an incident of Anne Boleyn's fervour for religious reform. She would read books which were banned, considered heretical by Cardinal Thomas Wolsey and the Catholic Church. A sixteenth-century source wrote that Anne had a copy of William Tyndale's *The Obedience of a Christian Man* which she lent to one of her ladies, Anne Gainsford, and told her to keep it hidden. However, her paramour, George Zouche, had taken it to read for himself. Cardinal Wolsey came upon him and confiscated the book, as he had called for heretical books to be seized and destroyed. Anne Boleyn went to the king to plead for assistance and when he replied kindly, she showed him the book and asked him to read it.[66] In Weir's novel, when Anne goes to Henry once the book has been taken, she says, 'for the Cardinal will think I dabble in heresy. All I sought was to understand why Master Tyndale is regarded as a heretic, when in fact his arguments make sense to me. Sir, I do beseech your Grace for your protection'.[67] Henry wanted to be seen as a protector and he did protect Anne, and the book was returned to her. She then gave it to Henry and urged him to read it, saying 'you will be surprised – and maybe impressed' and when Henry came to her next, he responded 'these are compelling arguments, darling'.[68] Another example of Alison Weir very obviously having used original sources in order to write her fictional narrative.

In the closing scenes of the novel, Anne Boleyn's execution plays out. In some novels, such as Suzannah Dunn's, the reader does not see or hear of the execution, but Weir has it playing out to the end graphically. Anne mounts the scaffold and says to herself, 'well, Henry should hear only of her courage. She would not criticise him or his justice – she had made her peace with God, and she wanted no retribution to fall upon her family'.[69] Anne was creating her own image even in her final moments facing a French swordsman. She always seemed to be cognisant of how history might see her and wanted the best for her daughter. She could not save her brother, or the other men, but she could protect her parents, sister, and daughter. Weir then relates Anne's final scaffold speech in full, as discussed in chapter four, so it does not need repeating here. Weir has Anne speaking to the ladies who accompanied her to the scaffold, declaring, 'Forget me not, and always be faithful to the King's Grace and to her whom with happier fortune you may look to have as your Queen and mistress'.[70] Anne was determined to die well, but not to be forgotten. She knows who will follow her on the throne, but Weir does not have Anne at the end being bitter, but wishing her well, knowing how difficult it can be to be queen, and particularly to be wife and queen to Henry VIII.

The final paragraph of the novel is difficult to read, describing what Anne might have felt as her head was decapitated from her body. Weir's description disagrees with William Kingston's assertion that 'it should be no pain; it was so subtle'.[71] It is haunting and upsetting to image what Anne may have gone through, and Weir conveys it wonderfully:

> She had believed Kingston when he had said there would be no pain and prayed that the blow would be instantaneous and bring immediate oblivion, but when it came there was a choking explosion of searing agony and a dreadful warm gush of blood. She was aware of tasting it in her mouth and

> of its flooding her nostrils as she felt her head, horribly light now, hit the scaffold with a painful thud and the blindfold fell away. She would have cried out, yet no sound came apart from terrible, silent gurgling, and she wanted to clamp her hands to the mortal wound that had been dealt her, yet she had no hands any more. They were attached to the dark, bloodied, crumpled thing that lay on the scaffold next to her. She blinked and tried to look away. Through her torment she could still see the blurred shapes of people around her on the scaffold. And then her eyes dimmed and the merciful darkness descended'.[72]

There have been suggestions that, in fact, the person retains consciousness for a short time once the head has been taken off. This is what Weir has played with here in Anne Boleyn's final scene; that she remains capable of seeing and understanding what is around her. Writing about death is always difficult but when it is written so emotionally like it often is in fiction, it makes it even harder. Weir has Anne able to see her crumpled body and feel the blow and the pain that killed her, knowing that this is what her husband wanted for her.

* * *

There will always be debates over the veracity and accuracy of historical novels, but that is a little beside the point. Although it is obvious writers have at least conducted some research, novels are intended to be entertaining rather than instructive. It is certainly a way for future historians to become interested in controversial and important historical topics. David Starkey's claim that 'the idea that [historical novelists] have authority is ludicrous' is rather beside the point.[73] Novelists are not claiming to have authority; their intention is to entertain, and perhaps to make people more interested in the history that is being fictionalised. Historical novels, as well as television and films, seem to be how lots of people find their interest in history as a subject, and it is that interest which can lead to a lifelong passion. There is more importance in novels than the historical authority and accuracy, though it is important to be aware of these issues when reading.

Of the five novels discussed in this chapter, only three are along the lines of more traditional historical fiction. Jean Plaidy, Suzannah Dunn and Alison Weir have written chronological fictionalised versions of Anne Boleyn's life. Laura Andersen has written an alternative what-if scenario, while Jennifer C. Wilson has written a modern-day ghostly spin on various historical figures, but not modernising the characters themselves. Wilson's and Andersen's are more loosely based on the historical record as it is more an imaginative viewpoint on how Anne Boleyn's character might have reacted to certain situations. Weir, Dunn and Plaidy have the actual historical sources to reference in their works and can be more easily judged on their historical accuracy.

Historical novels always dedicate time to Anne Boleyn's fall from power. No matter which other topics they cover or focus on, like the divorce in Hilary Mantel's *Wolf Hall* or Anne's earlier romantic relationships in Philippa Gregory's *The Other Boleyn Girl*, there is always time dedicated to her fall. Jean Plaidy's *Murder Most Royal* suggests even in the title a focus on her brutal end. Novels which have an alternative theme like Jennifer C. Wilson's *Kindred Spirits: Tower of London* or Laura Andersen's *The Boleyn King* both have their Anne Boleyn reflecting on her fate, and the danger she was in. It is what fascinates readers of fiction: the drama and the shock of what happened.

Chapter 12

Historiography

'She was no saint, but neither was she a villain. Anne was simply very human'[1]

There has been so much written about Anne Boleyn in the nearly 500 years since her death, that it is often difficult to distil it down into something a bit more manageable. But that means there is a lot to get your teeth into. In the twenty-first century, there is still plenty of debate and new research and discoveries being made. These new discoveries can help to change and enhance our understanding of Anne Boleyn, Henry VIII, and the Tudor court.

The historian who is probably most likely to be mentioned when asking for book recommendations about Anne Boleyn is Eric Ives. There is a good reason for this. He wrote what is generally considered to be one of the best accounts of Anne's life, focusing on analysis of contemporary sources. A very different account of Anne's life was published a few years later by G.W. Bernard. The pair have polarising opinions, which were played out in a written joust in *The English Historical Review* in the 1990s. It is worth examining the two arguments in detail here as they demonstrate why, even today, Anne Boleyn is such an enigmatic and divisive figure.

Discoveries made by Kate McCaffrey, castle historian and assistant curator at Hever Castle, regarding Anne Boleyn's printed Book of Hours on display at Hever Castle were made public in 2021. Hever Castle is currently putting on a series of exhibitions curated by McCaffrey, Dr Owen Emmerson, and Alison Palmer, to celebrate 500 years since Anne Boleyn made her debut at the English court in 1522. The first one, in 2022, was entitled 'Becoming Anne: Connections, Culture, Court', exploring Anne's beginning up to her debut, including her time at the courts of the Low Countries and France. The second one in 2023 was entitled 'Catherine and Anne: Rivals, Queens, Mothers' which examined the relationship between Katherine of Aragon and Anne Boleyn and how these two women may have had more in common than traditionally thought. These exhibitions have explored different parts of Anne's life, and more are planned.

This chapter will end with a summary of conclusions that different historians who have written about Anne have drawn. Was she a saint or sinner? A woman ahead of her time? And why have her 'spirit, her triumph, and her brutal death … lost none of their power to capture hearts and minds'?.[2] Anne Boleyn's life and tragic end keep people coming back, whether it's through film or novels, or someone who wants to find out the true history. Her legacy and controversy endures.

The importance of historiography in a cultural history like this cannot be overstated. It is not possible to truly understand how Anne Boleyn's image and perception has changed over time without discussing how historians view her, and how new discoveries are still being made. Perceptions will keep changing because opinions are always influenced by the time and society in which the writer lives:

> The society in which a text is written is as integral to its narrative as the past that it attempts to capture. Historians, biographers, and novelists are each influenced by the cultural conditions of their own present, and social mores and moral conventions have the potential to shape a narrative just as significantly as historiographical theory and extant evidence.[3]

It is interesting to think about how future generations of historians, biographers, novelists and filmmakers will view Anne Boleyn, and what might change from what we understand today. How historians of the future might sit and analyse our work, just as we sit and analyse the work of the past. This is why it is important to understand past works, so that we can try and recognise where our own work fits in, and where these different opinions have come from. Even if we do not agree with each other, a fuller understanding of historiography and how it has changed and developed can only be beneficial.

Eric Ives versus G.W. Bernard

Eric Ives is probably the most well-known of Anne Boleyn's many biographers, and well-respected as well. His book *The Life and Death of Anne Boleyn* is often seen as the bible in terms of writing on Anne. G.W. Bernard appears to be the only historian convinced of Anne Boleyn's guilt in the charges against her, a theory he expounds in his book *Anne Boleyn: Fatal Attractions*. Biography is a 'distinct genre of historical narrative', but it is sometimes thought that the focus on a single individual 'is seen to limit the commentary on broader political and social milieus'.[4] That is not necessarily true. A better understanding of individuals can help to explain why or how events happened, and where the individual's influence played its part. Ives and Bernard each submitted an article to *The English Historical Review*, beginning with Bernard in 1991, with Ives's response following in 1992. The pair 'directly address their conflicting interpretations' in this exchange of articles.[5] However, we will begin with their full-length biographies.

In his book, Ives attempts to uncover the truth behind the myth of Anne Boleyn's controversial life, making excellent use of contemporary sources and pulling apart the stories surrounding her to reveal that she 'deserves to be a feminist icon, a woman ...who broke through the glass ceiling by sheer character and initiative'.[6] Ives's argument is that Anne was essentially a modern woman in an early modern world, and that she managed to thrive in a male-dominated arena, at least until her sudden and unexpected fall. She attracted and kept a king at arm's length for seven years before their tumultuous three-year marriage, which ended in a king beheading his once entirely beloved wife.

The book's first twelve chapters' deal with Anne's life in largely chronological order, from her birth and childhood spent at the French court, up to her coronation in 1533. This section includes analysis of her romances with Henry Percy and Thomas Wyatt, and her role in the fall of Cardinal Wolsey and the King's Great Matter; controversial topics which have sparked much debate. However, Ives seems to dispel a lot of rumour and uses contemporary sources to put forward a concise argument, steering clear of conjecture. His conclusions are based on the interpretation of contemporary sources. Ives then takes a break from his chronological analysis to look at some of the most fascinating themes surrounding Anne. The chapters on 'Influence, Power and Wealth', 'Image' and 'Personal Religion' are some of the best in the book. This is because they go beyond the generally accepted perceptions of Anne and look at her in a new light. They are more of a deep dive into particularly important areas, as Ives goes into critical analysis of these often contentious issues, quoting from sources like the Lisle Letters, Hall's Chronicle and the Letters and Papers of the Reign of Henry VIII, including dispatches from Chapuys, the Imperial ambassador, and Thomas Cromwell, the king's first minister. These kinds of sources offer a first-hand insight, not just into the life of Anne herself, but into the world of the Tudor court in which she lived and died. The later chapters discuss the first half of 1536, and Anne's fall from power, in exceptional detail, analysing the evidence, the pitfalls, and the information that Anne herself supposedly divulged to indict her so-called 'accomplices'. Because Ives dedicates so many chapters to her fall, he really does wade through all the evidence to try and untangle the fact from the fiction. He puts forward the historical argument that Thomas Cromwell was to blame for engineering Anne's fall in the manner of a coup, although many historians (like G.W. Bernard) disagree with this view.

G.W. Bernard's biography of Anne is shorter than Ives's work, and the title certainly less clear. 'Fatal Attractions' implies that Henry's attraction to Anne was always doomed. It was destined to be stormy because Anne had struggled to move from the position of mistress, where she had a lot of power, to wife and queen, where she was expected to be subservient to her husband, but it did not have to be fatal from the beginning. Bernard's work is often cited less than Ives's in other works, but it is important not to dismiss it completely. Bernard puts forward the argument that it was not Anne who held herself off from Henry in terms of sexual relations, but the other way around. Henry held off in order to ensure that when Anne conceived a child it was undoubtedly legitimate, and worried that if it was obvious that it was his passion for Anne which fuelled his determination for an annulment, it would undermine his 'moral case'. Bernard describes the idea that it was Anne who held off Henry's advances for six years as 'nonsense' and that 'it was manifestly Henry, once he set off on his campaign for a divorce, not Anne, who then deliberately refrained from full sexual relations'.[7] His other main argument which places him at polar opposites to Ives, is his belief that Anne Boleyn was guilty of the charges for which she was executed, where Ives believes her innocent. Bernard argues that the 'plausible' explanation that Anne and her alleged lovers were framed 'is too hasty a response' and perhaps there was 'rather more substance' to the charges.[8] He raises this possibility in the first chapter before expounding on it towards the end of the biography. Like Ives and so many other historians who have written biographies of Anne Boleyn, Bernard's work is written in chronological order, though with a separate chapter on her religion, similarly to Ives. Also like Ives, Bernard devotes several chapters to Anne's fall from power, the circumstances of a possible coup, and a discussion of her guilt or innocence.

Some of Ives's conclusions have become the basis for future works. They are very convincing as he does not leave out critical evidence but discusses everything and explains that there is some evidence he does not believe is as convincing, which is important. Bernard argues against a lot of Ives's points, particularly about Anne's religion, as he believes she died a Catholic death, ignoring her earlier evangelical sympathies. However, works like Joanna Denny's *Anne Boleyn* and Alison Weir's *The Lady in the Tower: The Fall of Anne Boleyn* agree with a lot of Ives's conclusions, concurring on issues like religion and, in the case of Weir, the reason for her fall from power. Denny argues that Anne's was 'no superficial faith … she had an abiding interest in the New Learning and the religious reformation that was spreading like a revolution in thinking'.[9] Alison Weir describes Anne's fall from power as 'one of the most astonishing and brutal coups in English history'.[10] Firstly, Ives correctly sees Anne's fall from grace as a 'coup' and a 'tragedy', as it took less than three weeks from the arrest of the first suspect to Anne's death.[11] This rapid fall suggests that the protagonists were less than sure of their own arguments and that they were worried they would not succeed. Secondly, Ives sees Anne as a victim of the early modern court in which she lived as rumours and circumstance destroyed her without any real concrete evidence. Dates and places in the indictment could be disproved. As historians, we can understand the influence of rumours and stories about Anne because we also lack any concrete evidence as to her innocence or guilt, and the reasons behind her fall, so we rely on conjecture and interpretation of the surviving sources.

Turning to the articles written for *The English Historical Review*, G.W. Bernard wrote his article *The Fall of Anne Boleyn* which was published in July 1991 and Eric Ives responded with *The Fall of Anne Boleyn Reconsidered* in July 1992. Beginning with Bernard, he believes that a coup against Anne accusing her of adultery with five men, such an intimate crime, 'does not fit the evidence of Henry's own relationship with Anne'.[12] Bernard refutes the idea that Anne's fall was a coup engineered by Thomas Cromwell, saying that it 'depends heavily on the assumption' that Anne Boleyn and the men accused alongside her were innocent.[13] The notion that the events of May 1536 were a coup would mean that 'Henry VIII was essentially a weak king who was often the plaything of factions'.[14] The two are not mutually exclusive. Factional politics did exist at Henry VIII's court, but that does not mean that Henry was a weak king. Henry remained in control at court throughout his reign, and though Anne's fall may well have been a coup planned by Cromwell, it had to have been done with the king's permission, otherwise Cromwell himself was risking execution. Bernard's summary of the guilt or innocence of those accused is as follows:

> Perhaps the safest guess for a modern historian is that Anne had indeed committed adultery with Norris, and briefly with Mark Smeaton; and that there was enough circumstantial evidence to cast reasonable doubt on the denials of the others. It must also be remembered that not everyone involved was tried and punished. This reinforces the succession that the accusations were not indiscriminate.[15]

Bernard believes that Smeaton's confession was real, as he maintained his confession to the end, saying on the scaffold that he deserved death. His belief in Norris's guilt stems from flirtatious talk and the 'dead men's shoes' conversation.[16] The fact that not everyone was tried and punished could easily have been a ploy by Cromwell to try and reinforce the supposed guilt of the others. It cannot be forgotten that many of the dates and places in the indictment where the crimes supposedly took place can be disproven. If the crimes had really taken place, then why not use true dates and places?

Eric Ives begins his rebuttal paper by noting similarities of interpretation between himself and G.W. Bernard, that 'Henry's marriage to Anne was eventful rather than unhappy, and that her last miscarriage did not make her fate inevitable'.[17] Ives astutely notes that 'Anne could have been divorced and incarcerated. She was indeed divorced, which destroyed the accusation of adultery, but only when safely condemned. Clearly the treason route was chosen to have the Queen and her "lovers" dead'.[18] It is one of the things about the case against Anne Boleyn which is so controversial. If Anne had never been married to the king, then she could not have been guilty of adultery. This is why the annulment was delayed until after Anne was already sentenced to death. It is something which is difficult to get around if you believe Anne truly guilty of the charges, but it was likely intended to make sure that her daughter, Elizabeth, was declared illegitimate and unable to inherit the throne.

Ives writes a blistering rebuttal to Bernard's claims of Anne's guilt towards the end of his paper, having gone through all of the evidence, both prosecution and defence, including 'the evidence Dr Bernard prefers: news, rumour and reports'.[19] Ives summarises his own arguments, and his dismissal of Bernard's arguments as follows:

> Thus much for the data of Anne Boleyn's fall: powerful indications of innocence; inescapable evidence of a deliberate intention to destroy her and the others; a miscellany of court and popular story with little substance, but with the potential to be manufactured into a case against them; and apparent corroboration of the Crown's case which, on examination, turns out to be an elaborated repetition of it. This is palpably no justification for suggesting that 'Anne and at least some of her friends were guilty'. The hypothesis which does satisfy the evidence is that Anne's fall was the consequence of a political coup and a classic example of Tudor faction in operation. What in the event of guilt would be unnecessary chicanery then becomes the means to an end, the immorality charges merely a weapon and the evidence of innocent irrelevant.[20]

Ives has the most compelling argument, though as a direct response to Bernard, he has the benefit of Bernard's article to work from, and the opportunity to pull apart the evidence Bernard bases his conclusion on. Bernard posted a rebuttal to Ives's article called *The Fall of Anne Boleyn: A Rejoinder* in 1992, beginning with 'if self-citation is evidence of complacency, then Professor Ives must plead guilty' since his article cited his own book.[21] This is not necessarily unusual in a journal article, there is a smaller word count in an article than a book, so you can direct readers to the complete arguments. Bernard then says that the idea of Cromwell orchestrating a coup is 'extravagantly implausible speculation based on assumption and inference'.[22] But, there are 'powerful indications of innocence' in Anne's story, notably the fact that dates and times in the indictment can be disproven, and that only Smeaton professed his guilt, and then it was rumoured only after he had been tortured.

Eric Ives's and G.W. Bernard's articles give a real insight into the different sources and ways of interpreting them that illustrate why Anne Boleyn's life, and particularly her fall, is still so hotly debated. Even though the articles were written in the early 1990s, similar debates are still raging today, and in all likelihood will continue to inspire others to get involved. Whether you believe her innocent or guilty is valid and we will in all likelihood never know the truth.

Kate McCaffrey and Anne Boleyn's Book of Hours

Kate McCaffrey currently works as Chief Curator and Castle Historian at Hever Castle, the childhood home of Anne Boleyn. It was her master's research for her dissertation in her Medieval and Early Modern Studies course at the University of Kent that has now given additional insight into how Anne was seen after her death by other women, and how Anne's Book of Hours survived with its inscription, 'remember me when you do pray, that hope doth lead from day to day'. McCaffrey's research focused on the smaller printed Book of Hours rather than the manuscript Book of Hours which is the more famous of the pair. Legend suggests that Anne Boleyn handed the book to one of her ladies on the scaffold at her execution on 19 May 1536.[23] The research is fascinating, and it makes you wonder just how much more there might be to discover if we look a little closer and use modern methods to examine old sources.

McCaffrey wrote a series of posts on her website describing her research and how she made the discoveries. She explained how she began by leafing through and taking everything in, photographing all of the folios to take away and examine further later. A more detailed study found the first erased inscription on the page that the book is usually opened to when on display to the public. To the naked eye these erasures just look like water damage or smudges, but there are letters beneath the smudges when examined more closely.[24] McCaffrey has said that whoever erased the notes obviously wanted them gone, but for what reason is harder to discern.[25] She describes finding four different erased notes through examination with an ultraviolet torch initially, then a stronger ultraviolet light. She took photographs of the inscriptions under ultraviolet light and then began to try and decipher them.[26] She used different filters in Photoshop to bring out different things in the erasures, but they were often difficult to decipher as the women who wrote in the book used different abbreviations and shorthand which was probably familiar to those writing at the time, but not today.[27] Given that spelling was not standardised in the sixteenth century the same word could be spelt multiple different ways, which makes reading these kinds of inscriptions difficult. One example that McCaffrey gives is where one or more letters are omitted from a word to save space, like Anne Boleyn's inscription where 'remember me' is written as 'remeber me' to save space, given that it was written at the bottom of an illuminated page.[28] It is fascinating research and an interesting insight into what there may still be to uncover or discover in old books and manuscripts that has previously been overlooked, and not just about Anne Boleyn.

Hever Castle made the announcement on their website on the anniversary of Anne's execution, 19 May 2021, that McCaffrey had uncovered hidden inscriptions in the Book of Hours, and describing her research, McCaffrey said:

> It is clear that this book was passed between a network of trusted connections, from daughter to mother, from sister to niece. If the book had fallen into other hands, questions almost certainly would have been raised over the remaining presence of Anne's signature. Instead, the book was passed carefully between a group of primarily women who were both entrusted to guard Anne's note and encouraged to add their own. In a world with very limited opportunities for women to engage with religion and literature, the simple act of marking this Hours and keeping the secret of its most famous user, was one small way to generate a sense of community and expression.[29]

McCaffrey's research goes beyond Anne herself and into the realms of networks of women who wanted to protect Anne's legacy. Henry VIII appears to have destroyed so many things related to Anne, including her badges and emblems which were all over his palaces, quite possibly any portraits of her, and likely her letters to him in reply to the love letters he sent to her in the late 1520s. Henry's letters to Anne survive only because they were smuggled out of England to the Vatican, where they remain today. This Book of Hours is one of the survivals, and that is because it was not within the confines of the court but in the hands of local women working to protect the legacy of a maligned English queen.

One of the most important things to come out of Kate McCaffrey's research is that Anne Boleyn and Katherine of Aragon both owned a copy of the same printing of a Book of Hours. In addition, it has recently been proven that Thomas Cromwell also owned a copy of the same printing. The books were produced by French printer Germain Hardouin in Paris in 1527, given that there is a calendar at the beginning for 1528.[30] This was a pivotal time in both Anne's and Katherine's lives and we can date the printing because of a calendar in the front of the book for that year. Anne's surviving book is displayed at Hever Castle, Katherine of Aragon's in the Morgan Library in New York, and Thomas Cromwell's in the Wren Library at Trinity College, Cambridge. The discovery of links between these Books of Hours proves that, despite not being compatible in terms of their religious outlook, Katherine and Anne were both pious, highly educated, and with a love of beautiful books. The discovery has demonstrated that Anne and Katherine had more in common than might otherwise be assumed. It's a tangible connection between the two women divided by the love of a changeable and ultimately tyrannical king. It is a brilliant discovery which offers more to our understanding of these two queens who are constantly compared to each other, and to Thomas Cromwell who was pivotal in the lives of both Katherine of Aragon and Anne Boleyn. The link between the three is fascinating. As McCaffrey states, the ownership of these three books by Katherine, Anne and Cromwell, came at a pivotal moment when Henry had decided to annul his marriage to Katherine and marry Anne.[31] Cromwell would be the one who eventually made it happen, and it would hugely affect both Katherine and Anne, and the course of their lives.

There were four family names that McCaffrey discovered written then erased in the book: Gage, West, Shirley, and Guildford, all connected to the Boleyn family through kinship with Elizabeth Hill, one of Anne Boleyn's childhood companions.[32] McCaffrey explains that 'it really comes full circle. What makes the book so dangerous to preserve, its association with Anne, actually becomes the main reason for preserving it when Elizabeth I comes to the throne and wants her mother to be remembered'.[33] That the book has survived for 500 years is a testament to these Kentish women who kept it safe as, had they been found in possession of it, it could have been seen as treason. They risked their lives to preserve something that an executed and disgraced English queen had owned and written in, a very personal prayer book; 'the simple act of marking this *Hours* and keeping the secret of its most famous user, was one small way to generate a sense of community and expression' for women often limited in what they could engage with.[34] Elizabeth I may well have been able to hold this book and read her mother's inscription. The mother her father refused to talk about or even acknowledge, it seems, yet Elizabeth respected and loved her and her Boleyn connections.

Historian Conclusions About Anne Boleyn

There is a very rich historiography surrounding Anne Boleyn and her life and legacy. What this section aims to do is to look at the summary comments made by historians about Anne. Having looked at her life and legacy, what did they make of her? Many of the comments focus on Anne's prominence in Tudor history, her role in the English Reformation, and her victory and ultimate success in her daughter, Elizabeth. This section focuses on interpretation of comprehensive studies and biographies and how these historians who have written about Anne Boleyn see her, her legacy and her place in history.

In an online event run by The Tudor Trio (Owen Emmerson, Kate McCaffrey, and Nicola Tallis) in 2024, called *The Retrial of Anne Boleyn* where 125 people listened to a debate by the three historians and studied the primary sources, 114 people (91%) found Anne innocent of all charges, so it was not a unanimous verdict. One person believed she was guilty of all charges, seven people believed she was guilty of treason but not adultery and incest, one person believed her guilty of adultery and treason but not incest, and two people believed the charges were not proven either way.[35] It is an example of how divisive Anne Boleyn, and her fate, can still be, with people not entirely sure, or divided, over her guilt or innocence, and how the interpretation of surviving sources is still open. There have been a lot of biographies and interpretations of Anne Boleyn over the years, and examining the opinions of these historians can give an insight into how perceptions have changed.

G.W. Bernard said that he came to 'suspect that Anne's life had too unthinkingly been incorporated into a triumphalist account of how a formidable woman sparked off the English Reformation', and that she 'is neither the Anne of protestant legend, nor Anne as a modern heroine, [but] she nonetheless remains one of the most important figures in Tudor history'.[36] Bernard seems to be the only historian who believes that Anne was guilty as charged of adultery, incest and treason, saying that'most historians have too quickly decided that the very notion that a queen could have committed adultery, and with five men, is so preposterous that it is hardly worth considering seriously'.[37] He challenges notions that Anne was a heroine or legend, and that she might actually have been guilty, but still acknowledges her importance as someone who changed the course of English history. Her fall was 'not just a salacious whodunnit; it has implications for our understanding of early Tudor politics'.[38] Anne Boleyn had wider implications than her own life and death.

Historian and podcaster, Natalie Grueninger, wrote a detailed analysis of Anne Boleyn's fall and final year, saying that, 'Anne's death was a shattering and incomprehensible loss ... for the English people, whose lives she genuinely wanted to improve. Henry attempted to obliterate Anne's memory, but in the end he failed. Death would immortalise her'.[39] It is ironic that in his desperation to get rid of Anne and wipe out any mentions or signs of her, Henry VIII in fact made sure that her memory lived on, and historians have continued for 500 years to study her life and her relationship with the king, and Anne has come off better. Henry VIII has been vilified instead, often as a tyrant. Henry did not believe that a woman could rule England, but it was his daughter by Anne Boleyn, Elizabeth, who succeeded as Gloriana. Elizabeth I 'embraced and cherished her mother's memory and carried within her heart a spark of her bold spirit, courage, and vivacity'.[40] Anne had succeeded in giving Henry an unexpected heir in their daughter.

A new work by duo John Guy and Julia Fox focuses on the relationship between Henry and Anne and concludes that 'the tumultuous events of Henry and Anne's courtship and marriage had made them the cynosure of all eyes for the best part of a decade and changed England for ever. But Anne did not change Henry. He changed himself'.[41] It is an interesting thing to consider: how much of an influence did Anne Boleyn and her relationship with the king have on the king's perceived personality changes? Henry would still have become the tyrant he was without Anne. He had already started down that path before he began courting her. Perhaps it is the examination of the relationship between Henry and Anne that makes Henry come off worse than he would otherwise, because of how he treated her in the end. It was unexpected that Anne would actually be executed, even when she was arrested. The expectation was that she would be banished from court and live out her life in some kind of exclusion like Katherine of Aragon had. But Henry wanted rid of her, and he did not want the years of wrangling he had in getting an annulment from Katherine.

David Starkey's opinions are often controversial. His thoughts on Anne Boleyn are that 'it has been Anne's fate to be vilified rather than idealised', and her three years of marriage combined with her seven-year courtship with Henry VIII 'was the most momentous decade of English history since the Norman Conquest'.[42] Anne has certainly had her share of vilification over the centuries since her death, though in the last century and more this has started to shift. Anne is seen through a much more sympathetic lens in the twentieth and twenty-first centuries, considered by most to be innocent of the charges against her. In a similar vein to Starkey about the vilification and darkness surrounding Anne Boleyn, Josephine Wilkinson says that 'Anne's reach was as long as the shadows that fell upon the last days of her life' and men 'became entrapped in the darkness that engulfed her'.[43] It is important to remember that it was not just Anne who lost her life in May 1536, but five men, including her brother, as well. The evidence suggests that they went to their death innocent of the charges of which they were accused. It is their innocence which makes their ultimate fate harder to accept.

David Loades, in his book on the six wives, describes Anne Boleyn as 'a complication [Henry] could have done without' but that she 'held him to his purpose because she was a part of it, but she was not the whole of it'. She 'represented freedom ... from a whole framework of political thought'.[44] Anne appears to have made Henry's life more difficult, because of her role in the Great Matter, but that was more Henry's own doing; Anne provided the catalyst as someone that he wanted to bed and mother his sons. Anne gave Henry a reason to break with the Church of Rome and set himself up as head of the English Church, allowing him more freedom to act in spiritual and temporal matters. In his study of the Boleyn family, Loades describes Anne as 'unusually sophisticated, thanks to her training in France, but not distinguished in any other way', and says that it was Henry's desire to marry Anne which elevated her and her family into 'the status of a political party'.[45] Loades downplays the rise of the Boleyns up to this point, and that Anne's father, Thomas Boleyn, was already established as a courtier and talented diplomat. He also downplays Anne's allure and the effect of her education in the Low Countries and France to make her stand out. In that way, she was very distinguished, intelligent, astute, and different to the other English ladies.

Retha Warnicke, whose work popularised the idea that Anne gave birth to a deformed foetus, explains that when Anne's life was viewed within the framework of societal and cultural norms of the sixteenth century, 'the modern conception of her as a femme fatale must be discarded'.[46] Both she and Katherine of Aragon had more in common than is usually accepted, as both 'became the involuntary victims of the king's drive and ambition for his own lineage, and of the rules of their Church and society that drastically limited divorces'.[47] It is impossible to discuss Anne Boleyn without Henry VIII as he was so central to both her rise and fall, and her ultimate execution. She was only able to rise to the heights she did because Henry VIII was so desperate to have a son. Without this drive from the king himself, and Katherine of Aragon having only a daughter, Anne could not have become queen.

Lacey Baldwin Smith wrote that 'Anne is an exceptional case, for her life was a double helix intertwining extraordinary human drama with profound historical crisis'.[48] With these famous historical figures it is often easy to forget that they were real people, because they are so far in the past. But Anne Boleyn's story is devastating. She is not just someone to look up to and admire, but even to feel sorry for and sympathise with. She was executed at her husband's hand, leaving her infant daughter motherless. That is a very sad human story, combined with the political and religious upheaval that occurred because Henry VIII wanted to marry Anne in the first place. Smith claims that, in relation to Anne Boleyn, 'the historian does out of desperation what the fiction writer does by choice: indulge in make-believe'.[49] Because so many of the sources about Anne are missing, incomplete, or presumed destroyed after her death, writers since her death have indulged in speculation, sometimes presenting assumptions and interpretation as truth, rather than as one possible viewpoint of several. It is a trap to be wary of for any historian as the aim of history is to tell the facts and offer some possible interpretations where that evidence is sketchy but being clear where it is fact and where it is opinion. Nowhere is that more obvious than with Anne Boleyn, where the six-finger myth and deformed foetus is now so often seen as fact.

Marie Louise Bruce wrote that Anne Boleyn 'had gambled and won gloriously, and finally she had lost. She had paid the price she had known she might have to pay since the day she gave her adoring royal lover the symbolic jewel of a lady in a storm-tossed ship … Anne had been surrounded by such impossible hazards that she had only the slenderest chance of survival. Now she had met the doom she had been lucky to avoid for so long'.[50] Anne's fate was not inevitable. Had she given the king a son, it is probable that no one would have been able to unseat her. Her fate in the end was so unexpected – never had an anointed queen of England been executed before. She could never have guessed or foreseen that her fate would be beheading at the end of a sword. She had won and then lost, but we only see her fate now with the value of hindsight. At the time, no one could have guessed.

Carolly Erickson, in her biography of Anne Boleyn, claims that Anne's end made her 'a persecuted heroine, bright with promise and goodness as a young woman, beautiful and elegant. True, she was not guiltless, but the suffering the king caused her and the punishment he meted out to her redeemed her in the end and allowed her nobility of spirit to reveal itself'.[51] The Victorians would run with this idea of Anne as a persecuted, almost tragic, heroine. She caused problems for Henry VIII, Katherine of Aragon and Princess Mary, allegedly forcing the separation of the three of them, although Henry had a huge hand in that himself. Anne Boleyn was not popular with the people in the way that Katherine of Aragon was, and that did her great harm. The people were initially ready to believe that Anne was guilty as charged, but even they began to question, as the Imperial ambassador did, in the veracity and truth of the charges. She is a divisive figure, but in reality, neither entirely good nor entirely bad. Like the majority of humanity, she had both light and dark inside her.

Elizabeth Norton has combined many of the primary sources about Anne into a single book but has also written a biography of her. She describes Anne Boleyn as 'the most vibrant and exceptional woman of her generation and she had the personality and drive to change history … she was no saint, but neither was she a villain. Anne was simply very human'.[52] That often seems to be forgotten. Anne was a catalyst for a Reformation, the second of six wives to Henry VIII, and the mother of Elizabeth I, but she was also a woman who made mistakes and paid the ultimate price for them. Anne 'was no victim and she fought until the end for her political survival. Although ultimately, she lost the battle, Anne was the winner in the end' as Anne is the one of the six wives who is most remembered and 'left a truly lasting legacy'.[53] Anne triumphed over Henry in that, through her daughter, she proved that a woman could be a successful ruler and that Henry's determination to have a son was effectively all for nothing.

Joanna Denny opens her biography of Anne Boleyn with the lines 'no English queen has made more impact on the history of the nation than Anne Boleyn, and few have been so persistently maligned. In her lifetime she was traduced, shamed and butchered. Since her death she has been pursued beyond the grave, subjected to accusations and vilification'.[54] Vilification seems to be a common theme in modern descriptions and summaries of Anne Boleyn. Her character was assassinated after her execution, and her name effectively remained unspoken for over twenty years until the reign of her daughter, Elizabeth. Even in her lifetime she was not popular with the people once it became clear that Henry VIII intended her to replace the popular Katherine of Aragon. And even during Elizabeth's reign Anne was further vilified with the publication of Nicholas Sander's work which has been exaggerated right up to today, as a heretic and witch.

Alison Weir in her *The Six Wives of Henry VIII* describes Anne Boleyn as 'an ambitious adventuress with a penchant for vengeance'.[55] Anne was certainly ambitious, and quite possibly an adventuress, but a penchant for vengeance is far from proven. In a later book about Anne Boleyn called *The Lady in the Tower: The Fall of Anne Boleyn*, Weir writes that the pressure and stress of marriage to Henry VIII made her 'haughty, overbearing, shrewish, and volatile, qualities that were then frowned upon in wives'.[56] But also that Anne 'might have died in ignominy, but she left, all unwittingly, a rich heritage in her infant daughter'.[57] The idea that Anne's greatest achievement was her daughter, Elizabeth, seems to be widespread, but people generally do not acknowledge the relationship between Anne and Elizabeth, assuming that because Elizabeth was not yet 3 years old when her mother died, she did not really have a relationship or memories of her mother, and did not work to rehabilitate her reputation.

Tracy Borman goes into the relationship between Anne and Elizabeth, and the important link between them – that both were unusual women who broke the mould and had long-lasting legacies. She writes that:

> Both women broke the mould that Tudor society had created for queens – and, indeed, for women in general. Elizabeth became a ruler of whom Anne would have been inordinately proud – indeed, the sort of queen she herself might have become if her life had not been cut so brutally short. There is a delicious irony in the fact that the child who had been the bitterest disappointment to Henry VIII would go on to become by far the longest-reigning and most successful of his heirs. Her legacy would reverberate down the centuries and can still be felt today. And it was a legacy that derived primarily from her mother.'[58]

Anne Boleyn did leave behind an incredible legacy in her daughter, Elizabeth. And their relationship is often underestimated. This was discussed further in chapter three. But both women broke the mould of women and queens in the sixteenth century. Elizabeth I did not marry and ruled alone. Anne Boleyn was never meant to be queen and was not afraid to assert her opinions.

Amy Licence comments that 'Anne was vulnerable because she broached expectations of class and gender, stirring up deeply felt convictions about how women should relate to men, especially to their husbands', and that Anne's death 'was the result of Henry's choice, his caprice', and that she died as a result of Henry's psychology.[59] Anne and Henry will always be tied together. *SIX The Musical* brings the women into their own lives, and away from their ties to Henry VIII, but their fates were always intertwined with his decisions and wants. Anne had a great level of self-fashioning, and it is this which makes her so captivating. Licence opens her work on Anne Boleyn by saying that 'she had something like a genius for self-creation, the ultimate renaissance self-made woman who flew too close to the sun. And at the heliocentric Tudor court, that sun was the volatile, mercurial Henry VIII'.[60] Anne was an independently minded woman, but still subject to a man. She was limited by the expectations of the sixteenth century.

Estelle Paranque, whose latest work focuses on France's involvement in Anne Boleyn's life and eventual fate, wrote that 'Anne's tragic end – and France's involvement in her story – explains why her memory has lived on there as well as in England, and, I believe, will continue to live on, forever'.[61] Anne's story had wider implications than just in England. She had spent her formative years in France and continued throughout her queenship to try and gain their support, unsuccessfully. Had Anne gained the support of France, she could have had a powerful ally behind her, as Katherine of Aragon had with the Emperor Charles V. It may have made it harder for Henry VIII to unseat Anne, and certainly to have her executed. Perhaps she would have lived in exile instead.

But she is certainly remembered, and farther afield than the country where her body was buried and still lies.

There are two recent works on the history of the Boleyn family more generally, rather than the focus on Anne Boleyn. Clare Martin, in her *Heirs of Ambition*, wrote that 'despite the passage of centuries, Anne's spirit, her triumph, and her brutal death have lost none of their power to capture hearts and minds'.[62] It is because the trajectory of Anne Boleyn's life was so unusual, and her fall so sudden, unexpected and controversial, that historians continue to be fascinated by her. Owen Emmerson and Claire Ridgway, in *The Boleyns of Hever Castle*, argue that 'Anne had been [Thomas's] joy and had brought greater wealth and power to the Boleyn family than Thomas could possibly have aspired to. Anne's rise had been unthinkable and her end unspeakable'.[63] The history of the Boleyns seems to end with Elizabeth I, despite Thomas Boleyn having siblings. Although Anne Boleyn had a momentous rise and was the mother of a queen, her end effectively removed the Boleyns from court.

Eric Ives, who wrote what is still one of the best works on Anne Boleyn, *The Life and Death of Anne Boleyn*, wrote that 'Anne Boleyn was so much more important than the circumstances of her execution' and that 'awareness of that importance is steadily increasing over the years'.[64] In the years since Ives wrote those words, Anne has certainly become more of a visual figure, on screen and in novels, and countless more biographies and discoveries are being made about her life. It is impossible for us to really know Anne Boleyn, she lived 500 years ago, but Ives believes that:

> ... she does come through as more than two-dimensional, more than a silhouette. She was the most influential and important queen consort this country has ever had. Indeed, Anne deserves to be a feminist icon, a woman in a society which was, above all else, male dominated, who broke through the glass ceiling by sheer character and initiative.[65]

It is important to remember when writing about historical figures from any age, that they were real people, they are not characters in the pages of a novel. All, or parts, of them may feel shadowy to us because it is difficult to understand the society in which they lived, and the expectations and rules they had to live by. But Ives's work and his insightful views into the sources he discusses, although not everyone agrees with his conclusions, have shaped perceptions of Anne in the modern day.

* * *

John Guy and Julia Fox wrote that, 'Anne was an extraordinarily modern woman, a supremely talented, captivating spirit comfortable in her own skin and confident in her destiny'.[66] Referring to Anne Boleyn as a 'modern woman' can be problematic. Putting the expectations of the twenty-first century onto a sixteenth century woman is taking her actions and the consequences of those actions out of context. She was certainly talented, comfortable in her own skin, and confident, but that does not mean she is necessarily modern. Women through history have had these characteristics, but where they come to the forefront of the historical record is when they are in power, or in trouble, and Anne Boleyn was both in the end. She was not a modern woman but a sixteenth century one. It was her unusual education and time spent abroad which made her stand out and brought her to the attention of a selfish and pampered king. It was her inability to fit into the mould that the king fashioned for her on their marriage which divided the couple. He loved her fiery temper and their passionate reconciliations when she was his mistress, but he wanted a more settled wife. Anne's failure to produce a son, along with her temperament and natural ability to be at the centre of vibrant court circles, made the king suspicious of her. In the end, it was this which brought her down. Perhaps she was just too unique in the sixteenth century to be a good fit for Henry VIII.

Epilogue

This book has been so much fun to write, bringing together over a decade of my own research since my master's degree. There are so many people who seem to love, respect and admire Anne Boleyn, that it also feels like a responsibility to do her justice. In a lot of ways, it is easy to identify with Eric Ives's claim that 'once [Anne] interests you, fascination grows'.[1] There is so much to her life: her years in the Low Countries and France for which evidence is scarce, the tantalising glimpse in Thomas Wyatt's poetry of a young, beautiful and desirable woman, the untrammelled devotion of Henry VIII, her ambiguous religious views, and her tragic end. The debates surrounding her role in the Break with Rome and the development of Protestantism in England, and the circumstances of her death particularly, mean that Anne Boleyn will always be fascinating to study. In the words of Eric Ives:

> She had been a remarkable woman. She would remain a remarkable woman even in a century which produced many of great note. There were few others who rose from such beginnings to a crown, and none contributed to a revolution as far-reaching as the English Reformation.[2]

Anne Boleyn changed the face of English history because of her involvement with Henry VIII and she is primarily known today because of that connection. Would she have been so well known today without the love of a king? Probably not. But she was fascinating in her own right. Anne had the gumption and confidence to say no when Henry VIII wanted to make her his mistress and to hold out instead for a crown. She had the bravery to declare her innocence and face an executioner. She was spirited and outspoken in a time when that was not considered proper for a woman. Queen Victoria's fascination was with Anne, and not Henry, and she wanted Anne's grave marked, which it was not until the nineteenth century. She did not build the grand tomb for Henry VIII that he had envisioned for himself, which was never built. She chose to mark Anne's resting place. In many ways, there has been more interest in Anne Boleyn than there has in Henry VIII, and she is well and truly out of his shadow today.

Having some letters said to have been written by Anne's own hand, and letters to her from Henry VIII, as well as poetry supposedly written about her, means that we get a glimpse into Anne's own mind and actions. She is such a fascinating figure precisely because things are debated. Did she or did she not write them? Is this poem about her, or not? Fictional portrayals on screen, both big and small, the page, and the stage mean that Anne Boleyn and Tudor history is being brought to a new audience. It is encouraging the historians of the future to look further into this fascinating queen. Both documentaries and drama can be valuable, to introduce society as a whole to new people and subjects that they might not have much knowledge of. Novels then provide a way of immersing ourselves completely in the past, imagining how people might have acted and spoken, with customs often completely at odds with those we recognise and understand today. The common phrase, 'the past is a foreign country', is apt here, as too often modern values and expectations are applied to figures from the past, including Anne Boleyn. However, it is important to look at Anne's actions and experiences in the context of the time in which she lived. The sixteenth century values and customs are not comparable with the twenty-first century, particularly expectations of women. These later fictional portrayals give us leave to fill in the gaps, but we must always remember to go back to the original sources to find the truth, and not take fiction as fact. The contemporary sources are often more interesting than the fictional portrayals that people are likely more familiar with.

Toby Marlow and Lucy Moss in *SIX The Musical* have been 'self-consciously rewriting history to make it amenable to twenty-first century feminism' as Anne Boleyn's story is always filtered through a modern lens.[3] It is difficult to write about a person who lived 500 years ago without using the benefit of hindsight. Anne Boleyn's history will always be coloured, however unconsciously, by the person writing about her. It is unavoidable. When considering her story, we know how it ends, and that often colours how we think of events. That is why it is so important to examine the cultural history of Anne's story, and how new developments are coming to light even now, and different opinions are being formed. It has been argued that 'Anne has never achieved full-blown cult status; she attracts intense curiosity but only intermittent admiration'.[4] That opinion comes from a 2007 article, but in the time since it seems like Anne Boleyn has gained even more interest in her, due in large part to television shows like *The Tudors* with a brilliant performance by Natalie Dormer as Anne and, more recently, she has been brought to a new audience in *SIX The Musical*. On social media Anne Boleyn seems to be the most talked about of the six wives, with people debating which is their favourite screen interpretation, or asking for recommendations on the best books, either fiction or non-fiction. The usual questions are asked and debated – did she really have a sixth finger, and did she really sleep with her brother? Some debates are certainly more polite than others, and people can be very passionate and unmoveable on their views. But Anne does garner great admiration, largely for her bravery and fortitude at the end.

John Guy and Julia Fox write that Anne was, 'a voice determined to be heard in the cacophony of sound in Henry's court, she read her own books, framed her own opinions and was ready to defend them against all comers … her major character flaw was succumbing to the dizzying effects of power and hubris'.[5] Anne was a woman who stood out at the English court, enhanced by her years spent abroad at the courts of Margaret of Austria and Queen Claude of France which made her seem exotic on her return to England. To me, Anne Boleyn's main 'flaw', if you can call it that, was in being too outspoken, and failing to make the expected shift from mistress to wife. Usually accomplished at reading people and situations, it seems that she believed she could mould and continue to influence the king in the same way as she had before her marriage. That was her crucial and critical mistake.

By examining cultural perceptions through 500 years of history, from the letters Henry VIII wrote to her in the throes of first love, through letters and accounts of her fall and execution, to William Shakespeare and Francis Bacon. Then through the Victorian romanticism of Anne as a tragic heroine, and into the twentieth century where Anne gained a new lease of life, we can see that the general perception is that Anne Boleyn went to her death as an innocent woman, with her husband having signed the death warrant. Whether Henry VIII truly believed Anne guilty of the crimes of which she was accused and condemned is still up for debate. But the many films, television shows and novels have brought Anne's story to new audiences. Attention paid to Anne and her story shows no sign of dimming. This 'very human' woman, 'she was no saint, but neither was she a villain' is divisive.[6] There is so much evidence missing that there is freedom for people to come up with their own theories to fill in the gaps. New discoveries and innovations, like those by Kate McCaffrey with Anne's Book of Hours, and Lucy Churchill's reconstruction of the 1534 portrait medal, are being made. However, we will never be able to fully know or understand Anne Boleyn and her life because we are 500 years removed from it. But that is where the excitement and interest lies. If we knew everything then there would be nothing left to discover.

Dr Owen Emmerson and Claire Ridgway sum up our fascination with Anne Boleyn in their book *The Boleyns of Hever Castle*, by saying that, 'Anne's rise had been unthinkable and her end unspeakable'.[7] It is her meteoric rise and dramatic and devastating fall that keeps historians coming back to Anne. She is fascinating, with much-debated religious beliefs, an uncertain birth date meaning we cannot age her at various points of her life, and with so much evidence missing, including those tantalising letters for which we only have Henry's part of the conversation. New theories and debates will keep being put forward because there is so much that we do not know. And cultural perceptions will also keep coming because there are so many ways that Anne's life can be interpreted. Anne Boleyn was a fascinating, spirited, and brave woman, who made mistakes as we all do. It is only human, after all. But she has left us with a rich history to explore, and tantalising glimpses of the woman she was.

Remember me when you do pray, that hope doth lead from day to day.[8]

References

Introduction

1. Ives, Eric, *The Life and Death of Anne Boleyn* (2005) p.xv.
2. Emmerson, Owen and Ridgway, Claire, *The Boleyns of Hever Castle* (2021) p.101.
3. Borman, Tracy, *Anne Boleyn and Elizabeth I: The Mother and Daughter Who Changed History* (2023).
4. Greenblatt, Stephen, *Renaissance Self-Fashioning: From More to Shakespeare* (1984) p.1.
5. Licence, Amy, *Anne Boleyn: Adultery, Heresy, Desire* (2017) p.7.
6. Greenblatt, Stephen, *Renaissance Self-Fashioning: From More to Shakespeare* (1984) p.2.
7. Ibid, p.7.
8. Foxe, John, *Acts and Monuments* (1838) p.135.
9. Grenville, John, 'The Historian as Film-Maker II' in Smith, Paul (ed.) *The Historian and Film* (2008) p.132.
10. Paget, Hugh, 'The Youth of Anne Boleyn', *Historical Research* (1981) p.166.
11. Parker, Matthew, *Correspondence of Matthew Parker, D.D.: Archbishop of Canterbury* (1853) p.400.
12. Ives, Eric, *The Life and Death of Anne Boleyn* (2005) p.19.
13. Licence, Amy, *Anne Boleyn: Adultery, Heresy, Desire* (2017) p.60.
14. Ives, Eric, *The Life and Death of Anne Boleyn* (2005) p.37.
15. Guy, John and Fox, Julia, *Hunting the Falcon: Henry VIII, Anne Boleyn and the Marriage That Shook Europe* (2023) p.92.
16. Ibid, p.194–195.
17. 'Love Letter 12 from Henry VIII to Anne Boleyn' in Norton, Elizabeth, *Anne Boleyn: In Her Own Words and the Words of Those Who Knew Her* (2011) p.44.
18. Licence, Amy, *The Six Wives and Many Mistresses of Henry VIII* (2015) p.217.
19. Scarisbrick, J.J., *Henry VIII* (1988) p.247.
20. Strype, John, *Ecclesiastical Memorials* (1721) p.113.
21. Ibid, p.113.
22. Borman, Tracy, *Thomas Cromwell: The Untold Story of Henry VIII's Most Faithful Servant* (2014) p.150.
23. Gristwood, Sarah, *Game of Queens: The Women Who Made Sixteenth Century Europe* (2016) p.169.
24. Somerset, Anne, *Elizabeth I* (1997) p.7; Loades, David, *Henry VIII* (2011) p.237.
25. Grueninger, Natalie, *The Final Year of Anne Boleyn* (2022) p.173.
26. Ibid, p.133.
27. Licence, Amy, *Anne Boleyn: Adultery, Heresy, Desire* (2017) p.421.
28. Scarisbrick, J.J., *Henry VIII* (1988) p.350.
29. Ives, Eric, *The Life and Death of Anne Boleyn* (2005) p.xv.
30. Guy, John and Fox, Julia, *Hunting the Falcon: Henry VIII, Anne Boleyn and the Marriage That Shook Europe* (2023) p.xxix.
31. Martin, Claire, *Heirs of Ambition: The Making of the Boleyns* (2023) p.207.

Chapter 1: Portraiture and Image

1. Ives, Eric, *The Life and Death of Anne Boleyn* (2005) p.43.
2. Bordo, Susan, *The Creation of Anne Boleyn: In Search of the Tudors' Most Notorious Queen* (2014) p.30.
3. Loades, David, *The Tudor Queens of England* (2009) p.115.
4. Borman, Tracy, *Anne Boleyn and Elizabeth I: The Mother and Daughter Who Changed History* (2023) p.209.
5. Sander, Nicholas, *Rise and Growth of the Anglican Schism* (1877) p.25.
6. Norton, Elizabeth, *Anne Boleyn: Henry VIII's Obsession* (2009) p.14.
7. Wilkinson, Josephine, *Anne Boleyn: The Young Queen To Be* (2011) p.53.
8. Greenblatt, Stephen, *Renaissance Self-Fashioning: From More to Shakespeare* (1984) p.68.
9. Emmerson, Owen, McCaffrey, Kate and Palmer, Alison, *Catherine and Anne: Queens, Rivals, Mothers* (2023) p.11.
10. Greenblatt, Stephen, *Renaissance Self-Fashioning: From More to Shakespeare* (1984) p.1.
11. Bordo, Susan, *The Creation of Anne Boleyn: In Search of the Tudors' Most Notorious Queen* (2014) p.30.
12. Wilkinson, Josephine, *Anne Boleyn: The Young Queen to Be* (2011) pp.52–53.
13. Ives, Eric, *The Life and Death of Anne Boleyn* (2005) p.43.
14. Bernard, G.W., *Anne Boleyn: Fatal Attractions* (2011) p.20.
15. National Portrait Gallery, NPG 668, https://www.npg.org.uk/collections/search/portrait/mw00142/Anne-Boleyn.
16. Guy, John and Fox, Julia, *Hunting the Falcon: Henry VIII, Anne Boleyn and the Marriage That Shook Europe* (2023) p.281.
17. Bordo, Susan, *The Creation of Anne Boleyn: In Search of the Tudors' Most Notorious Queen* (2014) p.30.
18. Weir, Alison, *The Six Wives of Henry VIII* (1997) p.152.
19. Bernard, G.W., *Anne Boleyn: Fatal Attractions* (2011) p.199.
20. Ibid.
21. Weir, Alison, *The Six Wives of Henry VIII* (1997) p.152.
22. 'Accounts for Works at Hampton Court', *Records of the Exchequer and its related bodies*, The National Archives, E36/239. Thank you to Dr Owen Emmerson for drawing my attention to this.
23. 'Accounts for Works at Hampton Court', *Records of the Exchequer and its related bodies*, The National Archives, E36/244. Thank you to Dr Owen Emmerson for drawing my attention to this.
24. Emmerson, Owen and Ridgway, Claire, *The Boleyns of Hever Castle* (2021) p.119.
25. Weir, Alison, *The Six Wives of Henry VIII* (1997) p.152.
26. Bordo, Susan, *The Creation of Anne Boleyn: In Search of the Tudors' Most Notorious Queen* (2014) p.32.
27. Ives, Eric, *The Life and Death of Anne Boleyn* (2005) p.43.
28. Bernard, G.W., *Anne Boleyn: Fatal Attractions* (2011) p.20.
29. Weir, Alison, *The Six Wives of Henry VIII* (1997) p.153.
30. British Museum, M.9010.
31. Ives, Eric, *The Life and Death of Anne Boleyn* (2005) p.41.
32. Ibid.
33. Churchill, Lucy, 'Anne Boleyn: My reconstruction of The Moost Happi portrait medal' (n.d.). https://www.lucychurchill.com/anne-boleyn-moost-happi-medal-reconstruction/.

34. Churchill, Lucy, 'Anne Boleyn's Moost Happi Portrait Medal … Revisited' (2020). https://lucychurchill.wordpress.com/2020/11/21/anne-boleyns-moost-happi-portrait-medal-revisited/.
35. Ibid.
36. Churchill, Lucy, 'The 'Moost Happi' portrait of Anne Boleyn: A reconstruction by Lucy Churchill' (2012). https://lucychurchill.wordpress.com/2012/05/14/the-moost-happi-portrait-of-anne-boleyn-a-rec/.
37. Ibid.
38. Denny, Joanna, *Anne Boleyn: A New Life of England's Tragic Queen* (2004) p.20.
39. Borman, Tracy, *Anne Boleyn and Elizabeth I: The Mother and Daughter Who Changed History* (2023) p.1.
40. Ibid.
41. Bernard, G.W., *Anne Boleyn: Fatal Attractions* (2011) p.198.
42. Guy, John and Fox, Julia, *Hunting the Falcon: Henry VIII, Anne Boleyn and the Marriage That Shook Europe* (2023) p.408.
43. Bordo, Susan, *The Creation of Anne Boleyn: In Search of the Tudors' Most Notorious Queen* (2014) p.30.
44. Denny, Joanna, *Anne Boleyn: A New Life of England's Tragic Queen* (2004) p.20.
45. Borman, Tracy, *Anne Boleyn and Elizabeth I: The Mother and Daughter Who Changed History* (2023) p.1.
46. Ives, Eric, *The Life and Death of Anne Boleyn* (2005) p.43.
47. Denny, Joanna, *Anne Boleyn: A New Life of England's Tragic Queen* (2004) p.18.
48. Heard, Kate, *Holbein at the Tudor Court* (2023) p.64.
49. Rowlands, John and Starkey, David, 'An Old Tradition Reasserted: Holbein's Portrait of Queen Anne Boleyn', *The Burlington Magazine* (1983) p.91.
50. Emmerson, Owen and Ridgway, Claire, *The Boleyns of Hever Castle* (2021) p.119.
51. Royal Collection Trust, RCIN 600878.
52. Royal Collection Trust, RCIN 912189.
53. Guy, John and Fox, Julia, *Hunting the Falcon: Henry VIII, Anne Boleyn and the Marriage That Shook Europe* (2023) p.281.
54. Weir, Alison, *The Six Wives of Henry VIII* (1997) p.153.
55. Royal Collection Trust, RCIN 912189.
56. Ives, Eric, *The Life and Death of Anne Boleyn* (2005) p.41.
57. Heard, Kate, *Holbein at the Tudor Court* (2023) p.63.
58. Ibid, p.64.
59. Ibid.
60. Guy, John and Fox, Julia, *Hunting the Falcon: Henry VIII, Anne Boleyn and the Marriage That Shook Europe* (2023) p.282.
61. Bernard, G.W., *Anne Boleyn: Fatal Attractions* (2011) p.197.
62. Weir, Alison, *The Six Wives of Henry VIII* (1997) p.153.
63. Bernard, G.W., *Anne Boleyn: Fatal Attractions* (2011) p.197.
64. Rowlands, John & Starkey, David, 'An Old Tradition Reasserted: Holbein's Portrait of Queen Anne Boleyn', *The Burlington Magazine* (1983) p.91.
65. Ives, Eric, *The Life and Death of Anne Boleyn* (2005) p.43.
66. Denny, Joanna, *Anne Boleyn: A New Life of England's Tragic Queen* (2004) p.21.
67. Rowlands, John & Starkey, David, 'An Old Tradition Reasserted: Holbein's Portrait of Queen Anne Boleyn', *The Burlington Magazine* (1983) p.91.

68. 'Henry VIII: Privy Purse Expenses', *Letters and Papers, Foreign and Domestic, Henry VIII,* Volume 5, 1531–1532, No.f113 (1880).
69. Denny, Joanna, *Anne Boleyn: A New Life of England's Tragic Queen* (2004), p.22.
70. Fraser, Antonia, *The Six Wives of Henry VIII* (2002) p.151.
71. Ibid.
72. Denny, Joanna, *Anne Boleyn: A New Life of England's Tragic Queen* (2004) p.22.
73. Bernard, G.W., *Anne Boleyn: Fatal Attractions* (2011) p.196.
74. Weir, Alison, *The Six Wives of Henry VIII* (1997) p.153.
75. Ives, Eric, *The Life and Death of Anne Boleyn* (2005) p.43.

Chapter 2: Anne as Mistress

1. Wyatt, Thomas, 'Whoso List to Hunt', in Norton, Elizabeth, *Anne Boleyn: In Her Own Words and the Words of Those Who Knew Her* (2011) p.34.
2. Cavendish, George, *The Life of Cardinal Wolsey* (1890) p.54.
3. 'Letter from Anne Boleyn to Thomas Boleyn 1513' in Norton, Elizabeth, *Anne Boleyn: In Her Own Words and the Words of Those Who Knew Her* (2011) p.25.
4. Emmerson, Owen and McCaffrey, Kate, *Becoming Anne: Connections, Culture, Court* (2022) p.62.
5. 'Letter from Anne Boleyn to Thomas Boleyn 1513' in Norton, Elizabeth, *Anne Boleyn: In Her Own Words and the Words of Those Who Knew Her* (2011) p.25.
6. Emmerson, Owen & McCaffrey, Kate, *Becoming Anne: Connections, Culture, Court* (2022) p.34.
7. Norton, Elizabeth, *Anne Boleyn: Henry VIII's Obsession* (2009) p.18.
8. Cavendish, George, *The Life of Cardinal Wolsey* (1890) p.36.
9. 'Letter from Northumberland to Thomas Cromwell on 13 May 1536', *Letters and Papers, Foreign and Domestic, Henry VIII,* Volume 10, January–June 1536, No.864 (1887).
10. Cavendish, George, *The Life of Cardinal Wolsey* (1890) p.48.
11. Ibid.
12. Ibid.
13. Ibid.
14. Ibid, p.51.
15. Ives, Eric, *The Life and Death of Anne Boleyn* (2005) pp.59–60
16. Ibid, p.65.
17. Cavendish, George, *The Life of Cardinal Wolsey* (1890) p.54.
18. Ibid, p.55.
19. Ibid, p.56.
20. Ibid, p.135–136.
21. Wilkinson, Josephine, *Anne Boleyn: The Young Queen to Be* (2011) p.8.
22. Starkey, David, *Six Wives: The Queens of Henry VIII* (2004) p.572.
23. *The Tudors* [DVD]. Season 1, Episode 10 (2007–2010).
24. Wyatt, Thomas, 'Whoso List to Hunt' in Norton, Elizabeth, *Anne Boleyn: In Her Own Words and the Words of Those Who Knew Her* (2011) p.34.
25. Ibid.
26. Ibid.
27. Ibid.
28. Ibid.
29. Wyatt, Thomas, 'Sometime I Fled the Fire' in Norton, Elizabeth, *Anne Boleyn: In Her Own Words and the Words of Those Who Knew Her* (2011) p.35.

30. Ibid.
31. Walker, Greg, *Writing under Tyranny: English Literature and the Henrician Reformation* (2005) p.288.
32. Wyatt, Thomas, 'Whoso List to Hunt' in Norton, Elizabeth, *Anne Boleyn: In Her Own Words and the Words of Those Who Knew Her* (2011) p.34.
33. Wyatt, Thomas, 'Sometime I Fled the Fire' in Norton, Elizabeth, *Anne Boleyn: In Her Own Words and the Words of Those Who Knew Her* (2011) p.35.
34. Ibid.
35. Wyatt, Thomas, 'If Waker care; if sudden pale colour' in Norton, Elizabeth, *Anne Boleyn: In Her Own Words and the Words of Those Who Knew Her* (2011) p.34.
36. Ibid.
37. Ibid.
38. Norton, Elizabeth, *Anne Boleyn: Henry VIII's Obsession* (2009) p.41.
39. Loades, David, *The Boleyns: The Rise and Fall of a Tudor Family* (2011) p.74.
40. Wilkinson, Josephine, *Anne Boleyn: The Young Queen to Be* (2011) p.81.
41. Hume, Martin, *The Chronicle of King Henry VIII of England* (1889) pp.68–69.
42. Southall, Raymond, 'Love, Fortune and my Mind: The Stoicism of Wyatt', *Essays in Criticism* (1989) p.27.
43. Warnicke, Retha, 'The Eternal Triangle and Court Politics: Henry VIII, Anne Boleyn and Sir Thomas Wyatt', *Albion* (1986) p.579.
44. Norton, Elizabeth, *Anne Boleyn: In Her Own Words and the Words of Those Who Knew Her* (2011) p.39.
45. Vatican Archives, ref. Vat.lat.3731.pt.A.
46. Starkey, David, *Six Wives: The Queens of Henry VIII* (2004) p.278.
47. Warnicke, Retha, *The Rise and Fall of Anne Boleyn* (2008) p.78.
48. Starkey, David, *Six Wives: The Queens of Henry VIII* (2004) p.273.
49. Lindsey, Karen, *Divorced, Beheaded, Survived: A Feminist Reinterpretation of the Wives of Henry VIII* (1995) p.57.
50. 'Love Letter 4 from Henry VIII to Anne Boleyn' in Norton, Elizabeth, *Anne Boleyn: In Her Own Words and the Words of Those Who Knew Her* (2011) p.42.
51. Denny, Joanna, *Anne Boleyn: A New Life of England's Tragic Queen* (2004) p.57.
52. Loades, David, *The Boleyns: The Rise and Fall of a Tudor Family* (2011) p.79.
53. Ives, Eric, *The Life and Death of Anne Boleyn* (2005) p.89.
54. Bernard, G.W., *Anne Boleyn: Fatal Attractions* (2011) p.25.
55. Norton, Elizabeth, *Anne Boleyn: In Her Own Words and the Words of Those Who Knew Her* (2011) p.39.
56. 'Letter from Anne Boleyn to Henry VIII' in Norton, Elizabeth, *Anne Boleyn: In Her Own Words and the Words of Those Who Knew Her* (2011) pp.40–41.
57. Norton, Elizabeth, *Anne Boleyn: In Her Own Words and the Words of Those Who Knew Her* (2011) p.39 and 'Love Letter 1 from Henry VIII to Anne Boleyn' from the same, p. 41.
58. 'Love Letter 10 from Henry VIII to Anne Boleyn' in Norton, Elizabeth, *Anne Boleyn: In Her Own Words and the Words of Those Who Knew Her* (2011) p.44.
59. 'Love Letter 2 from Henry VIII to Anne Boleyn' in Norton, Elizabeth, *Anne Boleyn: In Her Own Words and the Words of Those Who Knew Her* (2011) p.41.
60. Lerer, Seth, *Courtly Letters in the Age of Henry VIII: Literary Culture and the Arts of Deceit* (1997) p.105
61. Denny, Joanna, *Anne Boleyn: A New Life of England's Tragic Queen* (2004) p.91.

62. 'Love Letter 5 from Henry VIII to Anne Boleyn' in Norton, Elizabeth, *Anne Boleyn: In Her Own Words and the Words of Those Who Knew Her* (2011) p.42.
63. Ibid.
64. Weir, Alison, *The Lady in the Tower: The Fall of Anne Boleyn* (2009) p.24.
65. Chaucer, Geoffrey, edited by Nicholas, Harris, *Chaucer's Romaunt of the Rose, Troilus and Creseide, and the Minor Poems* (1846) p.131.
66. Erickson, Carolly, *Mistress Anne* (1984) p.108.
67. 'Love Letter 16 from Henry VIII to Anne Boleyn' in Norton, Elizabeth, *Anne Boleyn: In Her Own Words and the Words of Those Who Knew Her* (2011) p.45.
68. Lerer, Seth, *Courtly Letters in the Age of Henry VIII: Literary Culture and the Arts of Deceit* (1997) p.101.
69. 'Love Letter 3 from Henry VIII to Anne Boleyn' in Norton, Elizabeth, *Anne Boleyn: In Her Own Words and the Words of Those Who Knew Her* (2011) p.41.
70. 'Love Letter 12 from Henry VIII to Anne Boleyn' in Norton, Elizabeth, *Anne Boleyn: In Her Own Words and the Words of Those Who Knew Her* (2011) p.44.
71. Weir, Alison, *The Six Wives of Henry VIII* (1997) p.186.
72. 'Love Letter 3 from Henry VIII to Anne Boleyn' in Norton, Elizabeth, *Anne Boleyn: In Her Own Words and the Words of Those Who Knew Her* (2011) p.41.
73. Ives, Eric, *The Life and Death of Anne Boleyn* (2005) p.100.
74. Smith, Lacey Baldwin, *Anne Boleyn: The Queen of Controversy* (2013) p.76.

Chapter 3: Anne as Queen and Mother

1. 'Nicholas Udall's verse in the coronation procession of Anne Boleyn' in Norton, Elizabeth, *Anne Boleyn: In Her Own Words and the Words of Those Who Knew Her* (2011) pp.136–137.
2. Borman, Tracy, *Anne Boleyn and Elizabeth I: The Mother and Daughter Who Changed History* (2023) p.3.
3. Guy, John and Fox, Julia, *Hunting the Falcon: Henry VIII, Anne Boleyn and the Marriage That Shook Europe* (2023) p.409.
4. Lloyd, Carol Ann, *The Tudors by Numbers: The Stories and Statistics Behind England's Most Infamous Royal Dynasty* (2023) p.107.
5. Ridley, Jasper, *A Brief History of the Tudor Age* (2002) p.36.
6. Denny, Joanna, *Anne Boleyn: A New Life of England's Tragic Queen* (2004) pp.194–195.
7. Anonymous, *The Noble Tryumphaunt Coronacyon of Quene Anne, Wyfe unto the Most Noble Kynge Henry VIII* (1885).
8. 'Letter from Eustace Chapuys to Emperor Charles V on 16 June 1533', *Calendar of State Papers, Spain,* Volume 14, 1531–1533, No.1081 (1882).
9. 'Nicholas Udall's verse in the coronation procession of Anne Boleyn' in Norton, Elizabeth, *Anne Boleyn: In Her Own Words and the Words of Those Who Knew Her* (2011) pp.136–137.
10. Ives, Eric, *The Life and Death of Anne Boleyn* (2005) p.221.
11. 'Nicholas Udall's verse in the coronation procession of Anne Boleyn' in Norton, Elizabeth, *Anne Boleyn: In Her Own Words and the Words of Those Who Knew Her* (2011) pp.136–137.
12. 'Letter from Eustace Chapuys to Emperor Charles V on 16 June 1533', *Calendar of State Papers, Spain,* Volume 14, 1531–1533, No.1081 (1882).
13. 'Nicholas Udall's verse in the coronation procession of Anne Boleyn' in Norton, Elizabeth, *Anne Boleyn: In Her Own Words and the Words of Those Who Knew Her* (2011) pp.138–139.
14. Weir, Alison, *The Six Wives of Henry VIII* (1997) p.250.
15. 'Act of Succession 1534' in Gee, Henry and Hardy, John William (eds.), *Documents Illustrative of English Church History* (1914) pp.232–243.

16. Ibid.
17. Ibid.
18. Ibid.
19. Ibid.
20. Elton, G.R., 'The Law of Treason in the Early Reformation', *The Historical Journal* (1968) p.222.
21. 'Act of Succession 1534', in Gee, Henry and Hardy, John William (eds.), *Documents Illustrative of English Church History* (1914) pp.232–243.
22. 'Letterfrom William Kingston to Thomas Cromwell on 3 May 1536', Letters and Papers, Foreign and Domestic, Henry VIII, Volume 10, January–June 1536, No.793 (1888).
23. Grueninger, Natalie, *The Final Year of Anne Boleyn* (2022) p.156.
24. 'Act of Succession 1534', in Gee, Henry and Hardy, John William (eds.), *Documents Illustrative of English Church History* (1914) pp.232–243.
25. Ibid.
26. Ives, Eric, *The Life and Death of Anne Boleyn* (2005) p.170.
27. 'Act of Succession 1534', in Gee, Henry and Hardy, John William (eds.), *Documents Illustrative of English Church History* (1914) pp.232–243.
28. 'Treason Act 1534' in Gee, Henry and Hardy, John William (eds.), *Documents Illustrative of English Church History* (1914) pp.247–251.
29. Ibid.
30. Thornley, I.D., 'The Treason Legislation of Henry VIII (1531–1534)', *Transactions of the Royal Historical Society* (1917) p.88.
31. Ives, Eric, *The Life and Death of Anne Boleyn* (2005) p.201.
32. 'Treason Act 1534' in Gee, Henry and Hardy, John William (eds.), *Documents Illustrative of English Church History* (1914) pp.247–251.
33. Borman, Tracy, *Anne Boleyn and Elizabeth I: The Mother and Daughter Who Changed History* (2023) p.1.
34. Ibid, p.239.
35. Ibid, p.153.
36. 'Letter from Eustace Chapuys to Charles V on 15 September 1536', *Letters and Papers, Foreign and Domestic, Henry VIII, Volume 6, 1533*, No.1125 (1882).
37. Ives, Eric, *The Life and Death of Anne Boleyn* (2005) p.184.
38. Hall, Edward, *Hall's Chronicle* (1809) p.805.
39. Ibid, p.806.
40. Borman, Tracy, *Anne Boleyn and Elizabeth I: The Mother and Daughter Who Changed History* (2023) p.41.
41. 'Letter from William Kingston to Lord Lisle on 18 April 1534', *Letters and Papers, Foreign and Domestic, Henry VIII, Volume 7, 1534*, No.509 (1883).
42. Borman, Tracy, *Anne Boleyn and Elizabeth I: The Mother and Daughter Who Changed History* (2023) p.57.
43. Ibid.
44. Ibid, p.65.
45. Warnicke, Retha, *The Rise and Fall of Anne Boleyn* (2008) p.244.
46. Soberton, Sylvia Barbara, '"Large wen" or "swelling"? Exploring Myths and Misconceptions about Nicholas Sander's Description of Anne Boleyn and its Link to Witchcraft', *Royal Studies Journal* (2023) p.245.
47. Norton, Elizabeth, *Anne Boleyn: In her Own Words and the Words of Those Who Knew Her* (2011) p.15.

48. Russo, Stephanie, *The Afterlife of Anne Boleyn: Representations of Anne Boleyn in Fiction and on the Screen* (2020) p.42.
49. Bordo, Susan, *The Creation of Anne Boleyn: In Search of the Tudors' Most Notorious Queen* (2014) p.142
50. Russo, Stephanie, *The Afterlife of Anne Boleyn: Representations of Anne Boleyn in Fiction and on the Screen* (2020) p.42.
51. Wyatt, George, *Extracts from the Life of the Virtuous, Christian, and Renowned Queen Anne Boleigne* (1817) p.18.
52. Ibid.
53. Fraser, Antonia, *The Six Wives of Henry VIII* (2002) p.428.
54. Wyatt, George, *Extracts from the Life of the Virtuous, Christian, and Renowned Queen Anne Boleigne* (1817) p.18.
55. Ives, Eric, *The Life and Death of Anne Boleyn* (2005) p.40.
56. Wyatt, George, *Extracts from the Life of the Virtuous, Christian, and Renowned Queen Anne Boleigne* (1817), p.19.
57. Ibid.
58. Ives, Eric, *The Life and Death of Anne Boleyn* (2005) p.xv.

Chapter 4: Anne as Traitor

1. Wyatt, Thomas, 'Innocentia Veritas Viat Fides Circumdederunt me inimici mei' in Norton, Elizabeth, *Anne Boleyn: In Her Own Words and the Words of Those Who Knew Her* (2011) p.237.
2. Smith, Lacey Baldwin, 'English Treason Trials and Confessions in the Sixteenth Century', *Journal of the History of Ideas* (1954) p.472.
3. 'Trial Documents of Anne Boleyn and Lord Rochford', *Letters and Papers, Foreign and Domestic, Henry VIII*, Volume 10, January-June 1536, No.876 (1888).
4. Weir, Alison, *The Lady in the Tower: The Fall of Anne Boleyn* (2009) p.166.
5. 'Letter from Sir Henry Wyatt to Thomas Cromwell on 11 May 1536', *Letters and Papers, Foreign and Domestic, Henry VIII*, Volume 10, January–June 1536, No.840 (1888).
6. 'Letter from Thomas Cranmer to Henry VIII on 3 May 1536', *Letters and Papers, Foreign and Domestic, Henry VIII*, Volume 10, January–June 1536, No.792 (1888).
7. Ibid.
8. Ibid.
9. Ives, Eric, *The Life and Death of Anne Boleyn* (2005) p.335.
10. 'Letter from William Kingston to Thomas Cromwell on 3 May 1536', *Letters and Papers, Foreign and Domestic, Henry VIII*, Volume 10, January–June 1536, No.793 (1888).
11. Souden, David, *The Royal Palaces of London* (2008) p.52; Jones, Nigel, *Tower: An Epic History of the Tower of London* (2012) p.216.
12. Weir, Alison, *The Lady in the Tower: The Fall of Anne Boleyn* (2009) p.137.
13. 'Letter from William Kingston to Thomas Cromwell on 3 May 1536', *Letters and Papers, Foreign and Domestic, Henry VIII*, Volume 10, January–June 1536, No.793 (1888).
14. Ibid.
15. Ibid.
16. 'Letter from William Kingston to Thomas Cromwell at beginning of May 1536', *Letters and Papers, Foreign and Domestic, Henry VIII*, Volume 10, January–June 1536, No.797 (1888).
17. Ibid.
18. Ibid.

19. 'Letter from William Kingston to Thomas Cromwell on 16 May 1536', *Letters and Papers, Foreign and Domestic, Henry VIII*, Volume 10, January–June 1536, No.890 (1888).
20. Ibid.
21. 'Letter from William Kingston to Thomas Cromwell tentatively on 18 May 1536', *Letters and Papers, Foreign and Domestic, Henry VIII*, Volume 10, January–June 1536, No.902 (1888).
22. 'Letter from William Kingston to Thomas Cromwell tentatively on 19 May 1536', *Letters and Papers, Foreign and Domestic, Henry VIII*, Volume 10, January–June 1536, No.910 (1888).
23. Foxe, John, *Actes and Monuments* (1838) p.135.
24. 'Letter from William Kingston to Thomas Cromwell tentatively on 19 May 1536', *Letters and Papers, Foreign and Domestic, Henry VIII*, Volume 10, January–June 1536, No.910 (1888).
25. Ibid.
26. Norton, Elizabeth, *Anne Boleyn: In Her Own Words and the Words of Those Who Knew Her* (2011) p.255.
27. Vasoli, Sandra, *Anne Boleyn's Letter from the Tower: New Updated Edition* (2023) p.27.
28. 'Letter supposedly from Anne Boleyn to Henry VIII from the Tower' quoted in Vasoli, Sandra, *Anne Boleyn's Letter from the Tower: New Updated Edition* (2023) pp.33–36.
29. Denny, Joanna, *Anne Boleyn: A New Life of England's Tragic Queen* (2004) p.310.
30. Ives, Eric, *The Life and Death of Anne Boleyn* (2005) p.310.
31. 'Letter from William Kingston to Thomas Cromwell', *Letters and Papers, Foreign and Domestic, Henry VIII*, Volume 10, January–June 1536, No.890 (1888).
32. 'Letter supposedly from Anne Boleyn to Henry VIII from the Tower' quoted in Vasoli, Sandra, *Anne Boleyn's Letter from the Tower: New Updated Edition* (2023) pp.33–36.
33. Ibid.
34. Ibid.
35. Ibid.
36. Vasoli, Sandra, *Anne Boleyn's Letter from the Tower: New Updated Edition* (2023) pp.7–8.
37. 'Letter supposedly from Anne Boleyn to Henry VIII from the Tower' quoted in Vasoli, Sandra, *Anne Boleyn's Letter from the Tower: New Updated Edition* (2023) pp.33–36.
38. Ibid.
39. Vasoli, Sandra, *Anne Boleyn's Letter from the Tower: New Updated Edition* (2023) p.48.
40. Ibid, p.7.
41. 'Trial Documents of Weston, Norris, and others', *Letters and Papers, Foreign and Domestic, Henry VIII*, Volume 10, January–June 1536, No.848 (1888).
42. Ibid.
43. Ibid.
44. Ibid.
45. Ibid.
46. Grueninger, Natalie, *The Final Year of Anne Boleyn* (2022) p.191.
47. 'Trial Documents of Anne Boleyn and Lord Rochford', *Letters and Papers, Foreign and Domestic, Henry VIII*, Volume 10, January–June 1536, No.876 (1888).
48. Grueninger, Natalie, *The Final Year of Anne Boleyn* (2022) p.191.
49. 'Trial Documents of Anne Boleyn and Lord Rochford', *Letters and Papers, Foreign and Domestic, Henry VIII*, Volume 10, January–June 1536, No.876 (1888).
50. Ibid.
51. Ibid.

52. 'Trial Documents of Anne Boleyn and Lord Rochford', *Letters and Papers, Foreign and Domestic, Henry VIII*, Volume 10, January–June 1536, No.876 (1888).
53. Ibid.
54. 'Letter from Eustace Chapuys to Charles V on 19 May 1536', *Letters and Papers, Foreign and Domestic, Henry VIII*, Volume 10, January–June 1536, No.908 (1888).
55. 'Trial Documents of Anne Boleyn and Lord Rochford', *Letters and Papers, Foreign and Domestic, Henry VIII*, Volume 10, January–June 1536, No.876 (1888).
56. 'Letter from Cromwell to Gardiner and Wallop on 14 May 1536', *Letters and Papers, Foreign and Domestic, Henry VIII*, Volume 10, January–June 1536, No.873 (1888).
57. Ibid.
58. Foxe, John, *Actes and Monuments* (1838) p.135.
59. Weir, Alison, *The Lady in the Tower: The Fall of Anne Boleyn* (2009) p.291.
60. Ibid.
61. Walker, Greg, *Writing under Tyranny: English Literature and the Henrician Reformation* (2005) p.290.
62. Russo, Stephanie, *The Afterlife of Anne Boleyn: Representations of Anne Boleyn in Fiction and on the Screen* (2020) p.34.
63. Wyatt, Thomas, 'Innocentia Veritas Viat Fides Circumdederunt me inimici mei' in Norton, Elizabeth, *Anne Boleyn: In Her Own Words and the Words of Those Who Knew Her* (2011) p.237.
64. Ibid.
65. Walker, Greg, *Writing under Tyranny: English Literature and the Henrician Reformation* (2005) p.290.
66. Russo, Stephanie, *The Afterlife of Anne Boleyn: Representations of Anne Boleyn in Fiction and on the Screen* (2020) p.34; Wyatt, Thomas, 'Innocentia Veritas Viat Fides Circumdederunt me inimici mei' in Norton, Elizabeth, *Anne Boleyn: In Her Own Words and the Words of Those Who Knew Her* (2011) p.237.
67. Wyatt, Thomas, 'Innocentia Veritas Viat Fides Circumdederunt me inimici mei' in Norton, Elizabeth, *Anne Boleyn: In Her Own Words and the Words of Those Who Knew Her* (2011) p.237.
68. Foxe, John, *Actes and Monuments* (1838) p.135.
69. Ibid.
70. Borman, Tracy, *Anne Boleyn and Elizabeth I: The Mother and Daughter Who Changed History* (2023) p.88.
71. Grueninger, Natalie, *The Final Year of Anne Boleyn* (2022) p.180.
72. Borman, Tracy, *Anne Boleyn and Elizabeth I: The Mother and Daughter Who Changed History* (2023) p.89.
73. Grueninger, Natalie, *The Final Year of Anne Boleyn* (2022) pp.181–182.
74. Marlow, Toby and Moss, Lucy, 'Ex-Wives', *SIX The Musical (Studio Cast Recording)* (2018).

Chapter 5: Anne Through Foreign Eyes

1. 'Letter from Eustace Chapuys to Charles V on 3 September 1533', *Letters and Papers, Foreign and Domestic, Henry VIII*, Volume 6, 1533, No.1069 (1882).
2. Mackay, Lauren, *Inside the Tudor Court: Henry VIII and his Six Wives through the eyes of the Spanish Ambassador* (2015) p.9.
3. Starkey, David, *Six Wives: The Queens of Henry VIII* (2004) p.360.
4. Russo, Stephanie, *The Afterlife of Anne Boleyn: Representations of Anne Boleyn in Fiction and on the Screen* (2020) p.21.

5. Norton, Elizabeth, *Anne Boleyn: In Her Own Words and the Words of Those Who Knew Her* (2011) p.261.
6. Mackay, Lauren, *Inside the Tudor Court: Henry VIII and his Six Wives through the eyes of the Spanish Ambassador* (2015) p.9.
7. Ibid, p.8.
8. 'Letter from Eustace Chapuys to Charles V on 4 September 1529', Calendar of State Papers: Spain, Volume 4, Part 1, No.135 (1879).
9. 'Letter from Eustace Chapuys to Charles V on 15 June 1530', Calendar of State Papers: Spain, Volume 4, Part 1, No.354 (1879).
10. 'Letter from Eustace Chapuys to Charles V on 5 September 1532', Calendar of State Papers: Spain, Volume 4, Part 2, No.993 (1882).
11. Ibid.
12. 'Letter from Eustace Chapuys to Charles V on 3 September 1533', *Letters and Papers, Foreign and Domestic, Henry VIII*, Volume 6, 1533, No.1069 (1882).
13. Ibid.
14. Mackay, Lauren, *Inside the Tudor Court: Henry VIII and his Six Wives through the eyes of the Spanish Ambassador* (2015) p.115.
15. 'Letter from Eustace Chapuys to Charles V on 2 May 1536', *Letters and Papers, Foreign and Domestic, Henry VIII*, Volume 10, January–June 1536, No.782 (1888).
16. Ibid.
17. Ibid.
18. Ibid.
19. 'Letter from Eustace Chapuys to Charles V on 6 June 1536', *Calendar of State Papers: Spain*, Volume 5 Part 2, 1536–1538, No.61 (1888).
20. 'Letter from Charles V to Eustace Chapuys on 15 May 1536', *Letters and Papers, Foreign and Domestic, Henry VIII*, Volume 10, January–June 1536, No.888 (1888).
21. 'Letter from Eustace Chapuys to Granvelle on 18 May 1536', *Calendar of State Papers: Spain*, Volume 5 Part 2, 1536–1538, No.54 (1888).
22. Ibid.
23. Cavendish, George, *The Life of Cardinal Wolsey* (1890) p.54.
24. 'Letter from Eustace Chapuys to Granvelle on 18 May 1536', *Calendar of State Papers: Spain*, Volume 5 Part 2, 1536–1538, No.54 (1888).
25. 'Letter from Northumberland to Thomas Cromwell on 13 May 1536', *Letters and Papers, Foreign and Domestic, Henry VIII*, Volume 10, January–June 1536, No.864 (1887).
26. 'Letter from Eustace Chapuys to Charles V on 19 May 1536', *Letters and Papers, Foreign and Domestic, Henry VIII*, Volume 10, January–June 1536, No.908 (1887).
27. Ibid.
28. Ibid.
29. 'Letter from Eustace Chapuys to Granvelle on 18 May 1536', *Calendar of State Papers: Spain*, Volume 5 Part 2, 1536–1538, No.54 (1888).
30. Mackay, Lauren, *Inside the Tudor Court: Henry VIII and his Six Wives through the eyes of the Spanish Ambassador* (2015) pp.40–41.
31. Paranque, Estelle, *Thorns, Lust and Glory: The Betrayal of Anne Boleyn* (2024) p.51.
32. Ibid, p.212.
33. Ibid.
34. 'Letter from Montmorency to the Bailly of Troyes on 16 March 1533', *Letters and Papers, Foreign and Domestic, Henry VIII*, Volume 6, 1533, No.242 (1882).
35. Paranque, Estelle, *Thorns, Lust and Glory: The Betrayal of Anne Boleyn* (2024) p.154.

36. Emmerson, Owen and McCaffrey, Kate, *Becoming Anne: Connections, Culture, Court* (2022) p.73.
37. 'Letter from the Bailly of Troyes to Francis I on 3 September 1533', *Letters and Papers, Foreign and Domestic, Henry VIII*, Volume 6, 1533, No.1070 (1882).
38. 'Letter from Francis I to the Bailly of Troyes on 17 September 1533', *Letters and Papers, Foreign and Domestic, Henry VIII*, Volume 6, 1533, No.1135 (1882).
39. 'Letter from Antoine de Castelnau to Bailly of Troyes, labelled Camusat 21', *Letters and Papers, Foreign and Domestic, Henry VIII*, Volume 9, August–December 1535, No.566 (1886).
40. Ives, Eric, *The Life and Death of Anne Boleyn* (2005) pp.199–200.
41. 'Letter from Eustace Chapuys to Charles V on 19 May 1536', *Letters and Papers, Foreign and Domestic, Henry VIII*, Volume 10, January–June 1536, No.908 (1887).
42. 'Letter from J. Husee to Lord Lisle on 13 May 1536', *Letters and Papers, Foreign and Domestic, Henry VIII*, Volume 10, January–June 1536, No.865 (1887).
43. Guy, John and Fox, Julia, *Hunting the Falcon: Henry VIII, Anne Boleyn and the Marriage That Shook Europe* (2023) p.52.
44. Russo, Stephanie, 'The Story of the Death of Anne Boleyn', *History* (2023) p.25.
45. Ibid.
46. Bordo, Susan, *The Creation of Anne Boleyn: In Search of the Tudors' Most Notorious Queen* (2014) p.101.
47. Ives, Eric, *The Life and Death of Anne Boleyn* (2005) p.333.
48. 'Letter from Thomas Cromwell to Stephen Gardiner and John Wallop on 14 May 1536', *Letters and Papers, Foreign and Domestic, Henry VIII*, Volume 10, January–June 1536, No.873 (1888).
49. Carles, Lancelot de, *The Story of the Death of Anne Boleyn*, in Norton, Elizabeth, *Anne Boleyn: In Her Own Words and the Words of Those Who Knew Her* (2011) pp.261–262.
50. Norton, Elizabeth, *Anne Boleyn: In Her Own Words and the Words of Those Who Knew Her* (2011) p.279.
51. Carles, Lancelot de, *The Story of the Death of Anne Boleyn*, in Norton, Elizabeth, *Anne Boleyn: In Her Own Words and the Words of Those Who Knew Her* (2011) p.263.
52. Ibid.
53. Ibid.
54. Russo, Stephanie, 'The Story of the Death of Anne Boleyn', *History* (2023) p.25.
55. Bordo, Susan, *The Creation of Anne Boleyn: In Search of the Tudors' Most Notorious Queen* (2014) p.233.

Chapter 6: Anne as Reformer

1. Foxe, John, *Actes and Monuments*, Vol. 5 (1838) p.135.
2. Soberton, Sylvia Barbara, '"Large wen" or "swelling"? Exploring Myths and Misconceptions about Nicholas Sander's Description of Anne Boleyn and its Link to Witchcraft', *Royal Studies Journal* (2023) p.261.
3. Bernard, G.W., 'Anne Boleyn's Religion', *The Historical Journal* (1993) p.20.
4. Bernard, G.W., *Anne Boleyn: Fatal Attractions* (2011) p.95.
5. Ibid, p.123.
6. Freeman, Thomas, 'Research, Rumour and Propaganda: Anne Boleyn in Foxe's "Book of Martyrs"' in *The Historical Journal* (1995) p.819.
7. Dowling, Maria, 'Anne Boleyn and Reform', *Journal of Ecclesiastical History* (1984) p.46.
8. Bernard, G.W., 'Anne Boleyn's Religion', *The Historical Journal* (1993) p.4.

9. Ives, Eric, 'Anne Boleyn and the Early Reformation in England: The Contemporary Evidence' in *The Historical Journal* (1994) p.390.
10. Bernard, G.W., 'Anne Boleyn's Religion', *The Historical Journal* (1993) p.2.
11. Bordo, Susan, *The Creationof Anne Boleyn: In Search of the Tudors' Most Notorious Queen* (2014) p.140.
12. 'Letter from Reginald Pole to Henry VIII on 27 May 1536', *Letters and Papers, Foreign and Domestic, Henry VIII*, Volume 10, January–June 1536, No.974 (1888).
13. Ibid.
14. Pole, Reginald, *Defense of the Unity of the Church* (1965) p.181.
15. Ibid, p.184.
16. Mayer, T.F., *Pole, Reginald,* Oxford Dictionary of National Biography, https://doi.org/10.1093/ref:odnb/22456.
17. Pole, Reginald, *Defense of the Unity of the Church* (1965) p.185.
18. Ibid, p.188.
19. Mayer, T.F., *Pole, Reginald,* Oxford Dictionary of National Biography, https://doi.org/10.1093/ref:odnb/22456.
20. Bordo, Susan, *The Creation of Anne Boleyn: In Search of the Tudors' Most Notorious Queen* (2014) p.139.
21. Freeman, Thomas, *Foxe, John*, Oxford Dictionary of National Biography, https://doi.org/10.1093/ref:odnb/10050.
22. Ibid.
23. Foxe, John, *Actes and Monuments*, Vol. 5 (1838) p.134.
24. Ibid, p.135.
25. Ibid, pp.135–6.
26. Freeman, Thomas, 'Research, Rumour and Propaganda: Anne Boleyn in Foxe's "Book of Martyrs"' in *The Historical Journal* (1995) p.819.
27. Bernard, G.W., 'Anne Boleyn's Religion', *The Historical Journal* (1993) p.2.
28. Foxe, John, *Actes and Monuments*, Vol. 5 (1838) p.135.
29. Bordo, Susan, *The Creation of Anne Boleyn: In Search of the Tudors' Most Notorious Queen* (2014) p.140.
30. Guy, John and Fox, Julia, *Hunting the Falcon: Henry VIII, Anne Boleyn and the Marriage that Shook Europe* (2023) p.321.
31. Foxe, John, *Actes and Monuments*, Vol. 4 (1838) p.657.
32. Ibid, p.658.
33. Foxe, John, *Actes and Monuments*, Vol. 5 (1838) p.137.
34. Soberton, Sylvia Barbara, '"Large wen" or "swelling"? Exploring Myths and Misconceptions about Nicholas Sander's Description of Anne Boleyn and its Link to Witchcraft', *Royal Studies Journal* (2023) p.239.
35. Warnicke, Retha, *The Rise and Fall of Anne Boleyn* (2008) p.247.
36. Hui, Roland, 'Anne of the Wicked Ways: Perceptions of Anne Boleyn as a Witch in History and in Popular Culture', *Parergon* (2018) p.104.
37. *Harry Potter and the Philosopher's Stone* [DVD], directed by Chris Columbus (2001).
38. Sander, Nicholas, *Rise and Growth of the Anglican Schism* (1877) p.132.
39. Highley, Christopher, '"A Pestilent and Seditious Book": Nicholas Sander's Schismatis Anglicani and Catholic Histories of the Reformation', *Huntington Library Quarterly* (2005) p.156.
40. Sander, Nicholas, *Rise and Growth of the Anglican Schism* (1877) p.132.
41. Ibid, p.133.

42. Highley, Christopher, '"A Pestilent and Seditious Book": Nicholas Sander's Schismatis Anglicani and Catholic Histories of the Reformation', *Huntington Library Quarterly* (2005) p.156.
43. Sander, Nicholas, *Rise and Growth of the Anglican Schism* (1877) p.134.
44. Ibid, p.135.
45. Ibid, p.136.
46. Soberton, Sylvia Barbara, '"Large wen" or "swelling"? Exploring Myths and Misconceptions about Nicholas Sander's Description of Anne Boleyn and its Link to Witchcraft', *Royal Studies Journal* (2023) pp.256–258.
47. Ibid, p.256.
48. Ives, Eric, *The Life and Death of Anne Boleyn* (2005) p.39.
49. Sander, Nicholas, *Rise and Growth of the Anglican Schism* (1877) p.25.
50. Ives, Eric, *The Life and Death of Anne Boleyn* (2005) p.40.
51. Hui, Roland, 'Anne of the Wicked Ways: Perceptions of Anne Boleyn as a Witch in History and in Popular Culture', *Parergon* (2018) p.105.
52. Warnicke, Retha, *The Rise and Fall of Anne Boleyn* (2008) p.245.
53. Soberton, Sylvia Barbara, '"Large wen" or "swelling"? Exploring Myths and Misconceptions about Nicholas Sander's Description of Anne Boleyn and its Link to Witchcraft', *Royal Studies Journal* (2023) p.244.
54. Highley, Christopher, '"A Pestilent and Seditious Book": Nicholas Sander's Schismatis Anglicani and Catholic Histories of the Reformation', *Huntington Library Quarterly* (2005) p.156.
55. Warnicke, Retha, *The Rise and Fall of Anne Boleyn* (2008) p.247.
56. Burnet, Gilbert, *The History of the Reformation of the Church of England* (1865) p.83.
57. Ibid.
58. Guy, John & Fox, Julia, *Hunting the Falcon: Henry VIII, Anne Boleyn and the Marriage that Shook Europe* (2023) p.170.
59. Burnet, Gilbert, *The History of the Reformation of the Church of England* (1865) p.151.
60. Ibid, p.264.
61. Ibid, p.390.
62. Ibid, p.393.
63. Norton, Elizabeth, *Anne Boleyn: Henry VIII's Obsession* (2009) p.110.
64. Warnicke, Retha, *The Rise and Fall of Anne Boleyn* (2008) p.107.
65. Norton, Elizabeth, *Anne Boleyn: Henry VIII's Obsession* (2009) p.91.
66. Natalie Grueninger, *The Final Year of Anne Boleyn* (2022) p.47.
67. Guy, John and Fox, Julia, *Hunting the Falcon: Henry VIII, Anne Boleyn and the Marriage the Shook Europe* (2023) p.319.
68. Licence, Amy, *Anne Boleyn: Adultery, Heresy, Desire* (2017) p.225.
69. Guy, John and Fox, Julia, *Hunting the Falcon: Henry VIII, Anne Boleyn and the Marriage the Shook Europe* (2023) p.287, 319.
70. Smith, Lacey Baldwin, *Anne Boleyn: The Queen of Controversy* (2013) p.57.
71. Ibid, p.90.
72. Ives, Eric, 'Anne Boleyn and the Early Reformation in England: The Contemporary Evidence', *The Historical Journal* (1994) p.393.
73. Ibid, p.389.
74. Bernard, G.W., 'Anne Boleyn's Religion', *The Historical Journal* (1993) p.20.
75. Borman, Tracy, *Anne Boleyn and Elizabeth I: The Mother and Daughter Who Changed History* (2023) p.24.

Chapter 7: Anne as Tragic Heroine

1. Bell, Doyne C., *Notices of the Historic Persons Buried in the Chapel of St Peter ad Vincula in the Tower of London* (1877) p.vii.
2. Queen Victoria, 'Journal entry 13 September 1834', *Queen Victoria's Journals*, Volume 5, 20 May 1834 – 4 November 1834. http://www.queenvictoriasjournals.org/.
3. Austen, Jane, *The History of England* (1995) p.7.
4. Burstein, Miriam Elizabeth, 'The Fictional Afterlife of Anne Boleyn: How to Do Things with the Queen, 1901–2006', *Clio* (2007) p.5.
5. Ibid, p.6.
6. Guy, John and Fox, Julia, *Hunting the Falcon: Henry VIII, Anne Boleyn and the Marriage That Shook Europe* (2023) pp.xxxi-xxxii.
7. Bell, Doyne C., *Notices of the Historic Persons Buried in the Chapel of St Peter ad Vincula in the Tower of London* (1877) p.19.
8. Ibid, p.vii.
9. Weir, Alison, *The Six Wives of Henry VIII* (1997) p.147.
10. Weir, Alison, *The Lady in the Tower: The Fall of Anne Boleyn* (2009) p.324.
11. Abbott, Geoffrey, *Severed Heads: British Beheadings Through the Ages* (2003) p.43.
12. Bell, Doyne C., *Notices of the Historic Persons Buried in the Chapel of St Peter ad Vincula in the Tower of London* (1877) p.52.
13. Emmerson, Owen and Ridgway, Claire, *The Boleyns of Hever Castle* (2021) p.125.
14. Emmerson, Owen and Ridgway, Claire, *The Boleyns of Hever Castle* (2021) p.99; Grueninger, Natalie, *The Final Year of Anne Boleyn* (2022) p.180.
15. Mitchell, Rosemary, *Strickland, Agnes*, Oxford Dictionary of National Biography. https://doi.org/10.1093/ref:odnb/26663.
16. Ibid.
17. Bordo, Susan, *The Creation of Anne Boleyn: In Search of the Tudors' Most Notorious Queen* (2014) p.154.
18. Strickland, Agnes, *Lives of the Queens of England, Volume II* (1909) p.176.
19. Ibid, p.178.
20. Emmerson, Owen and McCaffrey, Kate, *Becoming Anne: Connections, Culture, Court* (2022) p.46.
21. Ibid.
22. Strickland, Agnes, *Lives of the Queens of England, Volume II* (1909) p.178.
23. Ibid, p.180.
24. Emmerson, Owen and McCaffrey, Kate, *Becoming Anne: Connections, Culture, Court* (2022) p.67.
25. Strickland, Agnes, *Lives of the Queens of England, Volume II* (1909) p.187.
26. Cavendish, George, *The Life of Cardinal Wolsey* (1890) p.48.
27. Strickland, Agnes, *Lives of the Queens of England, Volume II* (1909) p.196.
28. Ibid, p.208.
29. Cavendish, George, *The Life of Cardinal Wolsey* (1890) p.54.
30. Strickland, Agnes, *Lives of the Queens of England, Volume II* (1909) pp.223–224.
31. Ibid, p.224.
32. Ibid, p.243.
33. Ibid, p.262.
34. Ibid.
35. Russo, Stephanie, *The Afterlife of Anne Boleyn: Representations of Anne Boleyn in Fiction and on the Screen* (2020) p.110.

36. Bordo, Susan, *The Creation of Anne Boleyn: In Search of the Tudors' Most Notorious Queen* (2014) p.153.
37. Friedmann, Paul, *Anne Boleyn* (2010) p.15.
38. Ibid, p.26.
39. Bordo, Susan, *The Creation of Anne Boleyn: In Search of the Tudors' Most Notorious Queen* (2014) p.160.
40. Ibid.
41. Friedmann, Paul, *Anne Boleyn* (2010) p.249.
42. Ibid.
43. Ibid.
44. Ibid, p.26.
45. Ibid.
46. Ibid, p.188.
47. Ibid, p.156, 188.
48. 'Letter from Eustace Chapuys to Charles V on 2 May 1536', *Letters and Papers, Foreign and Domestic, Henry VIII*, Volume 10, January–June 1536, No.782 (1888).
49. Friedmann, Paul, *Anne Boleyn* (2010) p.237.
50. Ibid.
51. Russo, Stephanie, *The Afterlife of Anne Boleyn: Representations of Anne Boleyn in Fiction and on the Screen* (2020) p.122.
52. Bordo, Susan, *The Creation of Anne Boleyn: In Search of the Tudors' Most Notorious Queen* (2014) p.155.
53. 'Letter from Eustace Chapuys to Charles V on 19 May 1536', *Letters and Papers, Foreign and Domestic, Henry VIII*, Volume 10, January–June 1536, No.908 (1887).
54. Ives, Eric, *The Life and Death of Anne Boleyn* (2005) p.357.
55. Wyatt, Thomas, 'Whoso List to Hunt' in Norton, Elizabeth, *Anne Boleyn: In Her Own Words and the Words of Those Who Knew Her* (2011) p.34.
56. Bordo, Susan, *The Creation of Anne Boleyn: In Search of the Tudors' Most Notorious Queen* (2014) p.155.
57. Smith, Lacey Baldwin, *Anne Boleyn: The Queen of Controversy* (2013) pp.14–15.
58. Burstein, Miriam Elizabeth, 'The Fictional Afterlife of Anne Boleyn: How to Do Things with the Queen, 1901–2006', *Clio* (2007) p.3.

Chapter 8: Anne on Stage

1. Shakespeare, William, *King Henry VIII* (2008) p.126.
2. Sharpe, Kevin, *Remapping Early Modern England: The Culture of Seventeenth Century Politics* (2000) p.420.
3. Russo, Stephanie, *The Afterlife of Anne Boleyn: Representations of Anne Boleyn in Fiction and on the Screen* (2020) p.57.
4. Holland, Peter, *Shakespeare, William*, Oxford Dictionary of National Biography. https://doi.org/10.1093/ref:odnb/25200.
5. Russo, Stephanie, *The Afterlife of Anne Boleyn: Representations of Anne Boleyn in Fiction and on the Screen* (2020) p.56.
6. Ibid, p.55.
7. Holland, Peter, *Shakespeare, William*, Oxford Dictionary of National Biography (2021). https://doi.org/10.1093/ref:odnb/25200.
8. Bordo, Susan, *The Creation of Anne Boleyn: In Search of the Tudors' Most Notorious Queen* (2014) p.147.

9. Russo, Stephanie, *The Afterlife of Anne Boleyn: Representations of Anne Boleyn in Fiction and on the Screen* (2020) p.61.
10. Weir, Alison, *The Lady in the Tower: The Fall of Anne Boleyn* (2009) p.303.
11. Shakespeare, William, *King Henry VIII* (2008) p.26.
12. Ibid, p.148.
13. Starkey, David, *The Reign of Henry VIII: Personalities and Politics* (2002) p.44.
14. Shakespeare, William, *King Henry VIII* (2008) p.167.
15. Ibid, p.126.
16. 'Letters 1, 2 and 5 from Henry VIII to Anne Boleyn' in Norton, Elizabeth, *Anne Boleyn: In Her Own Words and the Words of Those Who Knew Her* (2011) pp.41–42.
17. Shakespeare, William, *King Henry VIII* (2008) p.104.
18. Noling, Kim H., 'Grubbing Up the Stock: Dramatizing Queens in Henry VIII', *Shakespeare Quarterly* (1988) p.299.
19. Denny, Joanna, *Anne Boleyn: A New Life of England's Tragic Queen* (2004) p.193.
20. Loades, David, *The Six Wives of Henry VIII* (2010) p.63.
21. Fraser, Antonia, *The Six Wives of Henry VIII* (2002) p.240.
22. Shakespeare, William, *King Henry VIII* (2008) p.176.
23. Ives, Eric, *The Life and Death of Anne Boleyn* (2005) pp.177–178.
24. Weir, Alison, *The Six Wives of Henry VIII* (1997) p.231.
25. Shakespeare, William, *King Henry VIII* (2008) p.149.
26. Gallup, Elizabeth Wells, in the preface to Bacon, Francis, *The Tragedy of Anne Boleyn* (2012) p.iv.
27. Bacon, Francis, *The Tragedy of Anne Boleyn* (2012) p.147.
28. Foxe, John, *Actes and Monuments* (1838) p.135.
29. Strickland, Agnes, *The Lives of the Queens of England* (2011) p.71.
30. Bacon, Francis, *The Tragedy of Anne Boleyn* (2012) p.147.
31. Ibid, p.20.
32. Ibid, p.21.
33. Bernard, G.W., *Anne Boleyn: Fatal Attractions* (2011) p.20.
34. Weir, Alison, *The Six Wives of Henry VIII* (1997) p.151.
35. Bacon, Francis, *The Tragedy of Anne Boleyn* (2012) p.42.
36. Ives, Eric, *The Life and Death of Anne Boleyn* (2005) p.147.
37. Bacon, Francis, *The Tragedy of Anne Boleyn* (2012) p.42.
38. Ives, Eric, *The Life and Death of Anne Boleyn* (2005) p.91.
39. Bacon, Francis, *The Tragedy of Anne Boleyn* (2012) pp.116–117.
40. 'Letter from Eustace Chapuys to Charles V on 19 May 1536', *Letters and Papers, Foreign and Domestic, Henry VIII*, Volume 10, January–June 1536, No.908 (1888).
41. 'Trial Documents of Anne and George Boleyn', *Letters and Papers, Foreign and Domestic, Henry VIII*, Volume 10, January–June 1536, No.876 (1888).
42. Bacon, Francis, *The Tragedy of Anne Boleyn* (2012) p.117.
43. Bordo, Susan, *The Creation of Anne Boleyn: In Search of the Tudors' Most Notorious Queen* (2014) p.143.
44. Russo, Stephanie, *The Afterlife of Anne Boleyn: Representations of Anne Boleyn in Fiction and on the Screen* (2020) p.79.
45. Ibid.
46. Brayne, Charles, *Banks, John*, Oxford Dictionary of National Biography (2004). https://doi.org/10.1093/ref:odnb/1297.
47. Banks, John, *Virtue Betray'd* (1715) p.5.

48. 'Letter from Henry Percy to Thomas Cromwell on 13 May 1536', *Letters and Papers, Foreign and Domestic, Henry VIII*, Volume 10, January–June 1536, No.864 (1888).
49. 'Letter from Northumberland to Thomas Cromwell on 13 May 1536', *Letters and Papers, Foreign and Domestic, Henry VIII*, Volume 10, January–June 1536, No.864 (1887).
50. Banks, John, *Virtue Betray'd* (1715) p.50.
51. Wiesner-Hanks, Merry E., *Women and Gender in Early Modern Europe* (2008) p.285.
52. Mena, Paula de Pando, 'Emasculated Subjects and Subjugated Wives: Discourses of Domination in John Banks's *Vertue Betray'd* (1682)' in *Yearbook of the Spanish and Portuguese Society for English Renaissance Studies* (2006) p.164.
53. Ibid.
54. Miller-Tomlinson, Tracey, 'Pathos and Politics in John Banks's *Vertue Betray'd* or *Anna Bullen* (1682)', *Restoration and 18th Century Theatre Research* (2008) p.49.
55. Banks, John, *Virtue Betray'd* (1715) p.55.
56. Weir, Alison, *The Lady in the Tower: The Fall of Anne Boleyn* (2009) p.11.
57. Banks, John, *Virtue Betray'd* (1715) p.5.
58. Ibid, p.1.
59. Mena, Paula de Pando, 'Emasculated Subjects and Subjugated Wives: Discourses of Domination in John Banks's *Vertue Betray'd* (1682)', *Yearbook of the Spanish and Portuguese Society for English Renaissance Studies* (2006) p.169.
60. Starkey, David, *Six Wives: The Queens of Henry VIII* (2004) pp.366–367.
61. SIX The Musical (2023) *About Us*. https://www.sixthemusical.com/london/about.
62. Marlow, Toby and Moss, Lucy, 'The One You've Been Waiting For', *SIX The Musical (Live on Opening Night Original Broadway Cast Recording)* (2022).
63. Russo, Stephanie, *The Afterlife of Anne Boleyn: Representations of Anne Boleyn in Fiction and on the Screen* (2020) p.294.
64. Marlow, Toby and Moss, Lucy, 'Don't Lose Ur Head', *SIX The Musical (Studio Cast Recording)* (2018).
65. Russo, Stephanie, *The Afterlife of Anne Boleyn: Representations of Anne Boleyn in Fiction and on the Screen* (2020) p.294.
66. Marlow, Toby and Moss, Lucy, 'Don't Lose Ur Head', *SIX The Musical (Studio Cast Recording)* (2018).
67. Ibid.
68. Ibid.
69. Ibid.
70. 'Letter from Eustace Chapuys to Charles V', *Calendar of State Papers: Spain*, Volume 4 Part 1, 1529–1530, No.224 (1879).
71. Marlow, Toby and Moss, Lucy, 'Don't Lose Ur Head', *SIX The Musical (Studio Cast Recording)* (2018).
72. 'Letter from Eustace Chapuys to Charles V on 19 May 1536', *Letters and Papers, Foreign and Domestic, Henry VIII*, Volume 10, January–June 1536, No.908 (1888), translation from Guy, John and Fox, Julia, *Hunting the Falcon: Henry VIII, Anne Boleyn and the Marriage That Shook Europe* (2023) p.394.
73. Russo, Stephanie, *The Afterlife of Anne Boleyn: Representations of Anne Boleyn in Fiction and on the Screen* (2020) p.294.
74. Russo, Stephanie, *The Afterlife of Anne Boleyn: Representations of Anne Boleyn in Fiction and on the Screen* (2020) p.62.

Chapter 9: Anne on Film

1. *Anne of the Thousand Days* [DVD], directed by Charles Jarrott (1969).
2. Richardson, Glenn, 'Anne of the Thousand Days' in Susan Doran & Thomas Freeman, *Tudors and Stuarts on Film: Historical Perspectives* (2009) p.60.
3. Freeman, Thomas, 'Introduction: It's Only a Movie' in Susan Doran & Thomas Freeman, *Tudors and Stuarts on Film: Historical Perspectives* (2009) p.1.
4. Kershaw, Ian, 'The Past and the Box: Strengths and Weaknesses' in Cannadine, David, *History and the Media* (2004) p.121.
5. Saxton, Laura, '"She was dead meat": Imagining the Execution of Anne Boleyn in History and Fiction', *Parergon* (2020) p.105.
6. Chapman, James, *National Identity and the British Historical Film* (2005) p.7.
7. Russo, Stephanie, *The Afterlife of Anne Boleyn: Representations of Anne Boleyn in Fiction and on the Screen* (2020) p.267.
8. Hutcheon, Linda, *A Theory of Film Adaptation* (2006) p.18.
9. Watt, Donald, 'History on the Public Screen I' in Paul Smith, *The Historian and Film* (1976) p.169.
10. Freeman, Thomas, 'Introduction: It's Only a Movie' in Susan Doran & Thomas Freeman, *Tudors and Stuarts on Film: Historical Perspectives* (2009) p.11.
11. Freeman, Thomas, 'A Tyrant for all Seasons: Henry VIII on Film' in Susan Doran & Thomas Freeman, *Tudors and Stuarts on Film: Historical Perspectives* (2009) p.36.
12. Russo, Stephanie, *The Afterlife of Anne Boleyn: Representations of Anne Boleyn in Fiction and on the Screen* (2020) p.267.
13. Carles, Lancelot de, *The Story of the Death of Anne Boleyn*, in Norton, Elizabeth, *Anne Boleyn: In Her Own Words and the Words of Those Who Knew Her* (2011) p.261.
14. *The Private Life of Henry VIII* [DVD], directed by Alexander Korda (1933).
15. Ibid.
16. Ibid.
17. 'Letter from William Kingston to Thomas Cromwell tentatively on 19 May 1536', *Letters and Papers, Foreign and Domestic, Henry VIII*, Volume 10, January–June 1536, No.910 (1888).
18. *The Private Life of Henry VIII* [DVD], directed by Alexander Korda (1933).
19. Bordo, Susan, *The Creation of Anne Boleyn: In Search of the Tudors' Most Notorious Queen* (2014) p.190.
20. Freeman, Thomas, 'A Tyrant for all Seasons: Henry VIII on Film' in Susan Doran & Thomas Freeman, *Tudors and Stuarts on Film: Historical Perspectives* (2009) p.37.
21. *The Private Life of Henry VIII* [DVD], directed by Alexander Korda (1933).
22. 'Letter from Eustace Chapuys to Granvelle on 6 June 1536', *Letters and Papers, Foreign and Domestic, Henry VIII*, Volume 10, January–June 1536, No.1070 (1888).
23. *The Private Life of Henry VIII* [DVD], directed by Alexander Korda (1933).
24. *Anne of the Thousand Days*, IMDb, review entitled 'A Sixties Classic Reveals a Rare Achievement' (2007).
25. Canby, Vincent, 'A Royal Battle of the Sexes: "Anne of 1,000 Days" Bows at Plaza, Burton Cast as Henry, Miss Bujold Stars', *The New York Times* (1970).
26. Hui, Roland, 'Anne of the Wicked Ways: Perceptions of Anne Boleyn as a Witch in History and in Popular Culture', *Parergon* (2018) p.112.
27. *Anne of the Thousand Days* [DVD], directed by Charles Jarrott (1969).
28. Ibid.
29. Bordo, Susan, *The Creation of Anne Boleyn: In Search of the Tudors' Most Notorious Queen* (2014) p.192.

30. Russo, Stephanie, *The Afterlife of Anne Boleyn: Representations of Anne Boleyn in Fiction and on the Screen* (2020) p.273.
31. Ibid, p.274.
32. *Anne of the Thousand Days* [DVD], directed by Charles Jarrott (1969).
33. 'Letter from Northumberland to Thomas Cromwell', *Letters and Papers, Foreign and Domestic, Henry VIII*, Volume 10, January–June 1536, No.864 (1887).
34. *Anne of the Thousand Days* [DVD], directed by Charles Jarrott (1969).
35. Ibid.
36. Bordo, Susan, *The Creation of Anne Boleyn: In Search of the Tudors' Most Notorious Queen* (2014) p.180.
37. *Anne of the Thousand Days* [DVD], directed by Charles Jarrott (1969).
38. Ibid.
39. 'Letter from Eustace Chapuys to Charles V', *Calendar of State Papers: Spain*, Volume 5, Part 2, 1536–1538, No.55 (1888).
40. *Anne of the Thousand Days* [DVD], directed by Charles Jarrott (1969).
41. Ibid.
42. Bordo, Susan, *The Creation of Anne Boleyn: In Search of the Tudors' Most Notorious Queen* (2014) p.190.
43. *Anne of the Thousand Days* [DVD], directed by Charles Jarrott (1969).
44. Bordo, Susan, *The Creation of Anne Boleyn: In Search of the Tudors' Most Notorious Queen* (2014) p.180.
45. Wyatt, Thomas, 'Whoso List to Hunt' in Norton, Elizabeth, *Anne Boleyn: In Her Own Words and the Words of Those Who Knew Her* (2011) p.34.
46. Burstein, Miriam Elizabeth, 'The Fictional Afterlife of Anne Boleyn: How to Do Things with the Queen, 1901–2006', *Clio* (2007) p.17.
47. Freeman, Thomas, 'Introduction: It's Only a Movie' in Susan Doran & Thomas Freeman, *Tudors and Stuarts on Film: Historical Perspectives* (2009) p.20.
48. *Anne of the Thousand Days* [DVD], directed by Charles Jarrott (1969).
49. Bordo, Susan, *The Creation of Anne Boleyn: In Search of the Tudors' Most Notorious Queen* (2014) p.196.
50. Davies, Serena, 'David Starkey: It is "ludicrous" to suggest that historical novelists have authority', *The Telegraph* (2013).
51. Hui, Roland, 'Anne of the Wicked Ways: Perceptions of Anne Boleyn as a Witch in History and in Popular Culture', *Parergon* (2018) p.116.
52. *The Other Boleyn Girl* [DVD], directed by Justin Chadwick (2008).
53. Bordo, Susan, *The Creation of Anne Boleyn: In Search of the Tudors' Most Notorious Queen* (2014) pp.24–25.
54. *The Other Boleyn Girl* [DVD], directed by Justin Chadwick (2008).
55. Bernard, G.W., *Anne Boleyn: Fatal Attractions* (2011) p.25.
56. 'Letter from George Throckmorton to Henry VIII', *Letters and Papers, Foreign and Domestic, Henry VIII*, Volume 12, Part 2, July–December 1537, No.952 (1891).
57. *The Other Boleyn Girl* [DVD], directed by Justin Chadwick (2008).
58. Cavendish, George, *The Life of Cardinal Wolsey* (1890) p.48.
59. *The Other Boleyn Girl* [DVD], directed by Justin Chadwick (2008).
60. Ibid.
61. Ibid.
62. Ibid.
63. Ibid.

64. Fox, Julia, *Jane Boleyn: The Infamous Lady Rochford* (2007) p.315.
65. *The Other Boleyn Girl* [DVD], directed by Justin Chadwick (2008).
66. Ibid.
67. Ibid.
68. Foxe, John, *Actes and Monuments* (1838) p.135.
69. *The Other Boleyn Girl* [DVD], directed by Justin Chadwick (2008).
70. Ibid.
71. Bordo, Susan, *The Creation of Anne Boleyn: In Search of the Tudors' Most Notorious Queen* (2014) p.221.
72. Ibid.
73. Freeman, Thomas, 'Introduction: It's Only a Movie' in Susan Doran & Thomas Freeman, *Tudors and Stuarts on Film: Historical Perspectives* (2009) p.26.

Chapter 10: Anne on the Small Screen

1. *The Tudors* [DVD]. Season 1, Episode 2 (2007–2010).
2. Freeman, Thomas, 'Introduction: It's Only a Movie' in Susan Doran & Thomas Freeman, *Tudors and Stuarts on Film: Historical Perspectives* (2009) p.16.
3. De Groot, Jerome, 'Slashing History: *The Tudors*', in String, Tatiana & Bull, Marcus (eds.), *Tudorism: Historical Imagination and the Appropriation of the Sixteenth Century* (2011) p.242.
4. *The Tudors*, IMDb, review entitled 'Exciting, but Flounders on Miscast Henry and Historical Inaccuracy' (2007).
5. De Groot, Jerome, 'Slashing History: *The Tudors*', in String, Tatiana & Bull, Marcus (eds.), *Tudorism: Historical Imagination and the Appropriation of the Sixteenth Century* (2011) p.246.
6. *The Tudors* [DVD]. Season 1, Episode 1 (2007–2010).
7. *The Tudors* [DVD]. Season 1, Episode 9 (2007–2010).
8. 'Letter from Eustace Chapuys to Charles V on 27 November 1530', *Letters and Papers, Foreign and Domestic, Henry VIII*, Volume 4, 1524–1530, No.6738 (1875).
9. *The Tudors* [DVD]. Season 1, Episode 8 (2007–2010).
10. Cavendish, George, *The Life of Cardinal Wolsey* (1890) p.54.
11. *The Tudors* [DVD]. Season 1, Episode 10 (2007–2010).
12. *The Tudors* [DVD]. Season 2, Episode 3 (2007–2010).
13. Ibid.
14. Borman, Tracy, *Anne Boleyn and Elizabeth I: The Mother and Daughter Who Changed History* (2023) p.41.
15. *The Tudors* [DVD]. Season 2, Episode 5 (2007–2010).
16. *The Tudors* [DVD]. Season 2, Episode 10 (2007–2010).
17. Ibid.
18. Foxe, John, *Actes and Monuments* (1838) p.135.
19. *The Tudors* [DVD]. Season 2, Episode 10 (2007–2010).
20. Ibid.
21. Ibid.
22. Russo, Stephanie, *The Afterlife of Anne Boleyn: Representations of Anne Boleyn in Fiction and on the Screen* (2020) p.286.
23. Ibid, p.283.
24. *Wolf Hall* [DVD]. Season 1, Episode 1 (2015).
25. Russo, Stephanie, *The Afterlife of Anne Boleyn: Representations of Anne Boleyn in Fiction and on the Screen* (2020) p.286.

26. *Wolf Hall* [DVD]. Season 1, Episode 1 (2015).
27. Ibid.
28. *Wolf Hall* [DVD]. Season 1, Episode 2 (2015).
29. 'Letter from Mary Stafford to Thomas Cromwell, unknown date 1534', *Letters and Papers, Foreign and Domestic, Henry VIII*, Volume 7, 1534, No.1655 (1883).
30. *Wolf Hall* [DVD]. Season 1, Episode 2 (2015).
31. *Wolf Hall* [DVD]. Season 1, Episode 3 (2015).
32. *Wolf Hall* [DVD]. Season 1, Episode 2 (2015).
33. Ibid.
34. 'Letter from Eustace Chapuys to Granvelle on 6 June 1536', *Letters and Papers, Foreign and Domestic, Henry VIII*, Volume 10, January–June 1536, No.1070 (1888).
35. *Wolf Hall* [DVD]. Season 1, Episode 3 (2015).
36. Ibid.
37. Ives, Eric, 'The Fall of Anne Boleyn', *The English Historical Review* (1991) p.602.
38. *Wolf Hall* [DVD]. Season 1, Episode 5 (2015).
39. Ibid.
40. *Wolf Hall* [DVD]. Season 1, Episode 6 (2015).
41. Ibid.
42. Ibid.
43. Russo, Stephanie, *The Afterlife of Anne Boleyn: Representations of Anne Boleyn in Fiction and on the Screen* (2020) p.275.
44. Warnicke, Retha, 'Anne Boleyn in History, Drama, and Film', in Levin, Carole, Carney, Jo Eldridge, & Barrett-Graves, Debra, "*High and Mighty Queens" of Early Modern England: Realities and Representations* (2019) p.251.
45. Bordo, Susan, *The Creation of Anne Boleyn: In Search of the Tudors' Most Notorious Queen* (2014) p.168.
46. *The Six Wives of Henry VIII* [DVD]. Episode 2 (1970).
47. Ibid.
48. Ibid.
49. Russo, Stephanie, *The Afterlife of Anne Boleyn: Representations of Anne Boleyn in Fiction and on the Screen* (2020) p.278.
50. Bordo, Susan, *The Creation of Anne Boleyn: In Search of the Tudors' Most Notorious Queen* (2014) p.197.
51. *Henry VIII* [DVD]. Episode 1 (2003).
52. Ibid.
53. Ibid.
54. *Anne Boleyn* [DVD]. Episode 2 (2021).
55. Ibid.
56. Murrell, Morgan, 'Jodie Turner-Smith's Casting as White Historical Figure Anne Boleyn Has A Few People Upset', *BuzzFeed* (2020).
57. Carr, Flora, 'Why Channel 5's Anne Boleyn is a Black woman - a look at the real Anne', *Radio Times* (2021).

Chapter 11: Anne on the Page

1. Gregory, Philippa, *The Other Boleyn Girl* (2008) p.434.
2. Saxton, Laura, '"She was dead meat": Imagining the Execution of Anne Boleyn in History and Fiction', *Parergon* (2020) p.105.
3. Davies, Serena, 'David Starkey: It is "ludicrous" to suggest that historical novelists have authority', *The Telegraph* (2013).

4. Saxton, Laura, '"She was dead meat": Imagining the Execution of Anne Boleyn in History and Fiction', *Parergon* (2020) p.104.
5. Bernard, G.W., *Anne Boleyn: Fatal Attractions* (2011) p.ix.
6. Saxton, Laura, '"She was dead meat": Imagining the Execution of Anne Boleyn in History and Fiction', *Parergon* (2020) p.104.
7. Bordo, Susan, 'When Fictionalised Facts Matter: From *Anne of the Thousand Days* to Hilary Mantel's new *Bring Up the Bodies*', *Chronicle of Higher Education* (2012).
8. Saxton, Laura, '"She was dead meat": Imagining the Execution of Anne Boleyn in History and Fiction', *Parergon* (2020) p.117.
9. Hui, Roland, 'Anne of the Wicked Ways: Perceptions of Anne Boleyn as a Witch in History and in Popular Culture', *Parergon* (2018) p.98.
10. Ibid.
11. Gregory, Philippa, *The Other Boleyn Girl* (2008) p.434.
12. Saxton, Laura, '"She was dead meat": Imagining the Execution of Anne Boleyn in History and Fiction', *Parergon* (2020) p.117.
13. Plaidy, Jean, *Murder Most Royal* (2006) p.125.
14. Ibid, p.55.
15. Ibid, p.56.
16. Ibid, pp.209-210.
17. Ibid, p.211.
18. Hart, Kelly, *The Mistresses of Henry VIII* (2011) p.133.
19. Plaidy, Jean, *Murder Most Royal* (2006) p.125, 324.
20. Ibid, p.325.
21. Ibid, pp.325–326.
22. 'Letter from Eustace Chapuys to Charles V on 3 September 1533', *Letters and Papers, Foreign and Domestic, Henry VIII*, Volume 6, 1533, No.1069 (1882).
23. Ives, Eric, *The Life and Death of Anne Boleyn* (2005) p.358.
24. Plaidy, Jean, *Murder Most Royal* (2006) p.503.
25. Dunn, Suzannah, *The Queen of Subtleties* (2005) p.287.
26. Ibid, p.1.
27. Ibid, p.3.
28. Ibid.
29. Norton, Elizabeth, *Anne Boleyn: Henry VIII's Obsession* (2009) p.164.
30. Dunn, Suzannah, *The Queen of Subtleties* (2005) p.96.
31. Ibid, p.98.
32. 'Letter from Eustace Chapuys to Charles V on 15 June 1530', *Calendar of State Papers: Spain*, Volume 4 Part 1, 1529–1530, No.354 (1879).
33. Dunn, Suzannah, *The Queen of Subtleties* (2005) p.276.
34. Ibid, p.277.
35. Ibid, p.283.
36. Russo, Stephanie, *The Afterlife of Anne Boleyn: Representations of Anne Boleyn in Fiction and on the Screen* (2020) p.223.
37. Neale, J.E. *Queen Elizabeth I* (1957) p.5.
38. Andersen, Laura, *The Boleyn King* (2013) p.3.
39. Ibid, p.6.
40. Ibid, p.180.
41. Ibid, p.13.
42. Ives, Eric, *The Life and Death of Anne Boleyn* (2005) p.128.

43. Andersen, Laura, *The Boleyn King* (2013) p.13.
44. Ibid, p. 14.
45. Friedmann, Paul, *Anne Boleyn* (2010) p.184.
46. Ibid, p.15.
47. Ibid.
48. Ibid, p. 220.
49. Ibid, p.222.
50. Wilson, Jennifer C., *Kindred Spirits: Tower of London* (2020) p.3.
51. Ibid.
52. Ibid, p.4.
53. Grueninger, Natalie, *The Final Year of Anne Boleyn* (2022) p.162.
54. Wilson, Jennifer C., *Kindred Spirits: Tower of London* (2020) p.6.
55. Ibid, p.36.
56. Ives, Eric, 'The Fall of Anne Boleyn Reconsidered', *The English Historical Review* (1992) pp.652–653.
57. Wilson, Jennifer C., *Kindred Spirits: Tower of London* (2020) p.36.
58. Ibid, p.133.
59. Ibid, p.132–133.
60. Ibid, p.137.
61. Russo, Stephanie, *The Afterlife of Anne Boleyn: Representations of Anne Boleyn in Fiction and on the Screen* (2020) p.226.
62. Weir, Alison, *Anne Boleyn: A King's Obsession* (2017) p.150.
63. Ibid.
64. Ibid, p.153.
65. Wyatt, George, *Extracts from the Life of the Virtuous, Christian, and Renowned Queen Anne Boleigne* (1817) p.4.
66. Louthe, John, 'The Reminiscences of John Loude or Louthe, Archdeacon of Nottingham, addressed to John Foxe in 1579', *Camden Old Series* (1859) pp.52–56.
67. Weir, Alison, *Anne Boleyn: A King's Obsession* (2017) p.238.
68. Ibid, p.239.
69. Ibid, p.504.
70. Ibid, p.505.
71. 'Letter from William Kingston to Thomas Cromwell tentatively on 19 May 1536', *Letters and Papers, Foreign and Domestic, Henry VIII*, Volume 10, January–June 1536, No.910 (1888).
72. Weir, Alison, *Anne Boleyn: A King's Obsession* (2017) pp.506–507.
73. Davies, Serena, 'David Starkey: It is "ludicrous" to suggest that historical novelists have authority', *The Telegraph* (2013).

Chapter 12: Historiography

1. Norton, Elizabeth, *Anne Boleyn: Henry VIII's Obsession* (2009) p.164.
2. Martin, Claire, *Heirs of Ambition: The Making of the Boleyns* (2023) p.207.
3. Saxton, Laura, '"She was dead meat": Imagining the Execution of Anne Boleyn in History and Fiction', *Parergon* (2020) p.105.
4. Ibid, p.106.
5. Ibid, p.105.
6. Ives, Eric, *The Life and Death of Anne Boleyn* (2005) p.xv.
7. Bernard, G.W., *Anne Boleyn: Fatal Attractions* (2011) p.31.

8. Ibid, p.3.
9. Denny, Joanna, *Anne Boleyn: A new life of England's tragic Queen* (2004) p.93.
10. Weir, Alison, *The Lady in the Tower: The Fall of Anne Boleyn* (2009) p.7.
11. Ives, Eric, *The Life and Death of Anne Boleyn* (2005) p.xv.
12. Bernard, G.W., 'The Fall of Anne Boleyn', *The English Historical Review* (1991) p.584.
13. Ibid, p.595
14. Ibid, p.591.
15. Ibid, pp.605–606.
16. Ibid, pp.600–604.
17. Ives, Eric, 'The Fall of Anne Boleyn Reconsidered', *The English Historical Review* (1992) p.651.
18. Ibid, p.655.
19. Ibid.
20. Ibid, p.659.
21. Bernard, G.W., 'The Fall of Anne Boleyn: A Rejoinder', *The English Historical Review* (1992) p.665.
22. Ibid, p.668.
23. Hever Castle & Gardens, 'New research on prayer book unveils what happened after Anne's death', *Hever Castle & Gardens* (2021). https://www.hevercastle.co.uk/news/new-research-anne-boleyn-prayer-book/.
24. McCaffrey, Kate, 'Uncovering Inscriptions: The Process (Part One)'. (2021). https://kateemccaffrey.wordpress.com/2021/06/01/uncovering-inscriptions-the-process-part-one/.
25. McCaffrey, Kate, 'Uncovering Inscriptions: The Process (Part Two)'. (2021). https://kateemccaffrey.wordpress.com/2021/06/24/uncovering-inscriptions-the-process-part-two/.
26. McCaffrey, Kate, 'Uncovering Inscriptions: The Process (Part One)'. (2021). https://kateemccaffrey.wordpress.com/2021/06/01/uncovering-inscriptions-the-process-part-one/.
27. McCaffrey, Kate, 'Uncovering Inscriptions: The Process (Part Two)'. (2021). https://kateemccaffrey.wordpress.com/2021/06/24/uncovering-inscriptions-the-process-part-two/.
28. Ibid.
29. Hever Castle & Gardens, 'New research on prayer book unveils what happened after Anne's death', *Hever Castle & Gardens* (2021). https://www.hevercastle.co.uk/news/new-research-anne-boleyn-prayer-book/.
30. McCaffrey, Kate, 'One Book, Two Rival Queens'. (2021). https://kateemccaffrey.wordpress.com/2021/07/04/one-book-two-rival-queens/.
31. Ibid.
32. Kindy, David, 'Hidden Inscriptions Discovered in Anne Boleyn's Execution Prayer Book'. (2021). https://www.smithsonianmag.com/smart-news/hidden-inscriptions-discovered-anne-boleyns-execution-prayer-book-180977770/.
33. Ibid.
34. Ibid.
35. Emmerson, Owen, McCaffrey, Kate and Tallis, Nicola (aka The Tudor Trio), *The Retrial of Anne Boleyn*, Online Event (2023).
36. Bernard, G.W., *Anne Boleyn: Fatal Attractions* (2011) p.193, 195.
37. Ibid, p.184.

38. Bernard, G.W., 'The Fall of Anne Boleyn', *The English Historical Review* (1991) p.609.
39. Grueninger, Natalie, *The Final Year of Anne Boleyn* (2022) p.182.
40. Ibid, p.187.
41. Guy, John and Fox, Julia, *Hunting the Falcon: Henry VIII, Anne Boleyn and the Marriage That Shook Europe* (2023) p.414.
42. Starkey, David, *Six Wives: The Queens of Henry VIII* (2004) p.xxi, xxiii.
43. Wilkinson, Josephine, *Anne Boleyn: The Young Queen to Be* (2011) p.8.
44. Loades, David, *The Six Wives of Henry VIII* (2010) p.153.
45. Loades, David, *The Boleyns: The Rise and Fall of a Tudor Family* (2021) p.228.
46. Warnicke, Retha, *The Rise and Fall of Anne Boleyn* (2008) p.5.
47. Ibid.
48. Smith, Lacey Baldwin, *Anne Boleyn: The Queen of Controversy* (2013) p.9.
49. Ibid, p.193.
50. Bruce, Marie Louise, *Anne Boleyn* (1975) pp.332–333.
51. Erickson, Carolly, *Mistress Anne* (1984) p.259.
52. Norton, Elizabeth, *Anne Boleyn: Henry VIII's Obsession* (2009) p.164.
53. Ibid.
54. Denny, Joanna, *Anne Boleyn: A New Life of England's Tragic Queen* (2008) p.1.
55. Weir, Alison, *The Six Wives of Henry VIII* (1997) p.3.
56. Weir, Alison, *The Lady in the Tower: The Fall of Anne Boleyn* (2009) p.3.
57. Ibid, p.328.
58. Borman, Tracy, *Anne Boleyn and Elizabeth I: The Mother and Daughter Who Changed History* (2023) p.3.
59. Licence, Amy, *Anne Boleyn: Adultery, Heresy, Desire* (2017) p.432.
60. Ibid, p.9.
61. Paranque, Estelle, *Thorns, Lust and Glory: The Betrayal of Anne Boleyn* (2024) p.247.
62. Martin, Claire, *Heirs of Ambition: The Making of the Boleyns* (2023) p.207.
63. Emmerson, Owen and Ridgway, Claire, *The Boleyns of Hever Castle* (2021) p.101.
64. Ives, Eric, *The Life and Death of Anne Boleyn* (2005) p.xiii.
65. Ibid, p.xv.
66. Guy, John and Fox, Julia, *Hunting the Falcon: Henry VIII, Anne Boleyn and the Marriage that Shook Europe* (2023) p.409.

Epilogue

1. Ives, Eric, *The Life and Death of Anne Boleyn* (2005) p.xiv.
2. Ibid, p.359.
3. Russo, Stephanie, *The Afterlife of Anne Boleyn: Representations of Anne Boleyn in Fiction and on the Screen* (2020) p.294.
4. Burstein, Miriam Elizabeth, 'The Fictional Afterlife of Anne Boleyn: How to Do Things with the Queen, 1901–2006', *Clio* (2007) p.3.
5. Guy, John and Fox, Julia, *Hunting the Falcon: Henry VIII, Anne Boleyn and the Marriage that Shook Europe* (2023) p.409.
6. Norton, Elizabeth, *Anne Boleyn: Henry VIII's Obsession* (2009) p.164.
7. Emmerson, Owen and Ridgway, Claire, *The Boleyns of Hever Castle* (2021) p.101.
8. Boleyn, Anne, *Printed Book of Hours c.1528*, Hever Castle and Gardens.

Bibliography

Primary Sources

Archives

Calendar of State Papers, Spain. Edited by Pascual de Gayangos. London: Her Majesty's Stationery Office, 1882. British History Online, https://www.british-history.ac.uk/search/series/cal-state-papers--spain.

Letters and Papers, Foreign and Domestic, Henry VIII. Edited by James Gairdner. London: Her Majesty's Stationery Office, 1864–1920. British History Online, http://www.british-history.ac.uk/letters-papers-hen8/.

Queen Victoria's Journals, Bodleian Libraries, http://www.queenvictoriasjournals.org/.

Records of the Exchequer, and its related bodies, with those of the Office of First Fruits and Tenths, and the Court of Augmentations, The National Archives, https://discovery.nationalarchives.gov.uk/browse/r/h/C96.

Vatican Archives, ref. Vat.lat.3731.pt.A, https://digi.vatlib.it/view/MSS_Vat.lat.3731.pt.A.

Printed

Anonymous (Goldsmid, Edmund ed.), *The Noble Tryumphaunt Coronacyon of Quene Anne, Wyfe unto the Most Noble Kynge Henry VIII* (Edinburgh: Privately Printed, 1885; originally printed by Wynkyn de Worde, 1532–3).

Austen, Jane, *The History of England* (London: Penguin Books, 1995).

Bell, Doyne C., *Notices of the Historic Persons Buried in the Chapel of St Peter ad Vincula in the Tower of London* (London: John Murray, 1877).

Burnet, Gilbert, *The History of the Reformation of the Church of England* (Oxford: Clarendon Press, 1865).

Cavendish, George, *The Life of Cardinal Wolsey* (London: George Routledge and Sons Limited, 1890).

Chaucer, Geoffrey, *Chaucer's Romaunt of the Rose, Troilus and Creseide and the Minor Poems* (London: William Pickering, 1846).

Foxe, John (Townsend, George, ed.), *Actes and Monuments of these Latter and Perillous Days, Touching Matters of the Church* (London: Seeley, Burnside and Seeley, 1838).

Gee, Henry and Hardy, William (eds.), *Documents Illustrative of English Church History* (London: Macmillan, 1914).

Hall, Edward (Ellis, Henry, ed.), *Hall's Chronicle; Containing the History of England During the Reign of Henry the Fourth and the Succeeding Monarchs to the End of the Reign of Henry VIII, in Which are Particularly Described the manners and Customs of Those Periods* (London: J. Johnson, 1809).

Henry VIII (Phillips, J.O., ed.), *Love Letters of Henry VIII to Anne Boleyn* (London: Merchant Books, 2009).

Hume, Martin, *The Chronicle of King Henry VIII of England, Being a Contemporary Record of Some of the Principal Events of the Reigns of Henry VIII and Edward VI* (London: G. Bell & Sons, 1889).

Norton, Elizabeth, *Anne Boleyn: In Her Own Words and the Words of Those Who Knew Her* (Stroud: Amberley Publishing, 2011).
Parker, Matthew, *Correspondence of Matthew Parker, D.D.: Archbishop of Canterbury: comprising letters written by and to him, from A.D. 1535 to his death, A.D. 1575* (Cambridge: Cambridge University Press, 1853).
Pole, Reginald, *Defense of the Unity of the Church* (Pine Beach NJ: Newman Press, 1965).
Sander, Nicholas, *Rise and Growth of the Anglican Schism* (London:Burns and Oates, 1877).
Strickland, Agnes, *Lives of the Queens of England from the Norman Conquest, Volume II* (London: George Bell & Sons, 1909).
Strype, John, *Ecclesiastical Memorials: relating chiefly to religion and the reformation of it, and the emergencies of the Church of England, under King Henry VIII, King Edward VI and Queen Mary the First* (London: John Wyat, 1721).
Wyatt, George, *Extracts from the Life of the Virtuous, Christian, and Renowned Queen Anne Boleigne* (London: Richard and Arthur Taylor, Shoe Lane, 1817).

Secondary Sources

Books

Abbott, Geoffrey, *Severed Heads: British Beheadings Through the Ages* (London: Andre Deutsch, 2003).
Bernard, G.W., *Anne Boleyn: Fatal Attractions* (London: Yale University Press, 2011).
Bordo, Susan, *The Creation of Anne Boleyn: In Search of the Tudors' Most Notorious Queen* (London: OneWorld Publications, 2014).
Borman, Tracy, *Anne Boleyn and Elizabeth I: The Mother and Daughter Who Changed History* (London: Hodder & Stoughton, 2023).
Borman, Tracy, *Thomas Cromwell: The Untold Story of Henry VIII's Most Faithful Servant* (London: Hodder & Stoughton, 2014).
Bruce, Marie Louise, *Anne Boleyn* (London: Pan Books Ltd, 1975).
Cannadine, David (ed.), *History and the Media* (Basingstoke: Palgrave Macmillan, 2004)
Chapman, James, *National Identity and the British Historical Film* (London: I.B. Taurus & Co Ltd, 2005).
Chapman, Lissa, *Anne Boleyn in London* (Barnsley: Pen and Sword History, 2017).
Denny, Joanna, *Anne Boleyn: A New Life of England's Tragic Queen* (Chatham: Piatkus Books, 2004).
Doran, Susan and Freeman, Thomas (eds.), *Tudors and Stuarts on Film: Historical Perspectives* (Basingstoke: Palgrave Macmillan, 2009).
Emmerson, Owen and McCaffrey, Kate, *Becoming Anne: Connections, Culture, Court* (Exeter: Jigsaw Publishing, 2022).
Emmerson, Owen, McCaffrey, Kate and Palmer, Alison, *Catherine and Anne: Queens, Rivals, Mothers* (Exeter: Jigsaw Publishing, 2023).
Emmerson, Owen and Ridgway, Claire, *The Boleyns of Hever Castle* (Almeria: MadeGlobal Publishing, 2021).
Erickson, Carolly, *Mistress Anne* (New York: St Martin's Press, 1984).
Fraser, Antonia, *The Six Wives of Henry VIII* (London: Phoenix, 2002).
Friedmann, Paul, *Anne Boleyn* (Stroud: Amberley Publishing, 2010).
Gristwood, Sarah, *Game of Queens: The Women Who Made Sixteenth Century Europe* (London: Oneworld Publications, 2016).
Grueninger, Natalie, *The Final Year of Anne Boleyn* (Barnsley: Pen and Sword History, 2022).

Guy, John and Fox, Julia, *Hunting the Falcon: Henry VIII, Anne Boleyn and the Marriage That Shook Europe* (London: Bloomsbury Publishing, 2023).
Harrison, Helene, *Tudor Executions: From Nobility to the Block* (Barnsley: Pen and Sword History, 2024).
Heard, Kate, *Holbein at the Tudor Court* (London: Royal Collection Trust, 2023).
Hui, Roland, *Anne Boleyn: An Illustrated Life of Henry VIII's Queen* (Barnsley: Pen and Sword History, 2023).
Hutcheon, Linda, *A Theory of Film Adaptation* (Abingdon: Routledge, 2006).
Ives, Eric, *The Life and Death of Anne Boleyn* (Oxford: Blackwell Publishing Ltd, 2005).
Jones, Nigel, *Tower: An Epic History of the Tower of London* (London: Windmill Books, 2012).
Lerer, Seth, *Courtly Letters in the Age of Henry VIII: Literary Culture and the Arts of Deceit* (Cambridge: Cambridge University Press, 1997).
Levin, Carole, Carney, Jo Eldridge, and Barrett-Graves, Debra (eds.), *"High and Mighty Queens" of Early Modern England: Realities and Representations* (New York: Palgrave Macmillan, 2019).
Licence, Amy, *Anne Boleyn: Adultery, Heresy, Desire* (Stroud: Amberley Publishing, 2017).
Licence, Amy, *In Bed with the Tudors: The Sex Lives of a Dynasty from Elizabeth of York to Elizabeth I* (Stroud: Amberley Publishing, 2012).
Licence, Amy, *The Six Wives and Many Mistresses of Henry VIII: The Women's Stories* (Stroud: Amberley Publishing, 2015).
Lindsey, Karen, *Divorced, Beheaded, Survived: A Feminist Reinterpretation of the Wives of Henry VIII* (Cambridge MA: Da Capo Press, 1995).
Lipscomb, Suzannah, *1536: The Year That Changed Henry VIII* (Oxford: Lion Hudson plc, 2009).
Lloyd, Carol Ann, *The Tudors by Numbers: The Stories and Statistics Behind England's Most Infamous Royal Dynasty* (Barnsley: Pen and Sword History, 2023).
Loades, David, *The Boleyns: The Rise and Fall of a Tudor Family* (Stroud: Amberley Publishing, 2011).
Loades, David, *Henry VIII* (Stroud: Amberley Publishing, 2011).
Loades, David, *The Six Wives of Henry VIII* (Stroud: Amberley Publishing, 2010).
Loades, David, *The Tudor Queens of England* (London: Continuum UK, 2009).
Mackay, Lauren, *Inside the Tudor Court: Henry VIII and his Six Wives Through the Eyes of the Spanish Ambassador* (Stroud: Amberley Publishing, 2015).
Martin, Claire, *Heirs of Ambition: The Making of the Boleyns* (Cheltenham: The History Press, 2023).
Morris, Sarah and Grueninger, Natalie, *In the Footsteps of the Six Wives of Henry VIII* (Stroud: Amberley Publishing, 2016).
Neale, J.E., *Queen Elizabeth I* (New York: Doubleday & Co., 1957).
Norton, Elizabeth, *Anne Boleyn: Henry VIII's Obsession* (Stroud: Amberley Publishing, 2009).
Norton, Elizabeth, *The Boleyn Women: The Tudor Femmes Fatales Who Changed English History* (Stroud: Amberley Publishing, 2013).
Paranque, Estelle, *Thorns, Lust and Glory: The Betrayal of Anne Boleyn* (London: Ebury Press, 2024).
Ridley, Jasper, *A Brief History of the Tudor Age* (London: Constable & Robinson Ltd, 2002).
Russo, Stephanie, *The Afterlife of Anne Boleyn: Representations of Anne Boleyn in Fiction and on the Screen* (Basingstoke: Palgrave Macmillan, 2020).
Scarisbrick, J.J., *Henry VIII* (London: Meuthen London Ltd, 1988).
Sharpe, Kevin, *Remapping Early Modern England: The Culture of Seventeenth Century Politics* (Cambridge: Cambridge University Press, 2000).

Smith, Lacey Baldwin, *Anne Boleyn: The Queen of Controversy* (Stroud: Amberley Publishing, 2013).

Smith, Paul (ed.), *The Historian and Film* (Cambridge: Cambridge University Press, 2008).

Somerset, Anne, *Elizabeth I* (London: Phoenix, 1997).

Souden, David, *The Royal Palaces of London* (London: Merrell Publishers, 2008).

Starkey, David, *The Reign of Henry VIII: Personalities and Politics* (London: Random House, 2002).

Starkey, David, *Six Wives: The Queens of Henry VIII* (London: Vintage, 2004).

String, Tatiana and Bull, Marcus (eds.), *Tudorism: Historical Imagination and the Appropriation of the Sixteenth Century* (London: British Academy, 2011).

Vasoli, Sandra, *Anne Boleyn's Letter from the Tower: New Updated Edition* (London: GreyLondon Press, 2023).

Walker, Greg, *Writing Under Tyranny: English Literature and the Henrician Reformation* (Oxford: Oxford University Press, 2005).

Warnicke, Retha, *The Rise and Fall of Anne Boleyn* (Cambridge: Cambridge University Press, 2008).

Weir, Alison, *The Lady in the Tower: The Fall of Anne Boleyn* (London: Jonathan Cape, 2009).

Weir, Alison, *The Six Wives of Henry VIII* (London: Pimlico, 1997).

Wiesner-Hanks, Merry E., *Women and Gender in Early Modern Europe* (Cambridge: Cambridge University Press, 2008).

Wilkinson, Josephine, *Anne Boleyn: The Young Queen to Be* (Stroud: Amberley Publishing, 2011).

Articles

Bernard, G.W., 'Anne Boleyn's Religion', *The Historical Journal*, Vol. 36, No. 1 (1993) pp.1–20.

Bernard, G.W., 'The Fall of Anne Boleyn', *English Historical Review*, Vol. 106, No. 420 (1991) pp.584–610.

Burstein, Miriam Elizabeth, 'The Fictional Afterlife of Anne Boleyn: How to Do Things with the Queen, 1901–2006', *Clio*, Vol. 37, No. 1 (2007) pp.1–26.

Dowling, Maria, 'Anne Boleyn and Reform', *Journal of Ecclesiastical History*, Vol. 35, No. 1 (1984) pp.30-46.

Elton, G.R., 'The Law of Treason in the Early Reformation', *The Historical Journal*, Vol. 11, No. 2 (1968) pp.211–236.

Freeman, Thomas S., 'Research, Rumour and Propaganda: Anne Boleyn in Foxe's "Book of Martyrs"', *The Historical Journal*, Vol. 38, No. 4 (1995) pp.797–819.

Gairdner, James, 'Mary and Anne Boleyn', *English Historical Review*, Vol. 8, No. 29 (1893) pp.53–60.

Harrier, Richard C., 'Notes on Wyatt and Anne Boleyn', *The Journal of English and German Philology*, Vol. 53, No. 4 (1954) pp.581–584.

Highley, Christopher, '"A Pestilent and Seditious Book": Nicholas Sander's Schismatis Anglicani and Catholic Histories of the Reformation', *Huntington Library Quarterly*, Vol. 68, No. 1-2 (2005) pp.151–171.

Hui, Roland, 'Anne of the Wicked Ways: Perceptions of Anne Boleyn as a Witch in History and in Popular Culture', *Parergon*, Vol. 35, No. 1 (2018) pp.97–118.

Ives, Eric, 'Anne Boleyn and the Early Reformation in England: The Contemporary Evidence', *The Historical Journal*, Vol. 37, No. 2 (1994) pp.389–400.

Ives, Eric, 'Anne Boleyn on Trial Again', *Journal of Ecclesiastical History*, Vol. 62, No. 4 (2011) pp.763–777.

Ives, Eric, 'Faction at the Court of Henry VIII: The Fall of Anne Boleyn' in *History*, Vol. 57, No. 190 (1972) pp.169–188.

Ives, Eric, 'The Fall of Anne Boleyn Reconsidered' in *English Historical Review*, Vol. 107, No. 424 (1992) pp.651–664.

Locke, Hilary Jane, '"Go too far on Tudor-speak, all hey-nonnynonny, [and] you'll alienate your readers": Alison Weir, Historical Fiction, and the Representation of Tudor History', *Parergon*, Vol. 37, No. 2 (2020) pp.151–169.

Louthe, John, 'The Reminiscences of John Loude or Louthe, Archdeacon of Nottingham, addressed to John Foxe in 1579', *Camden Old Series*, Vol. 77 (1859) pp.1–59.

Mena, Paula de Pando, 'Emasculated Subjects and Subjugated Wives: Discourses of Domination in John Banks's *Vertue Betray'd* (1682)', *Yearbook of the Spanish and Portuguese Society for English Renaissance Studies*, Vol. 16 (2006) pp.161–178.

Miller-Tomlinson, Tracey, 'Pathos and Politics in John Banks's *Vertue Betray'd* or *Anna Bullen* (1682)', *Restoration and 18th Century Theatre Research*, Vol. 23, No. 1 (2008) pp.46–67.

Noling, Kim H., 'Grubbing Up the Stock: Dramatizing Queens in Henry VIII', *Shakespeare Quarterly*, Vol. 39, No. 3 (1988) pp.291–306.

Paget, Hugh, 'The Youth of Anne Boleyn', *Historical Research*, Vol. 54. No. 130 (1981) pp.162–170.

Parsons, W.L.E., 'Some Notes on the Boleyn Family', *Norfolk Archaeology*, Vol. 15 (1935) pp.386–407.

Prieto, Arranza, Jose Igor and Bastida-Rodriguez, Patricia, 'The Changing Faces of Anne Boleyn: An Analysis of Contemporary Historical Fiction by Philippa Gregory, Hilary Mantel, and Alison Weir', *Clio*, Vol. 48, No. 3 (2021) pp.299–324.

Rowland, John and Starkey, David, 'An Old Tradition Reasserted: Holbein's Portrait of Queen Anne Boleyn', *The Burlington Magazine*, Vol. 125, No. 959 (1983) pp.88–92.

Russo, Stephanie, 'The Story of the Death of Anne Boleyn', *History*, Vol. 51, No. 2 (2023) pp.24–25.

Saxton, Laura, '"She was dead meat": Imagining the Execution of Anne Boleyn in History and Fiction', *Parergon*, Vol. 37, No. 2 (2020) pp.103–124.

Saxton, Laura, 'Writing the concubine: Anne Boleyn, Eustace Chapuys and popular historiography in Hilary Mantel's Wolf Hall trilogy', *Rethinking History* (2023) DOI: 10.1080/13642529.2023.2269825.

Smith, Lacey Baldwin, 'English Treason Trials and Confessions in the Sixteenth Century', *Journal of the History of Ideas*, Vol. 15, No. 4 (1954) pp.471–498.

Soberton, Sylvia Barbara, '"Large wen" or "swelling"? Exploring Myths and Misconceptions about Nicholas Sander's Description of Anne Boleyn and its Link to Witchcraft', *Royal Studies Journal*, Vol. 10, No. 2 (2023) pp.239–266.

Southall, Raymond, 'Love, Fortune and my Mind: The Stoicism of Wyatt', *Essays in Criticism*, Vol. 34, No. 1 (1989) pp.18–28.

Thornley, I.D., 'The Treason Legislation of Henry VIII (1531–1534)', *Transactions of the Royal Historical Society*, Vol. 11 (1917) pp.87–123.

Walker, Greg, 'Rethinking the Fall of Anne Boleyn', *The Historical Journal*, Vol. 45, No. 1 (2002) pp.1–29.

Warnicke, Retha, 'Anne Boleyn's Childhood and Adolescence', *The Historical Journal*, Vol. 28, No. 4 (1985) pp.939–952.

Warnicke, Retha, 'Anne Boleyn Revisited', *The Historical Journal*, Vol. 34, No. 4 (1991) pp.953–954.

Warnicke, Retha, 'The Eternal Triangle and Court Politics: Henry VIII, Anne Boleyn and Sir Thomas Wyatt', *Albion*, Vol. 18, No. 4 (1986) pp.565–579.

Warnicke, Retha, 'The Fall of Anne Boleyn: A Reassessment', *History*, Vol. 70, No. 228 (1985) pp.1–15.

Online Articles

Bordo, Susan, 'When Fictionalised Facts Matter: From *Anne of the Thousand Days* to Hilary Mantel's new *Bring Up the Bodies*', *Chronicle of Higher Education* (2012). https://www.chronicle.com/article/when-fictionalized-facts-matter/.

Canby, Vincent, 'A Royal Battle of the Sexes: "Anne of 1,000 Days" Bows at Plaza, Burton Cast as Henry, Miss Bujold Stars', *The New York Times* (1970). https://www.nytimes.com/1970/01/21/archives/screen-a-royal-battle-of-the-sexesanne-of-1000-days-bows-at-plaza.html.

Carr, Flora, 'Why Channel 5's Anne Boleyn is a Black woman – a look at the real Anne', *Radio Times* (2021). https://www.radiotimes.com/tv/drama/anne-boleyn-channel-5-casting/.

Churchill, Lucy, 'Anne Boleyn: My reconstruction of The Moost Happi portrait medal'. (n.d.). https://www.lucychurchill.com/anne-boleyn-moost-happi-medal-reconstruction/.

Churchill, Lucy, 'Anne Boleyn's Moost Happi Portrait Medal … Revisited'. (2020). https://lucychurchill.wordpress.com/2020/11/21/anne-boleyns-moost-happi-portrait-medal-revisited/.

Churchill, Lucy, 'The 'Moost Happi' portrait of Anne Boleyn: A reconstruction by Lucy Churchill'. (2012). https://lucychurchill.wordpress.com/2012/05/14/the-moost-happi-portrait-of-anne-boleyn-a-rec/.

Davies, Serena, 'David Starkey: It is "ludicrous" to suggest that historical novelists have authority', *The Telegraph* (2013). https://www.telegraph.co.uk/culture/tvandradio/10049866/David-Starkey-it-is-ludicrous-to-suggest-that-historical-novelists-have-authority.html.

Hever Castle & Gardens, 'New research on prayer book unveils what happened after Anne's death', *Hever Castle & Gardens* (2021). https://www.hevercastle.co.uk/news/new-research-anne-boleyn-prayer-book/.

Kindy, David, 'Hidden Inscriptions Discovered in Anne Boleyn's Execution Prayer Book'. (2021). https://www.smithsonianmag.com/smart-news/hidden-inscriptions-discovered-anne-boleyns-execution-prayer-book-180977770/.

McCaffrey, Kate, 'One Book, Two Rival Queens'. (2021). https://kateemccaffrey.wordpress.com/2021/07/04/one-book-two-rival-queens/.

McCaffrey, Kate, 'Uncovering Inscriptions: The Process (Part One)'. (2021). https://kateemccaffrey.wordpress.com/2021/06/01/uncovering-inscriptions-the-process-part-one/.

McCaffrey, Kate, 'Uncovering Inscriptions: The Process (Part Two)'. (2021). https://kateemccaffrey.wordpress.com/2021/06/24/uncovering-inscriptions-the-process-part-two/.

Murrell, Morgan, 'Jodie Turner-Smith's Casting as White Historical Figure Anne Boleyn Has A Few People Upset', *BuzzFeed* (2020). https://www.buzzfeed.com/morganmurrell/jodie-turner-smiths-anne-boleyn-casting-controversy.

Theatre, Film, TV, CDs, Plays and Novels

Andersen, Laura, *The Boleyn King* (New York: Ballantine Books, 2013).

Anne Boleyn, written by Eve Hedderwick Turner (2021). Fable Pictures [DVD].

Anne of the Thousand Days, directed by Charles Jarrott (1969). Universal Studios [DVD].

Bacon, Francis, *The Tragedy of Anne Boleyn* (London: Forgotten Books, 2012).

Banks, John, *Virtue Betray'd* (London: R. Wellington, 1715).

Dunn, Suzannah, *The Queen of Subtleties* (London: HarperCollins Publishers, 2005).

Gregory, Philippa, *The Other Boleyn Girl* (London: HarperCollins Publishers, 2008).

Harry Potter and the Philosopher's Stone, directed by Chris Columbus (2001). Warner Bros. Pictures [DVD].

Henry VIII, written by Peter Morgan (2003). Granada Television [DVD].
Mantel, Hilary, *Bring Up the Bodies* (London: Fourth Estate, 2012).
Mantel, Hilary, *Wolf Hall* (London: Fourth Estate, 2010).
Marlow, Toby and Moss, Lucy, *SIX The Musical: Studio Cast Recording* (2018). Absolute Records [CD].
Marlow, Toby & Moss, Lucy, *SIX The Musical: Live on Opening Night, Original Broadway Cast Recording* (2022). Absolute Records [CD].
The Other Boleyn Girl, directed by Justin Chadwick (2008). Universal Pictures [DVD].
The Other Boleyn Girl, directed by Philippa Lowthorpe (2003). 2entertain [DVD].
Plaidy, Jean, *Murder Most Royal* (London: Arrow Books, 2006).
The Private Life of Henry VIII, directed by Alexander Korda (1933). ITV Global Entertainment Limited [DVD].
Shakespeare, Henry, *King Henry VIII* (Oxford: Oxford University Press, 2008).
The Six Wives of Henry VIII, written by various (1970). BBC Studios [DVD].
The Tudors, written by Michael Hirst (2007–2010). Showtime [DVD].
Weir, Alison, *Anne Boleyn: A King's Obsession* (London: Headline Review, 2017).
Wilson, Jennifer C., *Kindred Spirits: Tower of London* (London: Dark Stroke Books, 2020).
Wolf Hall, written by Peter Straughan (2015). Company Pictures [DVD].

Other Sources

British Museum, https://www.britishmuseum.org/collection.
Chequers Trust, https://artuk.org/visit/collection/the-chequers-trust-268.
Hever Castle & Gardens, https://www.hevercastle.co.uk/visit/hever-castle/.
Internet Movie Database (IMDb), https://www.imdb.com/.
National Portrait Gallery, https://www.npg.org.uk/collections/.
Oxford Dictionary of National Biography (ODNB), https://www.oxforddnb.com/.
Royal Collection Trust, https://www.rct.uk/collection.
SIX The Musical, https://www.sixthemusical.com/london/about.

Index